I0797438

THE HOUR OF REVENGE

Holocaust Survivors and Their Search for Revenge and Retribution

Katarzyna Person

In the immediate aftermath of the Second World War, the emotional landscape of postwar Europe was profoundly shaped by the intertwined notions of retribution and physical revenge, particularly for Holocaust survivors. While much scholarly attention has focused on extra-legal purges in post-war Europe, the experiences of individual Polish Jews have largely been overlooked.

The Hour of Revenge addresses this critical gap, exploring the particular journey of Polish Jews as they navigated the complexities of their post-conflict realities. Katarzyna Person examines how these individuals not only confronted their traumatic pasts but also actively contributed to the reconstruction of their communities.

Crossing the traditional historiographical divide between "West" and "East," Person illustrates how Polish Jews moved between these zones before the Iron Curtain descended, how they reconciled memories of the war and their former lives, and how they built emotional communities in the face of loss. The book contributes to a more integrative, multiethnic history of post-war Poland and to the global history of societal reconstruction in the wake of conflict. In an era of mass migration, *The Hour of Revenge* sheds light on connections to pre-war homelands as expressions of integration and exclusion.

KATARZYNA PERSON is a historian of the Holocaust and the deputy director of the Warsaw Ghetto Museum.

The Hour of Revenge

Holocaust Survivors and Their Search for Revenge and Retribution

KATARZYNA PERSON

UNIVERSITY OF TORONTO PRESS
Toronto Buffalo London

Toronto Buffalo London
utppublishing.com
Printed in Canada

ISBN 978-1-4875-6261-8 (cloth)
ISBN 978-1-4875-6262-5 (paper)
ISBN 978-1-4875-6264-9 (EPUB)
ISBN 978-1-4875-6263-2 (PDF)

Library and Archives Canada Cataloguing in Publication

Title: The hour of revenge : Holocaust survivors and their search for revenge and retribution / Katarzyna Person.
Names: Person, Katarzyna, author
Description: Includes bibliographical references and index.
Identifiers: Canadiana (print) 2024053204X | Canadiana (ebook) 20240532112 | ISBN 9781487562618 (cloth) | ISBN 9781487562625 (paper) | ISBN 9781487562632 (PDF) | ISBN 9781487562649 (EPUB)
Subjects: LCSH: Holocaust survivors—Poland. | LCSH: Jews, Polish. | LCSH: Holocaust, Jewish (1939–1945)—Poland. | LCSH: Revenge—Moral and ethical aspects. | LCSH: Retribution—Moral and ethical aspects.
Classification: LCC DS134.7 .P47 2025 | DDC 940.53/1809438—dc23

Cover design: Mark Byk
Cover image: Ruins of the Warsaw ghetto, July 1945. United States Holocaust Memorial Museum, courtesy of Israel Gutman.

We wish to acknowledge the land on which the University of Toronto Press operates. This land is the traditional territory of the Wendat, the Anishnaabeg, the Haudenosaunee, the Métis, and the Mississaugas of the Credit First Nation.

This project received funding from the European Union's Horizon 2020 Research and Innovation Program under the Marie Skłodowska-Curie grant agreement No. 893018.

Printed with the support of the Gerda Henkel Foundation, Düsseldorf.

University of Toronto Press acknowledges the financial support of the Government of Canada, the Canada Council for the Arts, and the Ontario Arts Council, an agency of the Government of Ontario, for its publishing activities.

Canada Council for the Arts
Conseil des Arts du Canada

Funded by the Government of Canada
Financé par le gouvernement du Canada

Only then will we start feeling the burden, the nightmare of the past days. How should I believe that even if this war ends in a "felicitous" way, the hatred among men shall disappear as with a magic wand. Perhaps just the opposite

...

The hate of the vanquished for the victors will persist, concealed, and almost every house will be filled with unceasing weeping, with pain, incurable pain for one's loved ones who fell in the war or were murdered. And the craving for revenge, swelling up in the millions of downtrodden will burst out, in an open, all-engulfing flame and incinerate the world.[1]

Warsaw Ghetto, Anonymous Writer.

Contents

Acknowledgments ix

Introduction 3

1 "He Wept and We Didn't": Liberation, Revenge, and a Survivor's Return 16

2 Holocaust Survivors and State Courts 51

3 Jewish Civic Court in Poland 66

4 Polish Jews and Germany as the Site of Revenge 83

5 Justice and Migrations 107

Notes 121

Bibliography 157

Index 169

Acknowledgments

My work on this book began when I came across a story of a man attacked on the streets of Paris for his actions during the Second World War. The account led me from the Warsaw Ghetto, through the forests of Lithuania, streets of destroyed Polish cities, and displaced-persons camp barracks, to new life in Israel, the United States, and South America. This work would never have taken shape without colleagues and institutions who helped me grasp at least a small part of it. For their wisdom and guidance, I would in particular like to thank friends and colleagues in the Wiener Wiesenthal Institut für Holocaust-Studien, the Ludwig-Maximilians-Universität in Munich, YIVO, the Jewish Historical Institute, and the Warsaw Ghetto Museum, where I wrote and presented parts of this book. My research was made possible thanks to the Research Fellowship in the Wiener Wiesenthal Institut für Holocaust-Studien, The Workers Circle/Dr. Emanuel Patt Visiting Professorship in Eastern European Jewish Studies at YIVO, a Marie Skłodowska-Curie Individual Fellowship, and a Gerda Henkel Postdoctoral Fellowship. Gerda Henkel Stiftung also generously provided additional publication funding. Finally, I would like to thank the University of Toronto Press, and especially Stephen Shapiro, for taking a chance on this complicated and often extremely difficult story.

THE HOUR OF REVENGE

Holocaust Survivors and Their Search for Revenge and Retribution

Introduction

Norman Salsitz, the youngest son from a well-to-do Jewish Orthodox family in Kolbuszowa in Poland, was 21 years old when, hiding in the neighbour's attic, he saw his father being shot in the courtyard of their family home. Over 50 years later, in Springfield, New Jersey, he recalled:

> Yes, yes. Revenge was very important for me, and the revenge was important for a few reasons, but the main reason was, when my father was shot in the ghetto, the 28th of April, 1942, I witnessed it. And when he was shot by the Gestapo, before he died, he said what a Jew usually says before he dies, [...] we call it the Shema Israel. And then he said – the last words were, "*Nekume, nekume, nem nekume.*" It means, revenge, revenge, take revenge. Now, he said it in such a voice, that it was not a natural voice, it was something that it came from heaven, an unnatural voice, which I – till today, it is already almost 70 years, I can still hear his voice yelling to take revenge. And this gave me strength to survive. I said, "I must survive to take revenge." For this reason, revenge was so important for me. [...] If they are in heaven, which I don't know if they are, this is a different story, if they are, and if they look down, and they said – and they looked at me and said, I was the survivor, the survivor to take revenge, and if wouldn't take revenge, I will be a traitor, I would be a disappointment for them, because I was the only one. So I had to take revenge.[1]

Writing in 1963 about the factors favouring postwar adaptation of survivors, Mark Dvorjetski, a medical doctor and survivor of the Vilnius Ghetto, named three, which he considered to be key: the desire to live; the thirst for vengeance on the Nazis; and solidarity among the survivors.[2] Two years earlier, Dvorjetski himself participated in the most iconic event unifying all three of these: the Eichmann trial, the event that became symbolic of survivors' involvement in seeking justice (and revenge) after the Holocaust.

Yet vengeance took many forms, and it was not only aimed at the Nazis. Among the complexity of the postwar search for retribution and revenge, Polish Jews also sought what they considered to be justice for crimes that seemed beyond the reach of the legal system. Stories of postwar revenge usually played out far away from the courtroom. These were stories of regaining agency but also of helplessness, frustration, and the fear of giving up in case the silence would somehow diminish the memory of those for whom justice was sought. They were about the search for justice for one's own pain and suffering, for suffering of individuals, and for suffering of the whole nation.

The Methodology of Postwar Revenge

Starting a new life and recovering from the traumas of war required confronting and facing the past. This involved the crucial task of holding wrongdoers accountable for their actions committed during the war in occupied Poland. For Polish Jews, with minimal access to any responsive state apparatus, revenge was often the only justice they could obtain. While in some spaces the new authorities attempted to facilitate individual participation in state-conducted trials, this system of accountability was not long-lasting and not structural. Individuals and the community could be made whole only through action unmediated by the mechanisms that the state normally provided for resolution of disputes or redress of grievances.

When discussing postwar revenge, one of the leaders of the Warsaw Ghetto Uprising, Yitzhak Zuckerman, wrote: "Such acts aren't done by groups, only individuals can do something."[3] This book expands upon this belief and looks primarily at individual actions, even if undertaken in group circumstances. It deals with actions, defined as revenge or as justice by those who carried them out, but that we, today, see as revenge. Revenge will be understood here as deliberate retaliation in return for harm caused, an interpersonal aggression in response to individual norm-violating behaviours.[4] Revenge can be defined as the act, or urge, to pay back wrongs. In this sense it can be seen as a core value, "rooted in the belief that those who hurt others deserve to be hurt in return."[5] It is, therefore, not only an action, but also a belief that wrongs deserve to be repaid. Revenge may be successful, or not, but there is always an attempt to take it, and it is the act of choosing to take revenge that matters.

In this sense revenge was the opposite of impersonal and measured justice, which must emanate and be carried out under the law. Thus, when those seeking revenge turned to state courts, we speak instead of retribution, or retaliation, rather than justice. The key aim of retribution was punishment. As in revenge, the intention is to see the transgressor suffer, though the punishment would be administered by a legal body.[6] Yet, as opposed to revenge, retribution focuses "always on what harm the wrongdoer deserves, independently of the needs and just deserts of the wronged party."[7] Thus, retribution practices, as discussed in this book, provided self-regulation and cohesion to Jewish communities in Eastern Europe, rather than simply ripping them apart.

The Question of "Jewish Revenge"

There is now a considerable amount of work discussing the many occurrences and the enormity of violence during the German occupation and the extra-legal purges omnipresent in postwar Europe in the immediate aftermath of liberation.[8] However, individual revenge acts carried out by Polish Jews were usually written out of this narrative.[9] Instead, Holocaust survivors were described as physically and emotionally incapable of revenge,[10] destroyed by grief, disoriented in the new postwar reality, leaving their former hometowns and then Poland, "crushed and broken in body, embarrassed and humiliated in spirit."[11] The only strength and resources they could mobilize were to build their future, rather than face their past. The redemptive story of surviving the Holocaust had no place for revenge.

In 2010, in his study of the Starachowice slave labour camp, Christopher Browning wrote of the identity of perpetrators of revenge killings as part of a "secret and communal" memory, shared only among the small community of Holocaust survivors, equal to that of collaboration or sexual violence.[12] There is no question that the desire for revenge – seeking gratification in the suffering of another – was considered vindicative and barbaric by nature. Revenge was considered inherently irrational. Violence was acceptable for reasons of defense, being actual physical defense or defense of honour, as in the case of young underground fighters, but not as revenge for the sake of moral satisfaction. Defense and revenge were thus constructed as two contrasting reasons for which someone might return violence for violence.[13] Of these two, revenge was attributed to the defects of human nature. Moreover, both during the war and after it, revenge became the key element of the antisemitic Nazi propaganda narrative of the "vengeful Jew."[14] Thus, the stories of Polish Jewish revenge were often silenced, both by individual survivors and by their own community.[15] Yet, this does not mean that revenge and retribution did not take place. On the contrary, as this book aims to demonstrate, it remained an important part of both individual and communal recovery of Jewish survivors after the Holocaust.

Revenge was taken not only to achieve emotional satisfaction, but also to restore self-worth after the extreme social degradation and an imbalance of power between non-Jews and Jews caused by the upheaval of the war. It was an attempt to restore the balance of suffering between the victim and the transgressor.[16] Moreover, revenge was also a matter of honour and ethnic pride. Not fulfilling a duty to avenge collective harms could be considered as harming the group and bringing shame both on oneself and on the community. In testimonies this is especially clear that the act of *not* taking revenge could be linked to the antisemitic stereotype of Jews passively accepting persecution during the Holocaust. Importantly, as John Kerrigan has written:

> Revenge is a cultural practice which arouses intense emotion, not only in those who exact or endure it but in those who stand by and judge. Much of its capacity to disturb stems from its paradoxical nature. A destructive impulse, it is mobilized by values and allegiances which would have to be called positive: a proper sense of self-worth, a willingness to strike back in defense of family or other social bonds. [...] Arguments about the merits of vengeance quickly become entangled with intractable debates about the validity of retributive punishment and the nature of justice itself.[17]

In this case, revenge as described in the post-Holocaust sources is a virtuous act. It is morally justified as it punishes immoral acts, for which there can be no proportional punishment.

Avengers

The story of the postwar search for what we would consider to be revenge, and what was understood by survivors to be justice, will be told through the narratives of survivors of the Holocaust, Polish Jews, and pre-war citizens of Poland. Some were survivors of concentration camps and ghettos, some were witnesses of the suffering of their family members, some were witnesses in the death of their communities, and some were not directly affected. Each of them dealt differently with their experience, but all at some point thought of, or attempted to carry out, some form of revenge. Thus, revenge was carried out by those who were themselves victims and those who acted in the name of those victimized, sometimes individuals, sometimes in the name of the entire community or ethnic solidarity.

Polish-Jewish Holocaust survivors are understood here as citizens of Poland at its pre-1939 borders, who under Nazi law were targeted as Jews during the Holocaust. This term should, of course, always be used with the full awareness of the complexities of identities and fates encapsulated in it as well as the geo-political backgrounds of those involved. Similarly, the terms "Poles," "Ukrainians," or "Byelorussians" will be used to refer to local non-Jews, thus underlining the diversity of wartime and postwar fate of the various ethnic groups. Again, here too, the vast majority of those discussed will be pre-war Polish citizens. As Polish Jews migrated out of Poland, their fate was linked to other national and transnational contexts as well as to various emotional communities, understood as groups – usually but not always social groups – that have their own values, modes of feeling, and ways to express those feelings. These communities were not only limited to the immediate postwar but existed for many years later. Emotions involved in revenge were, thus, a private response to the trauma of the Holocaust, yet they were also collectively constructed and sustained. That is why studying individual responses to harm will allow us to unravel the emotional scripts and needs of communities, in particular the need to feel in charge and shape one's own story. We will further see which communal practices led to fulfilling these needs and how they interacted with the limited, but nevertheless existing, presence of state authorities.

The time frame of this story dates from mid-1944 to 1948, the period when "the post-genocidal status quo solidified"[18]: from the Soviets crossing pre-1939 Polish borders to the establishment of the state of Israel, as well as the resolute establishment of Communist rule in Poland. These stories occur in places wherever Polish-Jewish Holocaust survivors found themselves at that time, with each chapter looking at a different form of individual revenge. This book is, thus, not a comprehensive look at the development of individual vengeance in postwar Europe; it is episodic and necessarily selective.

The geographical scope of cases in this book reveals the degree to which postwar revenge was an interplay between local and transnational entities.[19] It considers various dimensions of the locality: how local conditions and relationships before, during, and after the Holocaust determined the fate of Polish Jewish survivors. Most stories are of local, private revenge, such as acts taken against local collaborators, often pre-war acquaintances, in places where survivors had emotional ties. Carrying out these acts of revenge was thus contingent on knowledge of the local geography, and often contacts with local partisans. At the same time, people who are part of this story were also often involved in transnational projects: Communism and Zionism. These permitted the achievement of retribution either through a responsive communist apparatus (particularly in territories that after the war were located within the Soviet Union) or the network of Jewish honour courts. This account is, thus, about physical locations and ways in which they are imagined and re-imagined as spaces of revenge. It is about multiple identities of space and the dynamics of communities in relationship with them.[20]

Groups Targeted for Revenge

The range of conduct that is discussed in this book as revenge was not limited to physical violence. Vengeance took many forms, and was a complex, multi-faceted process.[21] As a result, German perpetrators, groups that most often appear in calls for revenge during the Holocaust, occupy relatively little space in testimonies regarding postwar revenge. Their crimes were often more remote; they often did not come into direct contact with the families of their victims. They were more difficult to identify when encountered on the street or other communal spaces. Retribution against them could, therefore, mainly (if at all) be sought in a court setting and was not possible to achieve for many.

Groups that could be more easily targeted for revenge were local collaborators: mainly Poles, Ukrainians, and Byelorussians. While many of those who survived the Holocaust in hiding did so with the help of the local non-Jewish community, it was also local collaborators who constituted the greatest threat to their survival. Betrayal and death were carried out by neighbours. Historian Mary Fulbrook, who writes about "facilitators and benefactors" of the Holocaust, and scholar Elżbieta Janicka, who discusses "participating observers,"[22] describe people who were directly involved in the Holocaust, playing key roles in the third stage of it, when after liquidation of the ghettos Jews were trying to survive in hiding both in cities and in the countryside. Unlike the experience of German death camps, suffering among non-Jewish locals was shared by all who survived the Holocaust in occupied Poland, including those from the formerly Polish part of Belarus and Ukraine.[23] As one survivor from David-Gorodok in pre-war Poland and now in Belarus recalled: "My hatred towards the locals was no less than my hatred towards the German and Lithuanian murderers who carried out the killings in Vilnius. My hatred of the Germans was general, not aimed at a specific German. But my hatred of the locals, who murdered my family, was personal."[24]

Revenge against them was sought here in many ways: through physical attacks, turning to the state system of justice, or if none were possible, as was often the case, through leaving testimony as evidence of the crimes committed by those individual(s). While most of the cases described will deal with Poles, they take place in historically diverse, profoundly multi-ethnic regions. Thus, they also concern Ukrainians and Byelorussians, in particular the stationary and mobile units of the Ukrainian police, along with the strong Ukrainian nationalist movement.[25]

The third group against whom revenge was sought were other Jews, those considered by their communities to be "collaborators," and by us today more often as people involved in "forced cooperation." Under Jewish religious law these were people who committed the crimes of *meshorah* (informing) by handing other Jews over to foreign authorities.[26] These were mainly those who exercised dominance over other Jews in camps and ghettos: members and co-workers of the Jewish councils, participating in various capacities in the deportation to death camps, and Jewish policemen (members of the Jewish Order Service), who looted or otherwise profited from the misery of others. A separate group consisted of functionary prisoners in concentration and forced labour camps. These positions were different from those in the ghetto, as in some cases they were taken on at the moment of a direct threat to one's life. Many of them remained, and wanted to remain, part of the Jewish community in order to ensure both their personal safety and their emigration prospects. They were thus the easiest to track, and survivors had the largest range of means at their disposal to punish them: from purely symbolic measures such as boycotts and denunciations, to the use of various types of honour and religious courts, and, finally, through allied military courts or Polish state courts. Yet, even within Jewish honour courts in the period under discussion, the term "collaboration" was never defined and depended on individual perception of the accusers, the public, and the jury. The Jewish community, as historian Tuvia Friling wrote, "had no experience in, and no moral and legal categories and language for, considering and judging the actions of people who had participated in an unprecedented mass murder machine."[27]

The definition of "collaboration" was not stable; it kept being revised according to changing attitudes of the community, even within the first postwar years. While every culture tags collaboration as a moral failure, Jewish collaboration during the Holocaust was identified as treason and an offence to national honour, but it also had much more intimate connotations as it related to individuals within a very small group of survivors.

Sources

The first months of liberation were a mosaic of events that were, to a large degree, not officially documented. Thus, this book is primarily based on the memory of victims in the aftermath of the Holocaust.[28] It shows collective and individual narratives, with all their variations in selection, narrativization, repression, displacement, or denial, as well as influence and competition with local and national memories of countries to which Jews had emigrated. Individual memory and collective memory will be differentiated, following Nancy Wood, by assuming that "while the emanation of individual memory is primarily subject to the laws of the unconscious, public memory – whatever its unconscious vicissitudes – testifies to a will or desire on the part of some social group or disposition of power to select and organize representations of the past so that these will be embraced by the individuals as their own."[29]

The majority of individual memories will be taken from the collection of over 7,000 testimonies (almost half of them collected by the end of 1947), gathered first by the *historishe komisye*, then the Central Jewish Historical Commission by the Central Committee of Jews in Poland, and then by its successor, the Jewish Historical Institute and their local branches. The *historishe komisye* was set up in Lublin, on August 29, 1944, five weeks after the entry of the Red Army,[30] with the specific aim of collecting Jewish testimonies of the Holocaust. It was to continue the Eastern European tradition of writing a response to the catastrophe and to help bring justice both to victims and perpetrators by naming the guilty.[31] The testimonies were recorded verbatim, without editing, later read out loud to the person submitting it, and then signed by the person testifying. The accounts were thus considered formally under the law as legal documentation, and only later as a historical source. The guidelines for those collecting testimonies stated clearly: "The lack of original documents – taken away or destroyed by the enemy – should not prevent us from uncovering the entire truth."[32] To achieve this aim, the commission collaborated with the Main Commission for the Investigation of German Crimes, the Ministry of Justice, and the Public Prosecutor's office, and the collected testimonies were also used during the trials of the Nazi perpetrators.[33]

These testimonies were submitted by survivors and written down by other survivors when memories were still fresh, in the face of the growing uncertainty of the Jewish future in Poland, and often just before their authors left the country. In their testimonies survivors often expressed the wish that they wanted their testimony to be preserved before they began the next phase of their lives. The fact that revenge was included in the accounts demonstrates, first, how important it was to those speaking and, second, that it was very much considered part of the experience of the Holocaust.[34]

Ruptures and continuities in collective memory will be reflected in the second group of sources, captured in Memorial Books (Yiddish: *Yizker Bikher*). Rooted historically in the *Memorbucher*, commemorating pogroms as early as the Middle Ages, testimonies were published in the postwar years by *landsmanshaftn* – mutual aid societies of immigrants from the same localities and dedicated to their lost communities.[35] Through landsmanshaft, as Rebecca Korbin noted, "East European Jews sought to remap their regional identities into a transnational terrain by continually drawing and redrawing the boundaries of their distinctive communal identities."[36]

Memorial books were mainly published in Israel, the United States, and Argentina, and written in Hebrew or Yiddish (most commonly in a combination of the two languages); these books spoke of the history of a Jewish community in a certain locality, providing a detailed, usually highly idealized, story of the interwar years. This was followed by history of the locality during the Holocaust, usually composed of survivor testimonies, and finally, which will be a key element in this book, stories of survivors returning to their hometown. An audience of fellow townsmen served as a collective "control mechanism" of the events described.[37]

Memorial books not only shared the same structural framework, but very often similar historical frames of reference, and despite how dispersed communities created them, they were part of the same memory culture. The narratives in memorial books are filled with emotions, both implied and expressed. Revenge, both symbolic and literary, is one of the most pervasive features in these accounts, and even as a symbolic element, revenge was a response to the emotional needs of the community and expressed an emotional state.[38]

Memorial books used revenge to build an image of a Polish Jewish community possessive of agency and shaping their own story. While the Polish Jewish community in postwar Poland was attempting to challenge the antisemitic stereotype of "Jewish revenge," communities abroad in the 1950s and 1960s were fighting the image of Jewish passivity in the face of destruction and in its aftermath. Stories of heroism, of survival, transmitted by memory books could not culminate otherwise than through the act of revenge. In memorial books created by Jewish communities outside Poland, revenge becomes the last act of justice, before leaving Poland as the country of the past. It is the last parting action aimed at the final cutting of ties with their former homeland.

Revenge was simultaneously the first step of the rebuilding of Jewish people. Some memorial books include cases of survivors or their descendants fighting in Israeli-Arab conflicts in the chapters dealing with postwar revenge.[39] The acts of setting up new families and building the state of Israel and the horrors of the atrocities of the Holocaust were balanced with positive stories of the aftermath.[40]

At the time of opening of the United States Holocaust Memorial Museum, Holocaust survivor Elie Wiesel famously remarked in a public address to political figures: "The survivors advocated hope, not despair. Their testimony contains neither rancour nor bitterness. They knew too well that hate is self-abasing and vengeance self-defeating. Instead of choosing nihilism and anarchy, they chose to opt for man."[41] This statement reflects the narrative prevalent in the next group of sources to be used in this book: oral histories submitted in 1990s in the United States, in particularly those collected by the Fortunoff Video Archive for Holocaust Testimonies (or Fortunoff Archive) at Yale University; the United States Holocaust Memorial Museum (USHMM) in Washington, D.C.; and the USC Shoah Foundation (or Shoah Foundation) in Los Angeles.[42]

Oral histories demonstrate not only how the story of revenge is negotiated many years after the event, but also how it is adapted by the interviewer to fit the cultural narrative of the United States as well as by the interviewee to fit the perceived expectations of the postwar American audience. In the vast majority of cases, the expected message of the testimony is the triumph of the human spirit: forgiveness and redemption.

It is often an over-dependence on these later testimonies, and little awareness still of the content of those testimonies submitted immediately after the war, that leads to a widespread belief in the absence of revenge in the Jewish narrative of the Holocaust. While these testimonies gave those speaking an opportunity to express emotions that have remained suppressed for many years, they should always be seen, as Dawn Skorczewski argues, as an "intersubjective field created by institutions, interviewer, and survivor"[43] and suffer from imposing on wartime reality a postwar moral code and the perception of revenge as irrational. In their oral testimonies, survivors often rationalize not taking revenge, seeing the act of being a testifying witness as the most effective method of obtaining justice. An important issue in their analysis is the category of the relevance of postwar violence. One survivor, a fighter in the Warsaw Ghetto Uprising, later a member of the underground revenge group, explained:

> If I could have spoken about it in 1946, 1947 … But today?!! There is no logic to it. What crazy people would have come up with such an idea?

> Such a revenge? Who could understand it?! The world today does not need our story, it is full of terror and violence anyway. Why would I give them more cruel ideas. I see no reason.[44]

Later on he added:

> We did not manage to achieve what we planned. Some things I do truly regret. But I can only be happy that our main action did not work out. I don't know how I could live with it, if it did work out. This was real insanity. Fifty years I looked at it differently.[45]

Thus, revenge undoubtedly goes against redemptive humanism expected of survivors' stories. Violence might not have fitted within the discourse of remembrance and morality.

Official documentation used in this book relates to the work of postwar judicial courts, both Jewish honour courts, which can be considered to be part of the internal Jewish narrative, and state courts. Documentations in court files vary from heavily mediated sources of documentation coming from the Polish state courts to fully independent sources, such as anonymous denunciations.[46] While such official documents are usually considered to be credible sources, as they were carried out under the threat of punishment for false testimony, the historical narration provided by them was to serve a very particular end. One cannot put aside the social and political background of the trial as a weapon of oppression, a method of reaffirming political control, and asserting the legitimacy of the new government through the use of fabricated evidence or forced confessions. Those testifying were often affected by the fear both of the authorities and possible retaliation of the community should they testify against its prominent members; and various types of formal and informal pressure could be applied. Thus, these documents require a nuanced approach, taking into consideration their specific qualities as historical sources. Yet, if approached with methodological caution and sensitivity to the context in which they were created, these normative sources can also open new levels in the history of the postwar search for retribution.

Most importantly, however, all these sources show us the continuity of history. They highlight how postwar revenge was linked not only to wartime, but also to pre-war individual histories and the complexities of human relations. This shows us that it is not only impossible to delineate between wartime and postwar times, but we must also always include the influence of pre-war times. They also reveal the complicated links between the private, the national, and the international, between interiority and sociality, and between conflict and its aftermath.

Historical Veracity

Writing the story of such emotional weight does pose methodological and historiographical challenges. Testimonies quoted in this book leave us with questions. How were wartime fantasies of revenge lived out in real human encounters? To what extent is individual memory the reflection of the dominant discourse of society? To what extent was the narrative of revenge used to create meaning in one's postwar life? As a result of the sources used, this book is to a large extent an undertaking in emotional microhistories. As Yitzhak Zuckerman wrote, describing the emotional landscape of immediate postwar Poland: "Ultimately, revenge was perverse romanticism, which totally unhinged a few people. It was simply a product of constant living with tension, ready for vengeance and killing – and not carrying it out. [...] In sum, there was no revenge. There were words, there was talk that went on for months and filled their whole existence."[47]

Official documents rarely bear traces of individual postwar revenge in rural areas and rarely give voice to non-elite protagonists. Thus, the story will be primarily based on the victims' memory transmitted in testimonies: diaries, letters, eye-witness statements, oral history collections, and memorial books. When analyzing these narratives, we must take into consideration how traumatic events involving revenge are remembered and recounted. Revenge fantasies can be a strong natural reaction to the traumatized survivor's experience of victimization, intertwined with a "human tendency to perceive reality as we construct it in our imagination as the natural compulsion to understand events by creating narratives about them, which then of course can be more or less factually accurate, and intentionally fictional or non-fictional."[48]

This comes across very clearly in memory books, where universal themes and certain patterns that emerge in the narrative reveal the topoi of revenge. Testimonies in memorial books were written and re-written. In many cases they are more than recollections of historical events and resemble literary fiction, with easily recognizable literary tropes, "based on living individual memory of members, which then becomes stylized and even standardized when repeatedly told in communities of remembrance, to solidify into a collective framework which then in turn is reinforced through collective rituals."[49] Acts of revenge, stories of self-empowerment, of achieving a sense of justice, become the focal points of the postwar stories and could often be exaggerated to meet the discourse expected from them.[50] As Monika Admczyk-Garbowska and Adam Kopciowski note, even in wartime stories in memorial books of resistance they "are presented in an exalted and somewhat inflated manner, and the participants are often pictured as indomitable and impeccable heroes."[51] It often remains difficult to establish to what extent individual memories of survivors were already shaped at that point through interactions with other survivors and to what extent they reflect the discourse of the community, rather than their own experiences. Consequently, the immediate postwar years should be seen as a continuation of the war, with the postwar history interpreted and nurtured in a way that we usually associate with wartime memory. Acknowledging this fact does not mean renouncing the validity of such testimonies.

Further subtleties are lost in translations from Polish, Yiddish, and Hebrew: the languages of the first testimonies of Polish-Jewish Holocaust survivors, and even more so in the later testimonies delivered in English.[52] This specific attribute of speaking in English, when it comes to a sensitive topic, was already noted by the pioneer of collecting oral histories among Holocaust survivors. David Boder carried out a series of interviews with displaced Holocaust survivors in 1946. He wrote how, during one of his interviews, a female Polish Jewish survivor provided an account in English of her life during the Holocaust. In the last words of her interview she suddenly switched to Polish and called all the Jews to "hate the Germans because of the wrongs that they did to us and our families, because they broke our hearts, broke our homes, and we ought never to forget that."[53] In this and other cases, messages aimed at the "Jewish audience" are better conveyed in the language of the community.

Today we are in no position to check the veracity of the details described in testimonies from 1946 or 1947. Most of these events left no trace in the archival sources available to us. Emotional reactions cannot be proved in historical terms. Yet, these testimonies are extremely valuable when it comes to assessing collective fears, values, and moral standards as well as the construction of a narrative when considering revenge. Therefore, instead of using them uniquely to establish facts, a more effective approach would be to employ a means of ethnography to analyze them, looking at them "above all, through the prism of their autonomous value, seeking testimonies of collective conceptions – fears, aspirations, dreams, phantasms, stereotypical reactions, and standards."[54]

1 "He Wept and We Didn't": Liberation, Revenge, and a Survivor's Return

Revenge Imagined

In 1944 a teenage Jewish boy hiding in Mińsk Mazowiecki near Warsaw wrote in his diary: "I promised myself that if I will ever be able to carry out revenge I will have no mercy, and, as in the past I couldn't stand the sight of blood, I will murder in cold blood, butcher without pardon."[1] Years later, another Holocaust survivor, a woman coming from a Hasidic family, recalled the time she spent in the Auschwitz-Birkenau concentration and extermination camp:

> The thoughts that we had and the ideas that we fed ourselves were sickening. What we were going to do to the Germans because of what we lived through. We're going to cut them – you've got to live to take revenge. And that's what made us go on and made us live. And we said we're going to cut them into pieces. We're going put salt on them. We're going to tie them to two horses and let the horses run, the most horrible, horrible things that could come to a mind, we fed ourselves with hatred, and that made us go.[2]

Diaries, letters, and notes written during the Holocaust show the extent to which revenge was in the minds of men and women in camps, ghettos, and in hiding, the only answer to what had befallen them. Yet, for most of the Holocaust victims, revenge had to remain imagined. Increasing physical exhaustion, lack of access to weapons, fear of retributory actions against the whole community, lack of clarity regarding Germans plans, and planned German policies of disinformation – all of these meant that physical revenge could not be carried out. Still, revenge, most often very abstract, against groups rather than individuals, helped them to cope and, paradoxically, gave them hope. One survivor explained: "So, we started thinking about uprising and about revenge, and I think that kept us going, although it was a senseless thought, but, you know, that gave us the courage to survive, to do, because we planned, we planned. The plans weren't worth it, maybe in the beginning, five cents, but we planned and we saw ourselves outside, and we saw all the Nazis killed and this kept us going."[3] The founder of the Underground Archive of the Warsaw Ghetto, Emanuel Ringelblum, noted that people trapped in the hell of the Warsaw Ghetto began reading books on the First World War and the fall of Germany, and thus were seeking revenge "in fantasy, in literature."[4]

For a few young Jewish fighters, revenge materialized in the 1943 Warsaw Ghetto Uprising. Satisfying the widespread desire for revenge was the Jewish underground's best way to establish itself in the ghetto's collective consciousness.[5] Next to the image of "restoring Jewish honour," revenge was the key force considered to be the motivation for Warsaw insurgents. Some of them saw these two concepts as synonymous: "We had only one slogan in common: revenge – to save Jewish honour, the honour of the Jewish nation. And with this we went into battle.[6] One of the fighters recalled that he purposefully stayed on the streets before the uprising, to watch German crimes, so that he could "hate strongly enough."[7] Revenge was also part of the postwar narrative of the uprising, with fighters described immediately after the war as motivated by the drive to avenge: "as one draws water from a deep well – the feeling of revenge against the Germans. Each day and each hour, and each minute and each second awake and asleep – REVENGE."[8] In this case, we can claim revenge was not only about getting even, but it became part of the partisans identity as "new" Jews, with seeking revenge considered as the opposite to passively going to one's death.[9] As historian Anita Shapira noted, the Warsaw Ghetto Uprising turned from a symbol of destruction to one of revival and resurgence, a link in the chain of age-old Jewish heroism "to avenge the blood of Israel, the establishment of the Jewish homeland, and to rebuild Masada."[10] The struggle, the Warsaw Ghetto Uprising, became part of the narrative of Jewish self-assertion through revenge and part of the ideological grounds for postwar acts of revenge.

Revenge became more than just abstract plans for the substantial group of individuals who managed to join partisan groups, consisting mainly of Jews located in the Eastern Polish borderlands. In the war, the forest, in what Timothy Snyder termed the "bloodlands," became a hiding place for many. They went to the forest to engage in resistance or to secure their survival, often both.[11] As Evgeny Finkel noted: "People who had been active in the underground often cited the desire to avenge the destruction of their family, friends, and the Jewish community as their reason for joining the partisans; people who were not involved in the ghetto underground often referenced revenge as a factor in their narratives only after they joined the partisans. For them, survival and evasion were the key motivators; the desire for revenge, even if important, arose only later, when an opportunity to exact it unexpectedly became a reality."[12]

Some of them acted independently, others formed a coherent partisan movement under the Soviet leadership.[13] Some, often under non-Jewish identities, joined Polish partisan units.[14] Among those who achieved revenge during the war were also those who remained in the so-called family camps: groups of a few families hiding together, with men, usually armed, providing the food. The most famous example was a group called *Nekamah* [Revenge] principally affiliated with the Jewish underground movement in Vilna, a separate Jewish armed partisan detachment of the Soviet *Voroshilov* brigade based in the Naroch Forest. By September 1943, when it was disbanded, 250 Jewish men and women were members of Nekamah.

All those who went into the forest faced considerable danger. There were cases of Jewish newcomers shot as alleged German spies,[15] while women and girls were additionally at constant risk of sexual violence.[16] For many reasons, including antisemitism, not all Soviet partisan units were happy to take in Jews, especially as they were often unarmed, and groups of escapees from a ghetto endangered the whole unit. Older people, women, and children had particularly little chance of joining a partisan group. They did not serve as fighters but nonetheless had to be clothed and fed.[17] There was also fear that Jewish partisans, looking for revenge on those who harmed their families, could worsen the already fragile relationships between the Soviet partisans and local population.[18] In occupied Poland the relationships between Polish partisans and villages were complex, ranging from open hostility to villages becoming bases of support. Partisans under Soviet leadership did not have the widespread support of the local population. Joining partisan units was far from straightforward and was often a combination of good contacts with the underground, as well as luck and personal circumstances allowing individuals or groups entry to the forest.

In comparison to those in town or village, those hiding in the forest were in a better position in their search for justice and revenge throughout the war. Thus, as Abba Kovner, himself a commander of a fighting Jewish unit in the Lithuanian-Soviet partisan organization, put it, it was the partisans' right to fight and to decide their own fate.[19] Part of this right was revenge. Being in a partisan group gave one access to weapons as well as training in how to use them. This was important, as it applied to both men and women. As one former partisan recalled:

"Everyone received a gun, bullets, and three grenades. We now felt the time had come for revenge and to punish those who wanted to murder us."[20] Resistance groups had the means to carry out this revenge but also gave their members a feeling of security, alleviating their feelings of weakness and helplessness, giving them confidence to take group or individual action – sometimes planned, sometimes spontaneous. It also gave them a group support setting, which could reinforce their conviction of the need for revenge.[21]

This was particularly pertinent when it came to Jews who joined the Soviet partisan groups, who were actively pursuing those considered collaborators, often shooting them together with their families.[22] According to one former partisan: "Those who reached the forest were accepted as full-fledged members; they therefore asked to be involved in any action. The desire for revenge blinded them and dulled their senses, and they went out on dangerous missions. There was real commitment among them. The Jews were among the first who volunteered, and for the most part also the initiators."[23] Another recalled: "And I, what was I feeling? I had no feelings; I did not cry and did not say anything. My heart turned to stone. In my soul the fire of revenge burned without ceasing. Then I reached the decision: only by joining the partisans would I be able to get revenge."[24] The revenge actions carried by partisan units were mainly aimed at local police forces (*Schutzmannschaften* and *Ordnungspolizei*) involved in the expropriation and killing of the local Jewish population as well as in anti-partisan operations. Therefore, actions against local police forces were also supported by unit leaders.

While it can be questioned whether or to what extent actions taken when carrying out orders can be individual acts of revenge, there is no doubt that this was the aim of many Jewish partisans, with some openly disobeying their leaders' orders. One such story was told by a survivor, who described his actions as part of the partisan unit from Vilnius ghetto:

> When our regiment was near Glinna, I looked for Simon Slavuk who had denounced Shimon Gendelman and Freger. I did this on my own. I knew that I might have to pay for it later because partisans cannot perform any operations without their commander's permission. There was a gypsy woman in Glinna who knew where this murderer was living, and she took me there. I told him that the commander of the partisans was asking for him. He did not recognize me and took the announcement at face value. On the way he started talking to me. He said: "I obey every authority. When the Germans made me kill Jews, I did it. Now I am called to the partisans, and I am going to them!" My blood boiled when I heard these words. I could not control myself and I shot him with my pistol. I used 30 bullets.

In his story, instead of being punished by the commander, he is commended for his deed and told that he should have killed the collaborator in front of other partisans. When shortly after, he encounters a Ukrainian policemen involved in killing Jews, he indeed brings him to the regiment so that others can witness the killing.[25] Another Jewish partisan described coming across a local house full of looted Jewish property: "After taking the things and beating them, we broke their arms and teeth. We had no permission to shoot them without a verdict from the specialized department. We left feeling we had avenged our people a bit."[26] Later on in his story, the author described killing two others who participated in the murder of Jews from the local ghetto, even though the area was under the control of another partisan group, and they were forbidden to do so. These, however, were rare exceptions. Again, the vast majority of Holocaust victims had no opportunity to take revenge.

In November 1942, just after almost 300,000 Warsaw Jews were murdered in Treblinka in the first deportation action, Jechiel Górny wrote in his diary: "'The hour of revenge' will come after the war. People greet each other with the wish that it might all end quickly, so that the few surviving Jews might live long enough to see the end of the plague of Hitlerism and to take revenge."[27] The need for revenge, so clearly expressed in the writings from camps and ghettos, depicted in songs and poems, screamed out at the concentration camps executions and scratched on prison walls, did not die out on the day of liberation.

Revenge on Liberation

"I realized that I am liberated; because you feel … you know, you don't really know. There is nobody to tell you what to do," stated one of the forced labourers liberated in Germany, in an interview conducted many years after the war, talking about the misty, unclear period of the first months and years after the war.[28] As historian Yaacov Lozowick noted, the story of the liberation is not a good ending to a bad story; it is a harsh story in its own right.[29] One of the most difficult parts of dealing with this "after," this brief period of time when there was nobody to tell anybody what to do,[30] was that of attempting to reconcile with what happened by searching for closure.

The first wave, most readily associated with the "era of revenge" took place where the crimes were committed: concentration and forced labour camps and death marches. They were preceded by armed actions by the Jewish underground in the ghettos and then the wave of vigilante justice taking place in camps just before and immediately after the liberation. These descriptions of attacks on Jewish policemen, prisoner functionaries, and other victims of privilege, carried out with various degrees of brutality, are not difficult to come by in narratives relating to the last remaining days of camp existence,[31] camp liberation, and final days of the death marches. As one of the camp survivors recalled: "[the revenge happened] before the Americans came. And afterwards too. Nobody cared. Nobody cared in those days."[32] As Tony Judt notes regarding 1945–8: "Most of the acts of retributive punishment which took place in this period happened before the countries in question had been liberated, or else at the very moment of that liberation, as German authority lapsed, and new powers had yet to be installed. Of the approximately 10,000 summary executions in France which marked the transition from Vichy to the Fourth Republic, about a third were carried out before D-Day and a further 50 per cent during the battles of the following weeks."[33] This normalization of violence at that point was described by another female survivor, who spoke about an attack on a German prisoner functionary, while other prisoners were eating a meal after being liberated during a death march:

> SURVIVOR: And on the [death] march, as I understand, he was horrible. So, a few men got together and lynched him in the middle of eating that soup. It didn't bother us one bit.
> INTERVIEWER: And then what happened?
> SURVIVOR: What happened? Nothing. They took him on a wheelbarrow and wheeled out the pieces. That's it.[34]

Even though liberation was expected, its moment was sudden. Survivors' actions on liberation were unplanned and mixed with extremely strong emotions. One former camp prisoner recalled stumbling on leaving the camp on a body of a camp guard:

> Looking at him I began to laugh very loudly; this laughter soon turns to crying … Yes this is revenge for our brothers and parents whom you murdered for all, all victims …
>
> For the millions of Polish Jews, for the crematoria hissing loudly and begged for mercy to be turned down, for those innocent Jewish talents which disappeared from the face of the earth, for that soap which you made from human fat.[35]

Revenge was aimed at all three groups of perpetrators and their helpers: Polish fellow prisoners and prisoner functionaries, Jewish prisoner functionaries, and German perpetrators and civilians. Survivors took revenge on their own, but in most cases as part of a group, joining both other Jews as well as other non-Jewish prisoners and sometimes soldiers from the allied armies.[36] Their actions were aimed at those perpetrators who were still within reach – that is, mainly prisoner functionaries, after the German guards have fled, and, to a lesser degree, at the local civilian population.

Revenge during liberation seems much more straightforward and morally much less questionable than the more premeditated revenge carried out later. Survivors, whether testifying immediately after the war or many years later saw it as natural part of the violence surrounding liberation. Yet, despite the perception of Eastern Europeans who had been liberated from camps as being filled with the need for vengeance, their participation in revenge action on the German population was, above all, noticeable by its scarcity. Lack of revenge against civilians demonstrates to what extent this was personal, aimed at specific perpetrators (usually prisoner functionaries) rather than an anonymous group. In this sense, postwar revenge was very different from the planned wartime revenge.

If survivors do speak of carrying out revenge, it is usually through the plundering of surrounding German towns and villages. One survivor, 16 years old at the moment of liberation, described how, together with other prisoners, "we would literarily break out of that camp and literally, while running, kill those one would come across [...] there were no conversations, no questions, whoever was on the road was an enemy. You would run into an apartment, break everything, like some wild people. One would hit the mirrors, some glasses, just to break as much as possible."[37] Another recalled: "We were plundering the villas and the farms, full of rage, where people were living like kings on all the goods they had stolen after torturing and starving all the countries they devastated. In their station houses, we found piles of military equipment; they had prepared everything to subject the world to their doctrine."[38]

The best-known work dealing with the revenge of liberated prisoners, Elie Wiesel's *Night*, the first version of which, *Un di velt hot geshvign* [And the World Stayed Silent], was written in 1955,[39] depicts scenes of night-time raids, which include also rape by Buchenwald survivors on neighbouring German settlements. Fantasies of rape as a way of exacting revenge on the Germans were not only limited to Allied soldiers.[40]

Yet, while rape as a weapon of revenge was omnipresent in postwar Germany, Jewish survivors did not leave testimony of participating in it, even if they trivialized it in their testimonies and saw it as fitting revenge, excusable in view of the atrocities perpetrated by the Germans, especially those enacted against Jewish women and children. One survivor recalled how

> a drunken Russian soldier raped a young German girl in full view of everyone. No one raised a hand to help her; there was no sound but her screams. So much for the Master Race, who, in Auschwitz, I had watched slam the head of a Jewish baby into the wall of a shower room. The baby had died instantly, his brain protruding and his blood spurting; they had laughed, full of triumph and swagger. Now they were too meek even to protect one of their own children. Nor did I intervene; these were people who had set me apart, told me I could not be one of them.[41]

Another survivor, a Polish Jew from Ostrowiec, liberated as a teenager in Theresienstadt, showed the moral hierarchy of revenge and normalization of rape as a weapon of revenge, when he explained:

> Once the Russians came to me because I was in charge of the German women. They asked me to let them in, and do to their women what they did to ours. I turned my back, and didn't want to see what was happening. I walked away and let them go in. They did what they wanted and it didn't bother me. I couldn't kill them. The Russians gave me a gun and told me to go kill some and feel better. I aimed but couldn't shoot.[42]

The majority of survivors speak only of witnessing revenge, often providing very graphic details of how it was carried out, but not participating in it due to sheer exhaustion and weariness, incapable of any form of physical exertion.[43] A young Polish Jewish female survivor liberated by the Red Army in Lichtewerden, in Czech Silesia, explained it simply: "The Russians entered, and we were in such a condition that no one moved, no one went out. We did not laugh, we were not happy, we were apathetic – and the Russians came. A general came in, he was Jewish. He told us that he was delighted, as this was the first camp in which he had found people still alive. He started to cry; but we didn't. He wept and we didn't."[44]

Despite obvious reasons for not taking revenge, survivors still clearly internalized the narrative of revenge as a duty (especially for men) and felt the need to explain why they did not partake in it. Later oral history interviews often underlined not seeking revenge as a specific "Jewish" quality, explained as a demonstration of strength rather than weakness. This image of Jews as not carrying out revenge was to a large degree the product of the stereotype of Jews as people who abhorred violence. This was also linked to the spirit of Judaism and forgiveness, which contrasted with an image of bloodthirsty non-Jewish Eastern Europeans and their tendency towards violence.[45] One of them, a man, liberated in his early twenties, said: "At first, we thought we could [take] revenge, but we could not do it. The Russians and the Poles tried to avenge. They got a cruel German foreman. They took a tank chain, put it around his head and they made him run until he died. That was the first and last revenge act I saw. I was a free man."[46] Another one claimed: "It's just that after living through the war, and I said to myself and my brother, too, that we lived only to take revenge and avenge. Yet when the time came, we were pussycats. We were just – I – I – I witnessed where some Russian prisoners have just taken – they said they knew the German. And they have just laid him down, tied him up, and they just took a – a regular saw and were just slicing him into pieces, working on him. Well, I – I couldn't do this."[47]

The fact that others took revenge may be of course explained by the fact that liberated concentration camps usually included Jewish prisoners, who reached them only in the last weeks before the liberation, following gruelling death marches. Non-Jewish prisoners who spent longer time in camps and were in better physical condition had more reasons to take revenge on guards and prisoner functionaries, who they were more familiar with.

While survivors saw acts of revenge as morally justified and in general described indifference towards the sight of the victims' suffering, the act of revenge was still traumatizing, even to those who had endured the horrors of life in concentration camps. Some survivors speak of their repulsion at the sight of guards or functionaries being tortured to death:

> They caught that guy, and he was hanged upside down. I won't go into details. And they called everybody that we should watch the execution.
>
> [Pauses for three seconds]
>
> And I had to go. Actually, I went willingly, you know.
>
> [Pauses for three seconds]
>
> And when I saw that scene, which was nothing compared to what I saw before, all of a sudden I started to throw up. I got physically sick. I looked at the mob, and I felt they, they remind me from French history, you know, like those twitches, you know, during hanging. And I started to throw up.[48]

Joining the Red Army

Not all Jewish survivors were completely powerless at liberation. At the other end of the spectrum were those who could fight: those who arrived in Poland as members of the Red Army or the First Polish Army, an army unit of the Polish Armed Forces in the East, formed in the Soviet Union.[49] The idea of "vengeful Jews" who had already joined the Red Army during the war became the staple of the antisemitic narrative in Eastern Europe. The Polish underground during the war warned of "millions of mostly young Jews [who] will come out of hiding, from ghettos, from the forests, and will return with the Soviet army when it approaches our borders. Jews will emerge at the critical moment, wreaking vengeance on us, trying to deprive us of the fruits of victory."[50] This fear materialized and was intensified by existing antisemitic myths and slogans, with the notion of Jewish Bolshevism and the rhetoric of an "existential Jewish threat"[51] predating the entrance of the Red Army into Poland and a central feature of political life already established in the interwar period.[52]

Writing in 1947, Jewish journalist Jakub Egit described the entry of the Red Army in Poland as the *Yom HaDin* (The Day of Reckoning), when the liberated survivors could finally take their revenge.[53] While some of them joined the Red Army during the war, many survivors recalled approaching the Red Army immediately after their liberation and requested to be enlisted. Thus, in their testimonies the Red Army appears not only as a liberating force, but also as an opportunity to finally take up arms. One female survivor, who survived in the Soviet Union, joined the army as a nurse immediately after returning to her hometown, once she learned about the circumstances of her father's death. She wrote:

> I remained seated and saw before my eyes my dear father in a pool of blood with torn out pieces of flesh and with the blood still dripping. His soul expires with the last drops of blood, and I hear his final words; "Rachel! Take revenge for my blood."
>
> For a long time after that, I wandered around the harvested fields and thought about what to do and to whom to turn. Suddenly and idea came to me: You have nothing more to do in Radzyn! Go to the front line and take revenge for your father's spilled blood and for the blood of all the Jews![54]

Similarly, one of the first testimonies submitted to the Central Jewish Historical Commission ends with a scene in which a survivor describes how once men from his partisan group enlisted into the Red Army, he went to the graves of his parents, murdered in the Holocaust, to tell them that their blood will now be avenged.[55]

For Jews who joined the Red Army, revenge on Germans was always considered to be a reason for their decision. One of them explained:

"In April 1942, when all the youngsters volunteered to help the men in the war for the country and for human pride, I joined them and was drafted into the Red Army in order to revenge our fathers, mothers, sisters, brothers, our innocent children, and all the people that were murdered by the Nazi animals."[56] Another one admitted that "I did not display any particular heroism, but I took revenge wherever I could. I saw it as my holy duty for those murdered, and for the Jewish people."[57] This was not a uniquely Jewish phenomenon. During the war the Red Army was an agent for revenge, revenge also for non-Jews. As no religious martyrdom was admissible, the motive for revenge became a key part of the framework of Soviet ideology.[58] It was also an answer to the personal experiences of the soldiers and their emotional needs.[59] While many survivors wrote extensively about the satisfaction they felt when witnessing revenge carried out by Soviet soldiers,[60] their own acts of revenge done in the name of collective responsibility against German civilians, seen as representatives of their nations rather than for crimes committed by them individually, is rarely described in detail. It is usually vague. Detailed descriptions are those of revenge not taken, a decision often made when faced with the humanity of individual Germans, in particular children.

Yet, there were many cases to the contrary. These included sending Jews encountered during the liberation of Poland to penal military camps, or forcibly enlisting people recognized as Jews, as well as individual soldiers acting against Jews singled out for plunder and violence. One official Polish government report from Przemyśl notes numerous instances of the plunder of valuables during raids on houses and forcing local Jewish inhabitants to provide soldiers with food and alcohol. As stated in December 1944: "Because of these occurring situations, the mood among the Jewish population is very restless and tense; Jewish men with Semitic appearances were fearful of leaving their homes, even though they were exempted from mobilization. There were cases of documents [proving exemption] destroyed by Red Army soldiers."[61] In the worst situations, individual Red Army soldiers assisted those who committed crimes involving Jews, including those who participated in train sabotage attacks.[62] Yet, it remained the only hope for revenge. One of those who chose to stay in the army after liberation explained:

> Lublin had been taken by the Russian forces and I arrived in Włodawa, a town near Lublin, with my division. From time to time, I traveled to Lublin, where the headquarters of the Polish military was located. One fine day as I was walking along the main street, I encountered a familiar face. I ran closer and recognized my cousin David Senderowicz. We kissed each

other with joy and wept as we recalled our near death. "Avraham," my cousin said to me, "Take off your uniform and let us escape to Romania, and from there to the Land of Israel." "No," I responded, "my conscience does not permit me to desert the military. I owe a debt to those who had been murdered: Revenge!"[63]

Return to Poland

An estimated 50,000 Polish Jewish survivors were liberated prisoners from concentration and forced labour camps located in occupied Poland, Germany, or Austria. They were, however, not the largest group of surviving Polish Jews. It is estimated that 30,000 to 60,000 survived in hiding. Some of them fled the ghettos or deportations, others were in hiding throughout the duration of the war.[64] Others – some 140,000 – returned as part of the Soviet Union repatriation plan, which ended in 1946.[65] This group consisted of various subcategories: those who had been deported by the Soviet regime from the parts of eastern Poland that Moscow annexed in 1939; those who left the occupied zone in search of jobs in the East; Soviet army conscripts; and those who had fled in the wake of the Blitzkrieg on Soviet Russia in 1941. From 1944 to 1946, most of them migrated to Poland's new borders. Several thousand came back as soldiers in the communist-led Polish army in 1944. Approximately 55,000 Jews resettled under population-exchange agreements between the new Polish government and the Soviet republics of Lithuania, Belarus, and Ukraine.

Not all Polish Jews returned. Some spent some time in Poland, but never set foot in their pre-war hometowns. Some, liberated abroad, never went back to Poland. There were also those Jews, mainly survivors in the Soviet Union and as parts of partisans groups, for whom repatriation to post-1945 Poland was not a return home. These were Jewish inhabitants of the so-called Kresy, the eastern borderlands of Poland, which, with the outbreak of the Second World War, came under Soviet control and whose homes remained after the change of borders in the Soviet territory. Many of them returned temporarily after the war to their town or villages.[66] The majority later left for Poland, and then abroad. Some stayed, either because they supported communism and saw the Soviet Army as their liberator or feared antisemitism in Poland or because they simply wanted to re-build their lives where they had always lived.[67]

Postwar Poland was a country on the move.[68] Ethnic Poles from areas east of the River Bug were moving to postwar Polish borders; Germans were being resettled from the so-called Recovered Territories; Ukrainians and Byelorussians were leaving Poland to go East; Poles were returning from concentration camps, forced labour camps, and army units abroad; people were moving from the countryside to the city; and Jewish survivors were returning to their prewar homes, both on their own and as repatriates and then leaving again.[69] In all cases the journeys were arduous and dangerous.

Wherever they were liberated, returning Polish Jews found themselves in the middle of a civil war, the aftermath of a multi-dimensional conflict involving the Soviets and Germans, their accomplices, and local representatives, as well as different nationalist partisans and quasi-partisan groups. With the political and the social chaos of the new powers that were being installed, no peaceful rebuilding of lives could be guaranteed. The area of pre-war Poland was riven by inter-ethnic violence, partisan warfare, and violent crimes. Another layer of uncertainty was added for Polish citizens liberated in the area annexed by the Soviet Union, a no-man's land between the new government and the guerrillas. Some of them were ready to be repatriated immediately, others still considered rebuilding their lives in their hometowns. Natalia Aleksiun wrote about "the period of uncertainty, insecurity, frustration, mourning and daily routines that came after the death of the shtetl."[70] A survivor recalling his return to the town of Navahrudak (Polish: Nowogródek) described it as "a nightmare of thought, a vortex of memories and one did not remember that in the end the enemy was defeated. The world of the enemies survived, but ours vanished forever."[71]

Emotions of individuals were expressed in specific spaces. These were what Andreas Reckwitz referred to as "affective spaces."[72] "Emotionally heightened spaces" were those directly linked to the crimes committed during the Holocaust or those with large concentrations of Holocaust survivors. They range from busy streets in Tel Aviv and Munich to the *lieux d'oubli*, avoided by public memory. Distinct spatial settings awoke different kinds of emotions, but these were also (and maybe more importantly) spaces that offered various practical ways of dealing with the past. In each of these spaces Polish Jews had different capacities for action. It was shaped by both external circumstances and their own willingness and physical ability to act. Thus, following Christopher Browning, we can differentiate between various post-Holocaust "landscapes," limiting people differently and allowing for different choices.[73] Some spatial arrangements facilitated physical revenge and revenge through retribution (most often by allowing the use of physical force or access to responsive security apparatus), while others hindered it. As will be made clear, while some such spaces were universal, where emotions were collectively constructed and sustained, each survivor additionally had his or her "unique personal geographies" of revenge.

At that point, at every centre of Holocaust survivors' "personal geographies of revenge" were rural areas, which, during the war, turned into sites of collective crimes against the hiding of Jews. Jews were killed by local inhabitants acting on their own as well as by those acting under German authority and handed over to the German-supervised Polish Blue Police or German gendarmerie. As numerous studies have now shown, this was an effort that included entire collectives. As Andrew Kornbluth wrote: "The extermination of those who remained in hiding had a solidarizing effect on several levels. Jewish property was redistributed, villages were ethnically cleansed, and the guilt was apportioned among the numerous participants. The effect of witnessing, joining in, and benefiting from the death of Jews who had escaped the major deportations continued to resonate after the war, when the phenomenon of communities closing ranks proved critical in the legal defense of the accused."[74]

Violence continued after the war, and it was omnipresent[75] – as in Johan Huizinga's seminal work on the "violent tenor of life" in the late Middle Ages, when "violence and emotions formed a reflexive relationship, in which strongly experienced (and typically negative) emotions led to violence, which forged in turn intense affective responses.[76] This "violent tenor of life," with its intensity and immediacy, was also part of the emotional landscape of postwar Poland. There was no stability that would give individuals a reasonable vision of a stable future, especially as the new era into which the country was transitioning remained unclear; and it was uncertain how much longer this hazardous situation would last.

In the chaos of immediate postwar violence, Jews returning home became a target, both for organized groups, especially partisan units, and individuals, with murderers distinguishing between Jews and non-Jews when committing their crimes.[77] Just in March 1945, a month before the war officially ended, 108 Jews were murdered in attacks in liberated Polish lands.[78] The violence also took the shape of hostile slogans written on walls and on posters, calling for pogroms; stones were thrown through the windows of private apartments and Jewish institutions; anonymous letters were sent, with death threats; and various other attacks were made both in private and public spaces. These happened both in large cities and small towns.[79]

The impunity with which these crimes were committed was linked to the weakness of the system of justice, in particular to a lack of control exercised by the central authorities over the lower echelons of power. Thus, the fear expressed in testimonies was much more than just an abstract, post-conflict anxiety, it was very much a part of everyday, personal experience and had immense influence on the everyday life of the wider population. Postwar anti-Jewish violence and its widespread acceptance in the community, went beyond simply postwar criminality. Jews were defined in popular consciousness as alien in postwar Poland. As some researchers claim, this period witnessed the internalization of virulent and incessant wartime antisemitic propaganda; recurring patterns of wartime behaviour towards the Jews and thus killing a Jew was not considered by the wider community to be murder.[80] The scale of postwar violence, taking place in the immediate aftermath of the war, fully backs up this assertion, especially as these anti-Jewish feelings encountered the circumstances in Poland: lack of control by the security apparatus, easy access to arms, and societal chaos. This resulted in violent attacks on those returning home and attempting to reclaim their property, attacks on Jewish orphanages or random attacks and murders on the trains (the so-called train actions) and on the roads. Groups of returning Jews were almost completely devoid of any security and became targets of both armed underground groups and individuals, in particular those who saw them as a source of possible income. Testimonies tell us of Jews murdered at the moment of their return: in their own homes, in the front yards of their houses,[81] in beds, when staying overnight with their neighbours.[82] Very commonly, they were murdered when attempting to retrieve their belongings or those belonging to their murdered family members, as historian Alina Skibińska writes, "the only remaining links between Jews and their former homelands and neighbours."[83] Antisemitic violence culminated in three pogroms: the first on June 14 and 15, 1945, in Rzeszów; the second on August 11, 1945, in Kraków; and the third and bloodiest, with 42 victims, on July 4, 1946, in Kielce. But violence occurred almost everywhere where survivors of the Holocaust were present.

Postwar violence did not come out of the void. It was a direct continuation of what happened before and during the war: in the pre-war antisemitic economic and physical violence, in the rhetoric of Jews being a "problem" that "needs to be solved,"[84] and in the widely acquiescent spread of the persecution and murder of Jews during the war. An additional factor was the combat against so-called Judeo-Communism and the need to "cleanse" Poland by either killing Jews or forcing them to emigrate.[85] This was accompanied by pre-war antisemitism, including the still widely held belief in blood libel (in all its varieties, including a popular rumour of the use of Christian children's blood to provide transfusions for weak survivors).

However, the vast majority of killings were devoid of any political objectives; very few of those killed were in any way linked to the new system. Most were ordinary people. As Joanna Tokarska-Bakir noted regarding pogroms in postwar Poland, "Although it declares itself against the Judeo Communism, the crowd – be it in Kielce, Rzeszów, or Kraków – for the most part refrains from crossing the line and instigating a real anti-communist guerrilla conflict. The primary objects of assault are the Jews.[86] The cry of "Jewish revenge" was ever-present during postwar pogroms, used as a way to counterbalance the sense of guilt relating to the local collaboration in the implementation of the Holocaust and justification for violence against Jews.[87] An important part of this concept was that of Jewish "posthumous revenge," on families of those who had harmed them, particularly present in rural communities.[88] A postwar Jewish visitor to Czyżew, in central Poland, noted down the following story told him by non-Jewish inhabitants of the village, speaking of "posthumous revenge," of murdered Jews on the local perpetrator:

> The old woman stood up moaning and spoke with interrupted words: "All of the misfortunes come to us because ... Ragajczyk's two children froze. The wind opened the windows at night. In the morning they were pieces of ice. The hand of God. He [Ragajczyk] had shown the Germans the bunker in which Jews were hiding in the forest. She left murmuring something with her face to the ground, as if she wanted to ask for forgiveness for the crimes about which she knew much more than she spoke."

She later enters a former Jewish house, whose inhabitant tells her:

> There is an epidemic every year or another misfortune. Kazimierczak mutilated his hand with an unusual nail and it had to be amputated. Is this not a punishment from God? He had stolen a little in the ghetto. Kazimierczak's bull went insane and trampled his daughter ... Who knows how many more misfortunes await us. The horseshoes, which we have placed over our thresholds, do not help. There are angry spirits in the *shtetl* that want to take revenge.[89]

This belief was strongly based in Catholicism, the concept of a vengeful Jewish God and the Old Testament concept of "an eye for an eye, a tooth for a tooth," as opposed to the Christian principles of forgiveness and turning the other cheek.

In response, Polish Jews began organizing armed self-defense units.[90] Unlike communal self-defense organized before the war against antisemitic violence,[91] these units were officially recognized and organized by the Special Commission by the Central Committee of Jews in Poland as well as grass-root initiatives. These were set up by the staff of orphanages, sanatoriums, dormitories, and apartment blocks housing larger groups of survivors and included guards placed at particularly vulnerable train lines.[92] Their members either had wartime experience in the use of arms or were trained on joining the units.[93] "More than once we have suffered armed attacks and pogroms of Jews, but our answer was always armed resistance against the enemy. This is how it was in tsarists times, this is how it was in the II Republic, not to mention the heroic struggle against the German thugs during the occupation. 'Are we to act differently this time?' stated a member of Bund during the party meeting of around 500 workers in Wałbrzych in August 1946."[94]

So, even if we look only at a few cases in the environs of Łódź, the most populous Jewish city in immediate postwar Poland, the Jewish community of Pabianice, in 1946 inhabited by 230 Jews, set up a defense unit of 28 (armed with one illegally acquired pistol). A smaller community of Tomaszów Mazowiecki, numbering 110 Jews, organized a self-defense unit of 10, though not armed. Fifteen Jews living in a small town of Żychlin had a defense unit consisting of seven men (out of the eight male Jews in the community). A group of 40 Jews living in Aleksandrów did not have an organized defense, but just in case defense was needed, acquired two illegal pistols. A community of 35 in Koło acquired three pistols, while the 37-strong community of Jews in Radomsko owned eight pistols for the needs of self-defense.[95] In larger cities the situation was much more serious. In Kraków at the end of 1946, self-defense units were armed with 76 assault rifles, 17 automatic weapons, 12 grenades, and 15 revolvers.[96]

In immediate postwar Poland, as during the war, it was the individual and not the state who became the agent of punishment. Thus, in the absence of a system of justice, revenge often became the only way to obtain satisfaction for crimes committed against the Jewish population.

Return to the Village

Despite the dangers they were facing, people still returned to their former homes. Many went in the hope of retrieving property they had left behind, others purposefully to the site of criminal acts against them, sometimes in an attempt to find the fate of those who were in hiding there, and sometimes to locate those who had abused or been involved in the murder or deportation of their family members. Arriving in the town or village, they often realized that the fate of those who had been murdered was public knowledge and that in order to find out what had taken place they had to confront their pre-war neighbours.

Violence had been committed not by anonymous individuals but often by people they had known all their lives. This was, truly, a very profound, intense violence, to use Natalia Aleksiun's term: Jews were being expelled from a local universe of empathy and obligations.[97] As one survivor elaborated: "I felt that we were betrayed by them more so than we were betrayed by the Nazis. Because from the Nazis, meaning the Germans, we expected certain things. But we never expected that our next-door neighbours, or our so-called friends that we attended school with, that we grew up with, that they would turn against us and point us out to the Nazis."[98] In testimonies people were as eager to name the local wrongdoers as they were to name their perished family members and neighbours. They were condemned, but, unlike anonymous Germans, also humanized. As Hannah Pollin-Galay noted, "Just as many witnesses emphasize the local milieu as fundamental to social belonging, so too do they seem most invested in testifying to violence that arose from within this same local scene. [...] Crimes within this local microcosm still matter to them, not as metaphors or broad historical lessons learned, but as singular, unjust events that should have been – and still could be – righted."[99] Revenge on local perpetrators, unlike that taken on the Germans, is described in their narratives as a very personal encounter, with often detailed descriptions of the familiar space in which it takes place.

What did those seeking revenge want? First, they wanted just retributive punishment for the wrongdoer. Second, they wanted to know the details behind what happened. With Jews remaining in hiding, the local non-Jews were often the only ones who had knowledge regarding the location of graves or circumstances surrounding any deaths.[100] Thus, revenge often became linked to the moral obligation to bury one's family members. One survivor from Gródek described, in the memorial book of his hometown, how he had been led, together with a friend, a Polish soldier, and by a local person to a potato field, to the grave of his brother:

> There I came across two older women, who recognized me as Mendel, son of the blacksmith. One of them said: "See how nicely the potatoes are growing. It's because dead people, who were killed by gendarmes from Gródek are rotting in this field. O, here your brother is buried."
>
> We began digging out the grave and immediately we uncovered a skull, a few bones, and a pair of rotting shoes. With shaking hands, I put together the earthly remains of my younger brother, put them in a box, placed them

> on a cart and apathetically sat with them on the side of the cart. The sun was going down behind the forest, the night was approaching. My friend took my hand and said: "Come on. Let us finish our mission and find the murderer. Once he finds out that were looking for him, he will escape, and we will never see him again."[101]

They indeed managed to locate the murderer and brought him to the security apparatus in Białystok. On their way to Białystok, the author of the testimony writes, he held the perpetrator by the hair and kept his head in the box with his brother's remains. Thus, revenge did not end with physical violence, and its fulfillment often included scenes of humiliation.

Like the story above, reports of countryside revenge usually begin with a journey, often very perilous, to one's former hometown. Yet in some cases those telling their stories portray themselves as homeless wanderers, rooted only in the shadows of a no-longer existent community. In their stories the need for revenge is very much a self-devouring force, which allows for no rest until vengeance is achieved. Like literary figures, they become the sole avengers where vengeance becomes a self-devouring obsession. This type of revenge crosses borders, as both victims and local perpetrators (including Ukrainians who moved to Poland and declaring Polish nationality) were repatriated from borderland territories into Poland.

Calling Upon the God of Vengeance

With the impossibility of revenge, some survivors found comfort in the vision of God avenging crimes committed against them. Since they could not take revenge on their own, it was for the God of Vengeance to act in their name, as they had expected him to do even during the Holocaust. In a poem based on the Book of Lamentation, written in Hebrew in the Warsaw Ghetto in September 1942, an anonymous writer wrote:

> Only the creator of the universe, the maker of body and spirit,
> He can create the world anew –
> And in a new world, this revenge will appear,
> He will impart His revenge and His hand will proclaim
> In the wicked kingdoms, in the evil government,
> He will issue the retribution, will incite the dispute,
> Will repay Edom many times over
> And will erase memory of its existence from under the heavens …[102]

In the Scriptures vengeance is part of the legal system and is related to justice, where the redress has to be proportional to the injury inflicted. Survivors who sought to justify their actions in religion referred to the notion of the vengeance of God, implying that revenge was sanctioned by God. Thus, acts of violence they carried out were no longer senseless aggression but rather demonstrations of their faithfulness as Jews.

Vengeance and revenge were used in this way to signify divine judgment. When explaining their need for revenge, writers often associate it with God, or imply that while this is their personal initiative, they carry it out on behalf of God. Thus, their vengeance becomes holy, and the avenger becomes the agent of God's vengeance against those "impure murderers who had lost their G–dly image."[103] One survivor recalled: "We must not forget the 'Amalek'; the hatred of the Nazi nation of Germany shall not diminish. The fire of revenge for the murderers shall not be extinguished – these are the last words in the testament of each Jew who was burned; therefore, the job of this notebook is not only to assemble a testament for the community and its martyrs; it has to evoke hatred, anger, and shame toward the murderers of our nation! Our wounds are still fresh. They have no cure; we have no consolation. Our only comfort is that the G-d of Vengeance will pay them back."[104]

When depicting the need for revenge, survivors often recalled it as an almost religious duty, to which they were called by their departed relatives.[105] Just as often, memorial books reflected the author's changed relationship with God following the experiences of the Holocaust. God, rather than providing needed vengeance, is in these stories indifferent – just as indifferent to the fate of the survivors as he was during the Holocaust.

A female survivor wrote in a memorial book about her decision to emigrate and, before leaving, visiting her town of Kolno for the last time. She walks through the town and then sits on the steps leading to her old home. There she is surrounded by visions of murdered members of her community:

> I hear the children crying, the young women and girls groaning, as they are raped and tortured; I hear the old men praying, the screams of the humiliated and flayed. I walk with them when the hangmen tell them to go; I accompany them on their last way. Like them and with them, I raise my questioning eyes to heaven, demanding: "Where art Thou, my G-d?" and G-d, if indeed he exists, is hiding behind the clouds.
>
> Together with them I shout: "Who will revenge our blood?! I hope that you, too, murderers, will know terror and pain when you die! I hope that you never know love, because you don't know what pity is!"[106]

In survivor testimonies the destruction of communities is often linked to desecration of sacral spaces. Testimonies speak of destroyed and plundered synagogues, mikvot and devastated cemeteries, with gravestones taken over as building material for paving the town's streets. This destruction begins during the German occupation and is continued by the local population after the war, with cemeteries turned into public dumps, used to graze cattle or repossessed for construction.[107] One survivor described going to the cemetery in Radzyń to bury a victim of a postwar murder:

> We hire a wagon to carry Mrs. Greenblatt to her place of eternal rest in the Radzyn cemetery, accompanied by a number of Russian soldiers with automatic weapons in their hands. We almost did not recognize the cemetery. Half the place was plowed up and had corn growing. Cows are grazing on the other half, and there is not a sign of a tombstone. In answer to our question as to why he is pasturing his cows there, the man answers: "There's good grass here."
>
> With great sadness, we leave the Jewish cemetery for the last time. What once was does not exist anymore. Our return has made it clear to us that we have nothing more to do here. The air is stifling. For years I dreamt about the shtetl, but now everything is strange to us, and we must escape from here."[108]

Another one wrote:

> What could they have against the dead? Thus was I thinking as I walked along the way to the place of eternal rest of our ancestors. However, there, an image unfolded before my eyes that remains etched in my memory forever, and that will always evoke hate and wrath against the desecrators of the graves of generations of Sochaczew Jews. I saw before me a field overgrown with wild grass, no grave markers, no monuments, and not one brick of the canopies over the graves of the great Sochaczew Rebbes. However, it was not empty. On the contrary, it was noisy and joyful, with horses running around and cows and goats grazing, defiling the holy ground in which the bones of our dear ones lie.

The story is accompanied by a photograph, presumably taken by the survivor, of animals grazing the destroyed Sochaczew cemetery.[109] As Natalia Aleksiun noted, Jewish cemeteries intensified the distance between the once-thriving community and the lonely survivor.[110] Thus, following Yehiel Weizman, we can speak of ritual sites becoming material metonyms for the Jewish communities, a "presence in absence."[111]

It is often in this setting that survivors directly address the God of Vengeance, *El Nekamot Adonoi*. Standing in the courtyard of his town's abandoned synagogue, one survivor reflected: "Now it is silent, silent as a grave. Everything turned to ruin. Only the Great Synagogue remains standing alone, as if immersed in deep mourning. It was weeping for its worshippers who were no more. It was as if echoes could be heard from inside: 'G-d is a G-d of Vengeance, G-d of Vengeance appear, rise up the Judge of the earth, pay back the arrogant. Where is the G-d of Vengeance who will take revenge for our pure blood that was spilled?'"[112]

The Gendered Aspect of Vengeance

Lamentation is frequently presented as a female-gendered activity.[113] In testimonies, those lamenting their communities are male, and their lamentations are often aimed at keeping the name of the dead alive and inciting acts of revenge. Yet, while their grief translates into wrath, wrath does not translate into active revenge. Instead, it is often women who take it upon themselves to take revenge.

Mariasza Botwinik recounts her story in an article entitled "On the Path of Revenge" in the memorial book of Kryvičy (Polish: Krzywicze), where she admitted that "I neglected everything, my husband, my daughter […] I wanted revenge with my whole body and life." Botwinik described how, with very little network support, "I did not go anywhere, I did not ask anyone for help, but quietly, step by step, I began tracing all murderers who took people out of their hiding places and handed them over to the Germans or [to the local collaborators] killed them themselves. I had to fulfill the promise I gave to my own heart. Yearning for revenge, which was often stronger than me, fully took me over, so I began my mission."

In her story Botwinik traces local collaborators, murderers of Jews in her village, and then hands them over to the security apparatus. Importantly, she is helped along the way by her female friends, who help her in locating the murderers. While Botwinik is successful in getting members of the security apparatus to arrest those she considers guilty, she still mentions in her testimony "bringing two bottles of vodka" to make sure they carry out their duties.[114]

Another woman, originally from Hrodna (Grodno), whose son was denounced by a Ukrainian, recalled immediately after the war: "I only had one aim: to survive and get my revenge on Wołoczko [Wełyczko]. After the liberation I looked everywhere in Lower and Upper Silesia [where they were both repatriated]. Finally, after a year of searching I found him in a village called Jawor near Legnica. That Ukrainian bandit got 15 years in prison, but it did not sooth my pain, and it will never lessen after the death of my two sons."[115] According to the newspaper coverage of the trial, Wełyczko was accused of murdering a nine-year-old child and turning in over 30 Jews hiding in Gródek Jagielloński to the Gestapo, among them a 12-year-old son of the women who led to his capture. The relatively low sentence of 15 years in prison was a result of Wołoczko being a minor when the crime was committed. As the newspaper reported, he kept claiming innocence, while he was confronted by very emotional statements of the mother.[116]

Both women wrote openly about crossing traditional gender lines, abandoning their families, and turning from mothers to avengers, thus becoming invested with "masculine" attributes, with revenge seen in a postwar narrative as a quintessentially masculine activity, a "manly" value (as in the postwar narrative revenge not only helped recovery from trauma, but also helped in reclaiming lost masculinity).[117] These stories, of course, still have "feminine" characteristics: women obtain their revenge through a network of connections, rather than through physical power; they hand over the perpetrators to the authorities, gaining revenge indirectly rather than on their own. Nonetheless, they are particularly interesting when put in the context of other women portrayed in Yizker Bikher. As Natalia Aleksiun noted, memorial books were a male enterprise, with most articles written by men, and with men, almost exclusively, serving on editorial boards and women portrayed "in accordance with preset ideas about family and community, education, and leadership – areas in which gender and gender roles are of particular importance,"[118] their images serving to create a "pious, meaningful, and dignified Jewish life before the Holocaust."[119]

Recognition and Justice in the City

There was no doubt as to the vulnerability of Jews returning to the prewar homes. Returning Jews and their property were an obvious target of postwar violence of both individual and organized crime. They were also victims of incidental violence, which was often ignored by the local security apparatus. Survivors, fearing to return to the village, naturally gathered in larger cities, where they fled to find safety in a larger group of survivors. Thus, the majority of Jews in postwar Poland chose to settle in cities and larger towns. In Poland, a large part of the community began rebuilding its life in Lower Silesia, which became the place with the largest concentration of Holocaust survivors. Survivors also gathered in major cities of Warsaw, Łódź, and Kraków. The city became a gathering space, a site of places where survivors could get help from the Jewish committees and support groups as well as Jewish aid organizations.

Cities were more complex organisms than villages. Networks of support were less obvious, links between individuals were less intimate. Already in testimonies regarding wartime violence, crimes were much less individual. Revenge taken in the town was thus different. With fewer support networks, it was easier to find a sympathetic member of the security. Thus, physical revenge was limited also due to the availability of institutional paths for the desire to act.

Anna Cichopek Gajraj wrote about the concept of "*na ulicy*" [on the street], as "an urban space between the intimacy of the home and the formality of the public where people's political and social lives unfold."[120] Postwar testimonies provide us with numerous scenarios regarding "uncovering" a person on the street, encountering someone who was considered to be a wartime perpetrator and taking the law into one's own hands. These acts were not planned or coordinated.

Unlike the village, the city was less of a site of memory and more of a place for the future: a site for building a new life. Yet, while a postwar city can be a neutral space, a clear backdrop against which people were beginning to rebuild their lives, it was also a site of dealing with the past. A non-Jewish Polish survivor recalled after he war: "You know, if it wasn't for the fact that more of us returned from Auschwitz, and I would have returned on my own, I would have been ashamed to go out on the street, show myself to people, because how can you explain that others died, and I didn't. They would have thought that maybe I was a kapo of some kind or some other prominent [person], or who knows what because I survived."[121] The three cities, which re-appear in such stories are Warsaw, Wrocław, and Łódź, three important gathering sites of Holocaust survivors.

Łódź, in the postwar years, became the major centre of Jewish life. In mid-1945, immediately after the end of the war, it became the location of a quarter of all Jews registered in Poland (78,500), twice as many as in Warsaw, which was at that point the second largest community.[122] Łodź became a place of settlement as well as a place through which Jews migrating passed on their way abroad. In Łódź, it was Piotrkowska Street. As Shimon Redlich described: "It was lined by stores, restaurants, and coffee houses. Most of the theatres and numerous cinemas were located on or around Piotrkowska. The oldest hotel in Łódź, the Hotel Polski, or Polish Hotel, was located on Piotrkowska, around the corner of Plac Wolności. In 1945 it served as the headquarters of the Soviet Army that was stationed in the city."

Józef Apelfeld, then 37 years old, witnessed a pogrom in Berestechko that resulted in the murder of 200 Jews. One of the leaders of the pogrom was a certain Dołajczuk. Just after the war Apelfeld came across Dołajczuk on the street in Łódź.

> When he saw me, he tried to make sure that I don't recognize him. However, when he noticed that I was watching him and I keep following him, he approached me and after greeting me he began to explain his behaviour. Then he said: "Don't inform the militia about it, I did not hurt you in any way." I then stopped a Polish Army captain and asked him for help and later made a deposition at the police precinct.[123]

Another survivor, in 1945, saw a Polish prison functionary outside the Jewish Committee:

> Now, I met this guy after the war, in Lodz. [Pauses for some seconds.] In 1945, I was in Lodz after I came back from Auschwitz. It was in March or April, and it was in front of the Jewish Committee, and he walks past me. And here I see a policeman, I mean he – as if he came out from under me. And I jumped on top of him and I told the police who he was.
>
> Of course, they arrested him right away. At that time, they kept on arresting people right and left. And they put him in jail. And they called me. He took my name. They called me. They kept on calling me back about two or three times.

The man was released as there were no other witnesses to his actions.

In October 1947, a gardener named Aleksander B. saw Stefan K.K., an owner of a shoe manufacturing business and a pre-war business partner of Aleksander's father, on the streets of Warsaw. Stefan was also a denouncer and, according to Aleksander, had a death sentence carried out on him by the Home Army. However, three years after liberation, Stefan was alive and walking on the streets of Warsaw. "Last week, completely by chance, I saw him on the street. I walked past and pretended not to see him. On seeing me, he became shaken. However, I walked on, even though I was very surprised to see him as I thought he was not alive," testified Aleksander.[124]

Another survivor recounted a similar experience in his immediate postwar testimony. He spoke of walking down a street in Bydgoszcz in the summer of 1946, when he came across a man whom he suspected of murdering Jews he had been hiding. The man, named Lisowski, couldn't give a clear answer when asked about the fate of the seven Jews he had been hiding. The survivor wanted to get Lisowski arrested in Bydgoszcz, but he was afraid of the revenge of his family. Nonetheless, he filed a testimony with the Jewish Historical Institute just before emigrating from Poland, as it became the only available form of revenge for him. As he testified, "I am certain that the blood of my family was shed by Aleksander Lisowski and that he is the murderer."[125] Even in a relatively large city like Bydgoszcz, the survivor feared for his safety if he were to turn in a non-Jewish Pole.

Security Apparatus and the "Righteous Gentile"

In most stories revenge cannot be carried out alone. Revengers are often accompanied by other Poles, friends, and acquaintances, usually members of the security apparatus, who are instrumental in carrying out acts of revenge. Many testimonies of successful revenge refer to the motive of the "righteous gentile," on whom the avengers are to a large degree dependent. They are accompanied by non-Jews who protected them from any violence and who become witnesses of the acts of revenge. These were often either non-Jewish acquaintances who were members of the security apparatus or soldiers from the Red Army stationed in the area in which survivors could point out collaborators.[126] Yet, even in this case, survivors preferred to take extra steps to ensure that their demands were carried out. While some wrote about bringing vodka to ensure cooperation, in some cases, unsure if the authorities would intervene, survivors sometimes falsely denounced the locals as also participating in anti-communist violence, acting against pro-Soviet partisans or Soviet POWs.[127] This was particularly the case with the NKVD divisions who had more time to engage with the local population.[128] One survivor wrote: "We made a list of all the Poles who had helped murder our dear ones and passed it to the NKVD leader, our best friend. I would spend long hours at his office, and he wrote everything in the protocol. We purposely emphasized in the protocols that they had murdered Russians [as well]. For Jews alone, nobody would do anything. I signed off on all the details and waited for their reaction."[129]

Acts of revenge in a society are often less prevalent when there is an external system that can prosecute the perpetrator on behalf of the victim. This was the case in Soviet-occupied territories, where dealing with collaborators was part of the process of integrating newly liberated territories into the Soviet Union. For instance, a Polish Jewish survivor recounted how a Soviet partisan unit captured some inhabitants of Velyki Mezhyrichi (Polish: Wielki Międzyrzec) in the Rivne oblast. One of the Jewish partisans identified 28 Ukrainian policemen to the commander, who executed them without trial. Another Jewish partisan participated in the execution by killing the policemen with his knife. His friend stated in an oral history interview that he "wanted to see them bleeding like they bled his parents."[130]

Miriam Jaszuńska, born in 1914, joined a group of Jewish partisans during the war.[131] She recounted the first days of the unit in Vilnius, when, after setting up a kitchen for city inhabitants, the partisans began checking people's IDs and bringing captured Germans to them. After questioning and recording their statements, the Germans were sent to the Soviet army headquarters. The unit was also seeking policemen from the Vilnius ghetto, hoping to pay them back for the suffering they caused their families. Miriam worked with enthusiasm, just as she done in fighting in the partisan units. Another member of the unit recalled that their task was to capture those who had collaborated with the Germans. These collaborators were judged and exiled to Siberia. The situation had reversed: previously, the collaborators lived in the city and searched for the partisans in the forests. Now, the partisans were looking for them, taking revenge on them in a way.[132]

Another former partisan recalled in an interview carried out after the war:

> SURVIVOR: It was nothing special. It was just a few Russians came to the forest, and they announced to us that we are liberated, that the Germans were no longer here. The Germans escaped. That's right. We would see, here and there, single Germans wandering around. And they were not strong anymore. And I remember that they were asking, saying that I have a wife and I have children, please spare me. And some of the partisans, they were so angry, and they said – one, especially one partisan – he said this is for my mother, this is for my father, for my sister, for my brother, and killed him. He killed him.
> INTERVIEWER: How did he kill him? Stabbing?
> SURVIVOR: Yes.
> INTERVIEWER: Who was that partisan?
> SURVIVOR: I couldn't do it. I just couldn't.
> INTERVIEWER: Who was that partisan?
> SURVIVOR: He lives in Israel now.[133]

This is, of course, not to say that the partisans were unrestricted in their actions. The state did not want any challenge to its monopoly on force and, after 1944, former partisans were no longer allowed to commit such acts of violence.[134] Yet it was still not uncommon for NKVD special units or even the Red Army soldiers to shoot collaborators without any trial. District police officers were also major agents of violence.[135] A woman at the end of the war, in her early 20s, who was a member of a partisan unit recalled: "But when we came back after the war, I asked some Russian officers who were on their way back to take revenge and kill him. And so they did, they hung him. After the Russians killed him, they told me that when they arrived at his house he was hiding, and his mother cried and yelled that he hasn't done anything. They said: All right, if he hasn't done anything then tell him to come out and we won't harm him. He came out, and they hanged him."[136]

Locals, both Christian and Jewish, were treated by the Soviet authorities as so-called Westerners (*zapadniki*), yet the authorities, as "outsiders," relied heavily on them, as local informers provided them with information. Soviet partisans and the local population, including Jews, were called on to point out traitors (*izmenniki*) and German accomplices (*posobniki*) such as Ukrainian police collaborators, to assist the Red Army military counter-intelligence operatives, military field tribunals, and interrogators.[137]

There are, therefore, numerous stories of Jews (as well as non-Jewish Poles) joining the NKVD to combat the Ukrainian Insurgent Army (UPA).[138] One of those who remained in his town as part of the security apparatus explained: "As much as possible, I tried to avenge the blood of our holy ones. Their cries of 'Revenge!' echoed in my ears constantly. Their suffering was in front of my eyes. I collected much evidence to accuse the Nazi helpers, and I handed it in. They were mostly eliminated, according to my instructions."[139]

Baruch Milch, from Galicia, recalled:

> We were also co-opted by the draft board into the Russian army for participation in operations against the Ukrainian nationalists. I took part in this activity willingly and showed them no mercy: I drafted them into the army or sent them to the Donbass coal mines for hard labor … I sat on medical committees with Soviet army personnel and Communist Party officials who were regularly falling-down drunk. Sometimes I joined in, to forget or to harden my heart toward the Ukrainian population which, here also, had collaborated with the Germans.[140]

People were also handed over to the military tribunals and the Soviet State Extraordinary Commission for Ascertaining and Investigating the Crimes Committed by the German-Fascist Invaders and Their Accomplices. These trials served the aim of Sovietization and brought the population under the stricter control of the state. However, locals, including Jews, also used the trials for individual or collective revenge. While the efficacy and sensitivity of Soviet courts to Jewish concerns should not be exaggerated, as Tanja Penter noted, "the trials seem to have satisfied a strong desire for revenge, order, and the re-establishment of social hierarchies inside local communities. They were not simply imposed on the population and directed from above: they also provided a locus for interaction between Soviet authorities and local communities."[141] This usually involved almost immediately carrying out death sentences in the presence of the local population. One Polish Jewish survivor recalled:

> And in Równe they had a big market, like a farmers' market. The villagers used to bring out their stuff, like eggs, butter, salamis. Whatever they make, they brought in for sale. In the same token, these Ukrainians used to come in to kill Polacks, Jews. They used to come and kill Jewish families, or Polish families, or Russian soldiers, by the same token. And we used to go around and discover them. And one day, we discovered quite a few of them. And the – and from the KGB, they surrounded the market. And they caught most of them.
>
> And a few weeks later, after a – a – a certain time, period of time, there was supposedly a case in court. But there was – the Russian court didn't mean nothing. The commander had the upper hand – the commander, the general that commanded that particular area.
>
> And 18 of them [were] hung in Równe in the market, where I happened to participate in that hanging.[142]

There were deep enough conflicts within most communities to be sure that those who had suffered in the past would gladly take the opportunity for revenge.[143] It helped that, unlike the Polish Blue Police, former policemen in reoccupied Soviet lands were also usually seen as outside the village community and were not protected by the internal network of support.[144]

This is not to say that everyone who sought justice in former Polish territories was able to obtain it. In fact, many of these cases followed repatriated Jews and Poles to post-1945 Poland, and in some cases, justice was only found in Polish courtrooms.[145] One survivor, who joined the NKVD, wrote:

> The thought that it might be within my capacity to exact revenge from the murderers moved me to accept the proposal of the head of the NKVD and to begin work in his office. [...] The leadership of the NKVD knew that my entire family had been killed, and as a partisan, I had participated in many missions. They accorded me full trust and were diligent in assigning to me a position with responsibility for issuing residence permits (Паспортная Отделенне) and for the general archives that had been seized from the Gestapo during the capture [of the city].[146]

In some memorial books from territories that were located in the Soviet Union after the war, these stories of revenge within the NKVD structures are placed alongside stories of people who were persecuted by the same structures.[147]

Jews and the Milicja

The situation within post-1945 Polish borders was different than in the territory annexed to the Soviet Union. Jews entering a town or village without backing from partisans had no means of support and nobody to turn to. Here many believed that individual revenge was the only means available for restoring justice. The postwar Polish security apparatus as narrated by Jewish survivors was characterized by defiance of any authority. There was loyalty above all to local original (non-Jewish) networks.

Testifying to the lack of control of the Communist state over its quickly expanding territory, the security apparatus was unlikely to intervene during attacks on Jews and sometimes participated in them themselves. The most infamous case was that of the largest antisemitic outbreak in Poland, the July 1946 Kielce pogrom. Members of the security apparatus, both Milicja, the state security office, Civic Militia Voluntary Reserve (ORMO), and individual Polish Army soldiers also participated in other attacks on Jews, including the "train actions."[148] It was unlikely that they would intervene on behalf of Holocaust survivors against non-Jewish Poles, especially members of their own community. Referring someone to the security services did not necessarily mean handing them over to face justice. Security Bureau (*Urząd Bezpieczeństwa*) behaved as "a law unto themselves,"[149] and testimonies of survivors seeking retribution often point to the pervasiveness of local ties and influences. There was also reason to be concerned, as its members often functioned within the tight web of local social relations and investigated their own communities. As Andrew Kornbluth noted: "If anything, the men of the UB and MO were representatives of the local societies in which they operated, both realistically and demographically, and consequently they too were susceptible to antisemitism … After all, who better to police the community than its own members?"[150] In fact members of the security services were in many cases suspected of wartime crimes against Jews.[151] As such, their cases were investigated by fellow officers, revealing a clear example of people investigating and self-policing their own local community.[152]

Local circumstances and social ties were thus key when it came to the enforcement of authority in the immediate postwar period in

Poland. The issue of strong community ties was one which for many proved to be impossible to surmount. Jews also had reasons to fear repercussions from the Polish community. In 1945 the president of the Jewish community advised a survivor from Skarżysko against taking to court the case of the Polish underground murdering Jews, because he was concerned about revenge being taken against those testifying.[153] In a report regarding anti-Jewish violence in the town of Irena, dated October 1945, the Jewish community noted that local Jews refrained from reporting anti-Jewish crimes both out of fear of the "reactionary underground" and the total passivity of the local security apparatus.[154] A month later the Jewish committee in Białystok announced that following a series of attacks against Jews in Siemiatycze "some in the Jewish population of Drohiczyn and Siemiatycze do not have the slightest trust in the local precinct of the Milicja Obywatelska, in their formation, and the sentiment present there, which was very much hostile towards the Jews."[155]

This phenomenon was also noted by the authorities. In an order on July 25, 1945, Franciszek Jóźwiak, commandant of Milicja Obywatelska, informed rank-and-file members of the service that they should "embark in as energetic a fight to protect the life and assets of the Jewish population," which included intervening in all types of attacks against the Jewish population and establishing a system that would enable the Jewish population to address the local Milicja units in cases of attacks against them.[156] Two months later they were much more explicitly informed that members of the Milicja participating in attacks on Jews, as well as those passively watching attacks on Jews and not intervening, would be penalized and face court proceedings. He also noted cases of members of the Milicja using antisemitic slurs against Jews. He referred to it as "against the principle of democracy, which orders one to respect people's dignity irrespective of their nationality and religion." Those committing such defamations were threatened with disciplinary action, including removal from the service.[157]

There were reasons to believe that the local agencies would not investigate crimes against Jews with full impartiality. One such case was described by Icek Lerner, a native of Komorówka Podlaska, who was seeking justice against a Pole who murdered a Jewish child and was paid to keep hidden. He reported the case to the security apparatus, yet the matter remained inactive. After his intervention, the local Milicja agreed to arrest the Pole, yet as he found out, functionaries "spent the night before the planned arrest drinking in his house and probably advised him to hide." The next day he accompanied the still drunk functionaries to the house of the Pole who, however, could not be found. He tried several times to move the case forward and gave statements to the prosecutor, yet with no result. Fear of the Pole and the likelihood of his revenge on Lerner as the only person still alive who knew of his secret pushed Lerner to emigrate. Even though he was scheduled to emigrate legally, he decided to leave Poland earlier and go to Sweden.[158] The situation was further complicated as in some cases members of the communist Milicja had acted against Jews during the Holocaust. Another survivor described how on returning to his hometown he went straight to the Milicja to turn in the murderers of his family, only to find them among members of the local Milicja unit.[159] It was not uncommon for reports from local Jewish committees to Warsaw to end the information about antisemitic attacks with a phrase, "MO intervenes unwillingly and without results"[160] and, consequently, for individuals to refrain from reporting crimes to the state apparatus.[161] As a result, instead of informing the local security organizations, some representatives of the Jewish community sent reports regarding anti-Jewish violence straight to the Ministry of Public Security in Warsaw.[162]

Joining the Apparatus

The protagonists often came back in uniform. This would signal their status as either military soldiers or members of organized partisan units. The uniforms were their own, or acquired especially for this purpose from friends or family members. These also served the purpose of concealing the "thin frames" of the men.[163] Yet, a large number of people chose to actually join the apparatus. For many young Jews returning to Poland with the Red Army, with no profession and no family to lean back on, joining the security apparatus became a natural choice. Already trained, both physically and ideologically, often pre-war Communists, with no links to the local community, and especially members of the anti-Soviet underground, they were also an attractive group for the system, which was very open to new recruits and initially took in almost all who wanted to join them.[164]

Many individuals applying to join the Milicja underlined their identification with the new order and saw participating in its implementation as their duty as communists. Following the trauma of the war, Jews, both men and women, were attracted to the new vision of historical progress proposed by communist ideology, and possibly also by the stability and work opportunities offered by party membership. However, those who joined the apparatus spoke not only of ideology but also of a desire for revenge.[165] Joining the apparatus on a local level often involved joining the partisans, being liberated by the Red Army, participating in Red Army activities to search for Germans or local collaborators, and then officially enlisting with the Milicja.

One survivor recalled arriving in Katowice, the capital of Silesia on January 20, three days after the liberation of Auschwitz. There he found himself working in a prison, where he was able to exert its own form of retribution.[166] As he recalled: "It was not an easy task for me to take over a position like that. I had no experience and no idea how to run it. My experience of fighting in the war was minimal as far as security was concerned – we could kill, fight, or run away, that was it. But you learn on the job, and I learned a lot. Silesia was an area where a lot of Volksdeutsche lived: Germans who lived in Poland and had Polish citizenship. There were a lot of collaborators there who were Nazis, but also a lot of Volksdeutsche who were not Nazis, so you had to be careful not to punish the innocent."[167]

Joining the apparatus, putting on the security apparatus uniform, getting legal access to weapons, was one of the few available ways of ensuring one's safety. It was also one of the only ways of getting revenge. Postwar files of policemen preserved in the Institute of National Remembrance show clearly that revenge for the death of closest family members was a common reason for joining the security apparatus. Many joined it straight from the Red Army, seeing "fighting the forest bands" as a clear extension of their wartime fight. Leon J., born in 1926, who joined Milicja in early 1945 as a 19-year-old, recalled how Germans entered the Soviet-occupied territories where he lived:

> In the first days of their rule, they killed my father, and we stayed without any protection. I could not watch the harm that the Germans caused us, so I escaped to the forest, where I came across Soviet partisans and soldiers who escaped German captivity. They understood me and took me in. There I began the forest life. There I had the opportunity to take revenge on German bandits.[168]

After his unit was destroyed, J. joined the group of Polish partisans and stayed with them until the liberation. On returning to his hometown of Lublin he joined the security apparatus. His superior noted that he still felt "great hatred towards the Germans" and that despite intelligence and enthusiasm for work, he still carried out his duties "as if he was among the partisans." Similarly, 20-year-old Aron A. wrote in his application that he wanted to join the Milicja as "the ideal of my life is honest work for Free Democratic Poland and a revenge on German man-eaters."[169] Revenge can often be inferred from these statements.

One member of Milicja wrote in his application of his aim to "serve the society, remove all evil, and re-building the country."[170]

Files of Jews who joined the Milicja usually speak of stories of people who join the unit for a few months and then leave Poland. Both Leon J. and Aron A. left Poland soon after; already in late 1945, J. asked to be released so he could join surviving members of his family in Palestine. Aron A. left the apparatus after five years of service, after witnessing antisemitic attacks in Radom and decided to move to another city to look after his brother, who he deemed at risk of attacks from the anti-communist underground. Others chose to leave due to mental exhaustion and physical illnesses, usually linked to their wartime experiences.[171] One noted the fact that his "Semitic-looking" family was no longer safe in Poland.[172]

There are stories of people who joined the apparatus with the specific aim of taking revenge, and sometimes this was part of a larger story of a fight. One such person was Tuviah Friedman, a concentration camp inmate and escapee. In January 1945, he joined the local Milicja, and later, on April 14, as a member of Urząd Bezpieczeństwa, he worked for a year in the interrogation unit in a prison in Gdańsk. While working in Gdańsk, Friedman remained under his non-Jewish identity of Tadeusz Jasiński. In his testimonies, he described with candour the emotional toll his work had on him:

> I readily admit now that I probably was quite merciless with my prisoners, beating them, trying to extract the truth from them. I took savage delight in entering a prison cell full of Germans and waiting for them to respond to my entrance. […] My heart was filled with hate. I hated them in defeat as I had hated them in their brutal moments of victory. Although I was happy in my work, and felt now for the first time that I was making an important contribution, I was not happy with myself. The more brutal I acted, the less I knew myself. I began to fear that my actions would change me, and that I would become one with those I sought to punish. […] I was beginning to be known as the unmerciful one, who beat and harangued his prisoners, and as one who showed little humanity to others.[173]

Friedman's proclaimed motivation is strongly backed up by his later history. After leaving Poland, he became an employee of the Documentation Centre in Vienna, where he was engaged in tracing Nazi perpetrators, and later played a key role in locating and capturing Adolf Eichmann.

Joining the apparatus re-affirmed a couple of themes, singled out by Joanna Tokarska-Bakir as key in the antisemitic narrative of postwar

Poland. The first was that of "Judeo-bolshevism" – the purported "natural" link between Jews and Communism[174] and the perceived Jewish support for the new regime as well as for the brutality of Soviet occupation. The second was the upward mobility of Jews taking over positions unavailable to ethnic minorities in pre-war Poland and their sudden visibility in public life.[175] This was a clear case of "us" (Poles) being threatened by "them" (Jews), with "them" no longer confined in either pre-war state-sponsored antisemitic policy or by Nazis in camps and ghettos. As Tokarska-Bakir writes, this was "something the dominant group experienced with humiliation and saw as a violation of the social contract that provided for the subordination of the subordinate"[176] With Jews changing their names to "Polish" ones to conceal their ethnic identity and acquire positions "reserved" for non-Jewish Poles, this perceived danger was considered to be even greater, and the need to remove them from Poland became even more immediate.[177] In this case Jews, brought in this narrative to power by the Soviet occupation, were seen as responsible for arrests and murders of members of the Home Army carried out by Urząd Bezpieczeństwa and NKVD, describing the zeal with which Jews were to serve the needs of the new communist authorities in persecution of non-Jewish Poles.

One of the most well-known cases of post-Holocaust revenge, which later became a staple of an antisemitic narrative, is that of Salomon Morel, a former member of the communist underground who, at the age of 26, became a commandant of a camp in Świętochłowice-Zgoda, a former sub-camp of Auschwitz.[178] The camp housed "traitors of the Nation," including men, women, and sometimes even their children, including *volksdeutsche* and *reichdeutsche*, mainly from Bytom and Gliwice. Morel gained notoriety for his cruelty towards those interned in the camp. Anne Appelbaum described Morel as follows: "a Holocaust victim, a communist criminal, a man who lost his entire family to the Nazis, a man consumed by sadistic fury against Germans and Poles – a fury which may or may not have originated from his victimhood, and may or may not have been connected to his communism."[179] This description also applies to other high-ranking members of the security apparatus, such as Julia Brystiger. These are stories of individuals that shaped the perception of Jewish revenge, not only against Germans but also against Poles. Piotr Forecki refers to them as iconic in Polish antisemitic discourse, with their apparent crimes, even if unfounded, taking on a life of their own.[180] They take revenge both privately as victims of the Holocaust and collectively as part of the monolith of Judeo-communism.[181]

2 Holocaust Survivors and State Courts

On April 15, 1948, 28-year-old Lejb Goldberg stood in front of the Jewish Historical Commission's branch in Łódź to testify regarding a German collaborator, a Jewish policeman from a ghetto in Międzyrzec Podlaski, near Lublin. Speaking about the policeman's postwar return to his hometown, he recalled:

> The Jews called the court of the ten [minyan] (I was among them). It was decided to kill him. I was the one who was to carry out the sentence. It was two days after we killed a Polish traitor, who handed out Jews, and the majority in court thought that it's not appropriate, when it comes to the Poles, that Jews should kill a Jew. We decided to lure him to the ghetto and kill him in secret. But Lubicz found out, or maybe someone told him, and he escaped.

The group then decided to kill other collaborators, who were gradually returning to Międzyrzec: "After a while other Jewish traitors returned: Szejmel; deputy chairman of the Judenrat, organizer of the Ordnungsdienst, policeman Topf and others. We decided to kill them all." In the end they were convinced by a representative of the local Jewish committee to instead hand over the men to the local militia. At the same time the men gathered documents detailing Lubicz's crimes and handed them to the Central Committee of Jews in Poland.

While this testimony speaks primarily of the horror of encountering a traitor among those few who survived, it also demonstrates that the search for revenge did not take place in the void. In all the stories that appear in the book, there are four parties: Jewish public/community, avengers, those targeted for revenge, and the non-Jewish public This last element was particularly important during the first few months after the war in Poland when the number of antisemitic attacks was rapidly increasing, and many survivors were still considering their future in their pre-war homeland. Thus, in this chapter, justice moves away from one-on-one meetings in a forest or a village and moves to the much larger space of the courtroom. Revenge stops being intimate and becomes public and, just as importantly, it is carried out through non-Jewish intermediaries.

Jews and Trials of German Perpetrators

An Auschwitz survivor, and one of the most astute commentators about camp survivors in postwar Poland, Tadeusz Borowski wrote that "for people who suffer unjustly, justice alone is not enough. They want the perpetrators to suffer unjustly too. Only this [is what] they will see as justice."[1] Chaotic and uncertain circumstances, such as those in the immediate postwar Poland, offered irresistible opportunities to harm everyday enemies.[2] For many, and especially for state authorities, rejection of permanent, impersonal mechanisms for adjudicating disputes and the search for justice made revenge or retribution outside the state system more than just morally condemnable. It was "wild," "uncivilized," and "barbaric." It displayed madness, stemming from an immature urge and constituted a burst of destruction. It could incite communal unrest and trigger a never-ending circle of the very wrongdoing it sought to end.[3]

Already in the first passages, the Manifesto of the Polish Committee of National Liberation, the 1944 political manifesto of the Soviet-backed administration and the funding document of Communist Poland called for "an hour of revenge for torture and suffering, for burned villages, for ruined cities, for destroyed churches and schools, for round-ups, camps and mass shootings, for Auschwitz, Majdanek, and Treblinka, for murdered ghetto."[4] The idea of "extermination" of Germans in postwar Poland was not just a popular sentiment, but was even brought up by individual officials in government meetings. Yet, allowing for unrestricted justice was troubling for the newly established Polish government. The new regime had to assert its authority while confronting political challenges ranging from armed opposition to foreign interference to conflicting priorities between leaders and citizens. Individual vindictive violence taking place in a political vacuum or turmoil, during and in the aftermath of mass violence, was the opposite of impersonal and measured justice emanating from the law, clearly challenging the state's monopoly on force, what Max Weber called "the monopoly of the legitimate use of physical force within a given territory,"[5] an action widely perceived to have no place in a "civilized" society.

In the constant state of civil war, mob justice added another lawyer of lack of control by the authorities. It was thus necessary to quickly create a system of state justice that would rule out the emotional need to search for revenge elsewhere and that would act in a way that would meet communal needs. Understandably, unresolved conflicts over the legacies of war, occupation, and collaboration proved central to post-war governments' claims to legitimacy. As a result, between 1944 and 1960, 18,000 people were tried by state courts in Poland for war crimes or collaboration, the majority of them between 1944 and 1950.[6]

Jews and German Perpetrators in the Polish Courts

The prosecution of Nazi war criminals was one of the Allied coalition's first undertakings. In October 1941, Roosevelt and Churchill publicly declared that retribution for Nazi crimes was a major objective of the war. In July 1943, the first public war crimes trial took place in the liberated territories of the Soviet Union in Krasnodar. Three months later, the United Nations War Crimes Commission was established (without the participation of the Soviet Union), and the foreign ministers of the United States, Britain, and the Soviet Union signed the "Declaration of German Atrocities" in Moscow. Finally, with the establishment of the International Military Tribunal (IMT) in 1945, the internationally sanctioned legal prosecution of Nazi war criminals took its final form. However, due to political concerns and clear anti-Jewish bias, the Jewish experience of the war was marginalized during the Nuremberg trial. Despite the involvement of Jewish organizations in aiding legal teams from various countries, there was no official Jewish representation in Nuremberg. Although many witnesses spoke of the Holocaust, only three out of 94 testifying in the courtroom were Jewish Holocaust survivors: a Vilnius poet, Avrom Sutzkever; a survivor of Treblinka extermination camp, Szmuel Rajzman; and Izrael Eizenberg, a Polish Jew who worked as a mechanic expert for SS officers in Lublin and testified on their role in the murder of Jews in Lublin. Additionally, only a few written affidavits were submitted by Jews who did not appear during the trial. The key testimony regarding the Holocaust, which the tribunal relied on, came from non-Jews, including the perpetrators: Nazis imprisoned by the allied forces and the documentation that they produced during the war. As a result, the Holocaust was discussed during the trial through the eyes of the perpetrators and witnesses rather than the victims themselves.

As a result, to quote historian Hanna Yablonka: "The Jews were [portrayed during the trial as] string puppets in historical events – the subject of decisions made by others."[7] This reflected postwar attitudes towards survivors. Jewish testimony was considered to be "unobjective," and they were not seen as reliable witnesses to the fate of their kin. The evidence presented during the trial was to a large degree limited to documents, focusing mainly on the perpetrators and their sources, while it gave only marginal attention to the victims' experiences. The voice of the victims was certainly not heard.

This became an opportunity for the new Polish government. Bringing German perpetrators to trial was undoubtedly the most publicly visible and government-sanctioned form of revenge in postwar Poland. The hatred towards Germans was one of the few elements that unified the new Poland, and the authorities took full advantage of it. This was mainly directed towards ethnic Germans who had signed the ethnic German register (*Volksliste*), including inhabitants of pre-1939 Polish territories annexed by the Third Reich who were often forced to sign. In April 1945, 35,000 Volksdeutsche amounted to 70 per cent of all those incarcerated in Poland. However, only the trials of major perpetrators could satisfy the need for revenge.

The role of the "Polish Nuremberg," the first highly publicized group trial reflective of the mood in the newly liberated country, was played by the first Stutthof trial that took place between April 25, 1946, and May 31, 1946. The trial resulted in 12 death sentences for overseers and prisoner functionaries of the Stutthof concentration camp in Sztutowo and its Bromberg-Ost subcamp for women. The majority of those tried were locals involved in the implementation of Nazi policy, including in the Holocaust. Members of the occupational apparatus usually managed to escape to the Reich with the approach of the Soviet Army.

The trials evoked extreme emotions both with the audiences in the courtrooms and the wider public. The most striking aspect of the vengeance element of these trials was the public executions. Contemporary commentators noted that these executions went beyond the need for revenge, "a feeling which we should respect," and turned into a cruel public spectacle aimed at entertainment.[8] The Stutthof execution was watched by up to 100,000 spectators, with public transport rerouted to take them to the site, and some workplaces shortening work hours to allow their employees to arrive by 5 p.m.[9]

While the newsreel distributed in Polish cinemas during the Stutthof camp trial praised the nation's "gentle nature," which sought justice through the legal system rather than revenge, the idea of public execution was deemed by the authorities to be too risky.[10] During the subsequent high-profile trial of Arthur Greiser, Gauleiter and Reichsstatthalter of the German-occupied territory of Wartheland, held before the

Supreme National Tribunal in June and July 1946, authorities feared that the crowd might lynch Greiser before the execution took place. In order to prevent that, the site was cordoned off by two army units. This fear was not unfounded, as attempted lynching had occurred during earlier trials of Majdanek camp staff. To prevent public unrest, in contrast to the execution in Gdańsk, Greiser's death was scheduled for 7 a.m. on a Sunday, partly to ensure that children stayed home, and spectators were asked to "retain an appropriate seriousness and refrain from demonstrating any feelings they may have toward the criminal."[11] Public executions were subsequently banned.

These trials were rare occurrences where individual German crimes were described in detail, and Germans appeared as individuals rather than as nameless, "hazy, distant, almost inanimate force,"[12] or as an event or a system rather than as people.[13] However, in the majority of cases, perpetrators were anonymous to the victims, and survivors could rarely identify the names of their killers in camps or during death marches. These perpetrators quickly melted into postwar society, and the survivors were left to grapple with their trauma and loss without the satisfaction of justice being served.[14]

In some instances, Germans could still be recognized in Poland, such as during evacuation marches[15] or at Red Cross aid points.[16] However, the majority of trials were linked to perpetrators who had already left Poland and were recognized in Germany.

One American soldier recalled an instance of how survivors liberated in Germany took revenge on Nazi perpetrators encountered there:

> This was down at Deggendorf [in Bavaria]. It was night. And there was a barn over there. And we saw some lights. So, curious, we walked over and went in. And there was a group of DPs, Displaced Persons. And they had four SS. Now, they made sure they showed us the tattoos. We couldn't have done anything anyway. Didn't have any guns. We couldn't stop them. And they were holding court. I mean, we couldn't understand the language. But we knew what they were doing. And then they must have convicted them, because they started to beat them, just like, probably, the Germans had done to them.

Survivors already living abroad were also actively participating in trials taking place in Poland. In the case of Fritz-Adolf Fischer, the head of Security Police (SIPO) in the Radzyń district, four Jewish survivors from Międzyrzec Podlaski were called to testify. Additionally, testimonies from nine more survivors, who had already emigrated abroad, were read out. One of them stated, "I swear an oath to the truth of all the foregoing statements. I am informed about the penal consequences of a false statement and would be glad to participate in the trial against Fischer, since I would like to demonstrate in several details the murderer who shot Jews and acquaintances and relatives of mine."[17]

Another example is that of Eustachij Prindyn, an auxiliary policeman in the SIPO in Drohobycz. In March 1946, he was recognized in Buchloe, Bavaria, by a group of Polish and Jewish displaced persons, two of whom were relatives of individuals murdered by Prindyn himself. The displaced persons, who had worked as electricians in Drohobycz's *Sicherheitspolizei* (security police), were able to easily identify him. Prindyn was then extradited to Poland and tried there.[18]

As those captured after the end of the war in occupied Germany were often initially tried there and later had to undergo an extradition process, these cases demonstrate the transferability of witnesses and testimonies across international borders. Often, Jewish witnesses gave depositions in Germany or Austria, where the suspect was arrested by military authorities, and then in Poland, where they were tried by Polish authorities. In this way, trials were able to bring together survivors from different parts of the world who had dispersed after the war.[19]

Revenge on individual German perpetrators in Poland by individual Jews was close to impossible, unless they were discovered by chance. An exception and a particular site of revenge was Lower Silesia, with a capital in Wrocław (Breslau), which became the key settlement place for Jews resettled from the Soviet Union. In 1946, when Wrocław was still a predominantly German city, survivors described meeting war criminals on Matthias (Drobner) Strasse, in the first "Polish enclave" of the Odertorviertel, one of the least destroyed parts of the city. In the Landsberger Lager-Cajtung one of the survivors later recounted recognizing Heinrich Kestner, one of the liquidators of the ghetto in Częstochowa:

> After the liberation, I was in Breslau several times. Walking on one of my favorite streets, Matthias Street, the sudden appearance of a passerby who was strolling accompanied by an unfamiliar woman figuratively slapped me in the face. Our gazes met. Instantly, the thought flashed in my brain: this is him! I did not spare any effort; I ran after him to again be face to face with him, and I was certain that my visual memory had not fooled me: walking by, I had recognized Kestner. I almost had an attack of madness. I really could not contain myself. A flood of thoughts flashed through my brain. Yes, this is him. Yes, this is me who recognized him. This was my dream, our dream, this was our highest vow, the holiest oath; this was our most fervent, most incandescent desire: revenge!

The survivor, afraid to approach Kestner, later gathered other survivors from Częstochowa and handed him over to the security apparatus. As he later wrote:

> There ignited and burned in me the feeling of unlimited revenge against this evildoer! Revenge for the martyred death of our dearest, best, and most beautiful. Revenge for insulting the human family, the image of God. I lived through the strongest emotions of my life. I became drunk with good fortune. It seemed to me that this fact would, to a certain extent, improve the chances of my survival of the terrible storm. Revenge is sweet…[20]

Heinrich Kestner indeed stood trial in 1946 and was sentenced to death by hanging.

As more Nazi war criminals were handed over to the Polish state, based on the Moscow Conference Declaration, the Polish Jewish community members and Jewish communal institutions played a crucial role in getting retribution by organizing public campaigns for their extradition, gathering documentation of their crimes, and serving as witnesses. In the autumn of 1945, the Jewish Historical Commission by the Central Committee of Jews in Poland issued a call in Yiddish and Polish, urging people to "collect all documents of the human bestiality, horrifying barbarism, sadism, and bloodthirstiness which the 'cultured' German people showed in these years."[21] The commission also emphasized the need to compile a complete indictment for the world's public, as a series of trials were being opened against German criminals. In response, individuals prepared lists of fellow survivors ready to testify in trials of Nazi perpetrators.[22] Numerous Jewish witnesses actively participated in recognizing Polish and German guards and prisoner functionaries, testifying in the first, highly publicized trial of Stutthof camp staff.

However, within the complex of national purges and great power-influenced supranational politics, Jews could only press for a legal reckoning for crimes committed against them by proxy, using the Polish state courts, which sometimes proved reluctant to comply. As Donald Bloxham has written, "these instances do not undermine the generalization that Nazi anti-Jewish policy was not subjected, in its specificity, to systematic judicial examination directly after the war."[23]

Trials of Jews and Local Collaborators

According to historian Leszek Kubicki, almost three-quarters of the 18,000 people tried in postwar Poland for wartime crimes and collaboration were Polish citizens, including Jews, Ukrainians, Belarusians, and others.[24] Although the trials of Nazi perpetrators fully involved Holocaust survivors, when it came to Polish state courts trying local collaborators, it became questionable to the newly established government if the specific interests of Jews could be reconciled with the "common good." Trying the crimes of the Holocaust was not in the interest of the Polish authorities, particularly since the crimes of Polish perpetrators did not constitute part of the usable history of the Second World War. Just like the local security apparatus, postwar trials in Poland demonstrate how difficult it was to prosecute people when their actions were backed by public sympathy. Especially striking cases were those in which returning Jews refrained from physical violence to turn those guilty over to the court system, only to see them acquitted. In one such case, one of the first survivors to return to a village in east-central Poland, Jankiel Mendelson, faced a man who, during the war, together with another villager, raped Mendelson's wife and then killed both her and his eight-year-old son. Although Mendelson had an opportunity to kill him, he instead chose to turn him over to the security apparatus. The man was tried, but finally only sentenced to six years in prison and released even earlier on amnesty.

The trials regarding wartime crimes, including crimes against Jews committed both by other Jews and non-Jewish local collaborators, were carried out by Special Penal Courts, established in September 1944 as a key element in the Communist takeover of power. The Special Penal Courts were set up with the progress of military operations, with the Special Criminal Court in Gdańsk, the jurisdiction of which covered nearly the entire north of Poland, from Olsztyn to Szczecin, established as late as June 10, 1945.

Their functioning was based on the retroactive August decree, which dealt with "anyone who, assisting the German occupation authorities, (a) took or will take part in the commission of murder of civilians or prisoners of war, in their mistreatment or persecution, [or] (b) acts or acted to the detriment of individuals pursued or sought by German occupation authorities for any reason (except for the commission of a common crime) by denouncing, capturing, or deporting them."[25] Thus, the decree was used to punish war crimes, crimes of collaboration, and crimes against humanity (i.e., participation in criminal organizations) committed from September 1, 1939, to May 9, 1945. With respect to those subject to martial courts, article 185 of the Criminal Code of the Polish Army of September 12, 1944, applied, while all other crimes committed in this period were punishable according to the Criminal Code of 1932, which was still in force then.

The courts consisted of one judge and two assessors, and their legislative process was extremely simplified to deal with wartime crimes as quickly as possible. The indictment was to be brought within 14 days of capturing the suspect, and the date of the court hearing was to be announced within 48 hours of the indictment. Their sentences could not be appealed. Due to time constraints, only evidence investigation was carried out. In addition to taking revenge on war crimes, the statute of the courts allowed for passing swift sentences on all those who were considered dangerous to the building of the new system. As a scholar of the Stutthof camp noted, at that period there were no documents; there was only memory, "sometimes careful and fact-based, sometimes chaotic, sometimes with an underlying of revenge or hatred."[26]

For many of those who turned to the courts, they failed to provide them with any satisfaction. The trials were hastily done, often missing details of the crimes. They rarely focused on Jewish victims, in many cases failing even to establish their names (which were established when it came to non-Jewish victims) or the number of those murdered. Crimes against Jews were not important for the new government and interested them only as far as it could incriminate members of the anti-Communist underground. Finally, the punishment proved far from satisfactory. Yet, with no other route available, Holocaust survivors did turn to Polish state courts. Their stories told in front of courts showed that they often began by looking for them themselves, asking around, and trying to establish as many facts as possible before turning to the court.[27]

Both the courts and witnesses faced difficulties in establishing the circumstances of the crimes, the number, and especially the identity of the victims. In one case of a kapo tried in Katowice, the witnesses' estimates of the number of his victims ranged from 10 to 1,500 people (the latter number was considered an exaggeration by the court).[28] Due to the outside pressure to ensure the swiftness of proceedings, especially initially, punishments imposed by the Special Penal courts were often either very severe (often involving the death penalty) or acquittal or a very short period of imprisonment, which was often forced due to the lack of time to prepare appropriate documentary evidence or witness statements. This was very much an issue of accepting one word against the other. Following an interrogation of Rudolf Webber, the interrogator noted matter-of-factly that: "The subject is a typical Nazi policeman, and being aware of the fact that no evidence can be obtained as to his activities in Lublin, Poland, he keeps on denying the facts he is charged with."[29]

Importantly, as the state court system increasingly became a weapon in the fight against political opposition, those imprisoned were often treated very badly.[30] Prisoners were frequently held without any information regarding their cases and had no way of contacting their families or hiring their legal aid. As one Jewish prisoner wrote in a complaint to the court, the questioning in his case "towered over German methods in Auschwitz."[31] In a statement, which he claimed to have signed only because of torture, the accused owned up to all he was accused of and claimed that he returned to Łódź tormented by guilt, subconsciously hoping that someone would recognize and turn him in. The court must have believed his claim that his confession was made under duress, as it finally cleared him of all accusations.

Administering justice through vigilante means may have felt empowering, but for those at the bottom rung of power relations who had no other options, Polish state courts were their only recourse. This was particularly true for Jews, who, as outsiders to the local community even before the war, were not part of the power structure, and remained outside the structure of power in postwar Poland. Jewish victims in Poland were peripheral to the proceedings of postwar retribution, with their voices often absent from court documents. As a result, many Jews were understandably hesitant to turn to the Polish state system. As one survivor put it, "We were not notified, we were not asked to testify, we were ignored as much as we ignored them – we expected nothing from the proceedings and received nothing."[32]

What the trials demonstrated, above all, was the conspiracy of silence that existed in towns and villages where anti-Jewish violence took place. Investigators found it difficult to locate witnesses who were willing to discuss what had transpired in their localities and, in particular, to point out those responsible. All blame was frequently placed on individuals who were already deceased or people who had left the area. The most infamous set of testimonies demonstrating the "outside" status of Jewish survivors pertains to the massacre in Jedwabne, a small town in northeastern Poland. Witnesses recounted how on July 10, 1941, Jewish residents of Jedwabne were burned alive in a barn by their Polish neighbours – fellow inhabitants of Jedwabne and neighbouring villages. Several hundred Jews were murdered, often after being subjected to torture. This was likely the largest pogrom against Jews perpetrated by Poles during the Second World War. The testimonies provided extremely graphic details of the crimes committed against the Jewish inhabitants of Jedwabne by their Polish neighbours. Those who submitted them spoke of gangs of murderers roaming the villages, killing Jewish men, women, and children whom they had often known their entire lives. In the case of Jedwabne, as historian Krzysztof Persak has suggested, "the prosecuting agencies were aware that a thorough investigation would inevitably have led to a trial of the entire town."[33]

Thus, the postwar trials fell short of delivering justice. Despite the August decree stipulating the possibility of a death sentence for those involved in the pogrom in Jedwabne, only one person was ultimately sentenced to death. The rest received prison sentences, with some later being acquitted in appeal trials. The court's verdict was that the local population was compelled to cooperate by the Germans who held the real responsibility for the murders.

One survivor, Dora, 10 years old upon liberation, recounted her experience of losing her entire family at the hands of Polish villagers who were members of an underground unit. She recalled her aunt returning from a camp and encouraging her to turn in those she knew to be guilty: "Pola Milstein told me that the Russians arrived and told the rest of the survivors, 'If you have someone to inform on, do it.' But who thought about informing on others then? I didn't trust anyone any more to complain."[34] Dora's fears proved to be fully grounded. Despite murderers of her family being found guilty, based on the August decree in 1950 and receiving the death penalty, they were soon granted clemency and released by 1957.[35]

These cases highlight the inadequacies of the postwar trials in delivering justice for Jewish victims in Poland. Despite the August decree, the reality of limited accountability for the perpetrators and the lack of trust in the justice system for survivors meant that justice remained elusive for many.

Jews seeking retribution against other Jews found more success in cases where they were willing to cooperate with non-Jewish legal processes and testify against their fellow Jews in a non-Jewish court, particularly in Poland. Nearly 30 Jewish collaborators were convicted in Polish courts based on the August 1944 Decree.[36] It is safe to assume that most of these cases were brought by Holocaust survivors seeking justice and demanding that it be provided by a Polish court, often with the participation of Jewish witnesses and historians.[37]

In one such case, a survivor called for the trial of a member of the Jewish Order Service who had remained at large, stating that "such a bandit ... should be subjected to the most awful punishment. This is called forth by the death of innocent 13,000 Boryslaw Jews. In the name of these murdered, I call for the above-mentioned bandit to be tried in the place where the crimes were committed, according to the ruling of the International Commission for trying Hitlerite criminals."[38] This call was answered, and the accused was sentenced to death. To spur the court to action, the witnesses had claimed that the person they testified against was "worse than the Germans."[39]

Another case involved a man who arrived in the city of Dzierżoniów in Lower Silesia in 1947 and recognized a kapo from a camp where he had spent nine months during the war. He decided to turn him over to the local security, and the man was arrested. As Dzierżoniów was a major Jewish settlement, there were many witnesses at hand who had survived the same camp. The kapo admitted to bribing his way to become a prisoner functionary, claiming that he did so to gain access to ammunition that he could then hand over to the Polish communist underground, with whom he had established a relationship before the war. He claimed that he did not beat the prisoners any more than was necessary to maintain his position and not seem suspicious, and that he never denounced anyone to the camp commandant, preferring to hit them himself.

Not everyone was turning to the courts looking for justice. There were several clear-cut cases when special courts were purposefully used by people looking for revenge. One teenage boy, born in 1928, was arrested in 1945 for his role as a prisoner functionary in the concentration camp in Gleiwitz.[40] In the short proceedings he was accused by two witnesses of beating them up in the camp, and on that basis he was sentenced to ten years in prison. Despite being very young and straight out of concentration camp in Gleiwitz, he spent two years in prison before his trial took place. As his attorney noted, with no family in Poland, he could not rely on any aid from the outside and became severely malnourished. Numerous witnesses confirmed that he served only as the kapo's aid and had received extra portions of food, but he had no capacity to harm other prisoners. In the sentence the court noted that the baseless accusations might have been made because prisoners were jealous of extra food rations and referred to it as "personal revenge."[41] The court also saw as mitigating circumstance that the accused, still very young, was more likely to be demoralized by the conditions in the camp and relationships with other prisoners.

Another prisoner, an overseer in the forced labour camp in Kreising petitioned the court: "I survived the horrors, sharing the fate of all Jews, known to the whole world. Through beatings and constant torture by the occupying enemies, through tears and corpses of my family, I finally reached long-awaited liberation, only to find myself again behind bars. And on what basis? Based on slander by a degenerated human being, a man who only wants to fulfill his personal need for revenge."[42] As later re-told, H. was denounced to the Polish apparatus on the day when he returned from Germany to Poland in May 1945 and went to register in the Jewish committee in Łódź, where he was recognized by another former prisoner in the camp.[43] He was immediately arrested and did not leave prison until two years later, in May 1947, when he was cleared of all charges. Interestingly, already in the denunciation statement, his denouncer was open about his motives. He wrote that he was pushed to it by recalling those being executed in the camp, who in their last words called for revenge, and urged the court to "finish him off, like he finished off the other prisoners"[44] In another case, the accused was accused of brutality as a kapo by people, he claimed, who were leaving Poland and wanted to delay his emigration by keeping him arrested.[45]

In many ways, the special courts satisfied the first wave of the need for revenge and justice, especially against prisoner functionaries in camps. In their case, the courts already had ways of proceeding following a stormy public discussion of the topic and tried them as they did non-Jewish prisoner functionaries.[46] Jewish prisoner functionaries also underwent amnesty in the 1950s. There are moments when the court is trying to understand the uniqueness of Jewish experience, such as the case of a policemen from the Łódź ghetto, where it took into consideration the environment of "complete physical and moral dependence on the Germans."[47] As the regional court in Sosnowiec stated in the verdicts on the commandant of the Jewish Order Service in Będzin: "It is obvious, that even though the Jewish Order Service, or the Jewish police, on German orders participated in a number of repressions against the Jewish community, it cannot be considered to be a criminal organization, and participation in it cannot alone be considered a crime."[48]

In general, however, the Polish government, as other national legal systems, expressed little interest in persecuting Jewish collaborators after the war. Crimes against Jewish Polish nationals were considered to be an internal Jewish matter.

Despite all their shortcomings, postwar procedures were a way of establishing agency by the survivor community. They gave Jews a voice: they provided them with access to a public platform and sanctioned their role as members of the postwar Polish community. The trials and interrogations served as spaces where memories of Holocaust participation and responses to violence could be articulated, reframed, or repressed. As Joanna Tokarska-Bakir noted, when it comes to giving testimony in Polish institutions, "the language element was by no means unequivocal, since a conversation conducted in Polish could have signaled detachment from the Jewish experience, but alternatively it might have been an affirmation of the equality of rights in a democratic postwar Polish society. Also, by abolishing or creating distance to the witness's narrative, the recorder of the testimony could determine, in a subtle yet unavoidable manner, the discursive framework within which the narrative was related."[49]

Participation in the state court system can also be seen as an element of Jewish negotiations with the postwar state, as an aspect of struggle for agency within the new system. At the same time, as Anna Cichopek Gajraj noted: "After the war, ethnic minorities relied on the state more than usual. The Talmudic rule – *dina d'malchuta dina* (the law of the land is the law) – never seemed more vital for Jews than in the face of destruction and danger."[50] The trials show clearly that, at least initially, the Polish government did support the Jewish community, and many were ready to risk being involved in its proceedings to carry out retribution against those who harmed them.

When it comes to Polish state courts, the key concept is that of trust and the legitimacy of the courts. The question that arose is to what extent can the interests of Jews be reconciled with the "common good." Could Jews trust the courts to represent their interests? The answer is complex. As already shown, they had no reason to have confidence in the system of security on the local level, unless they were linked personally to its representatives.

Once Jews entered the space of the court, their agency was no longer personal but was now also officially legitimated. Testifying against Poles, Jews became legitimate interlocutors in the discussion of the memory of war. Postwar trials were to serve justice, but they were also to serve real political needs, and all involved in them were fully aware of it. The links between Polish state courts and the formation of the new state and the new historical memory to serve it also did not aid Jews attempting to engage in the procedures and practices of accountability through it.

To be accepted, these voices had to fit publicly accepted (and expected) language of victimhood. One survivor, testifying after the war, ended his testimony by saying: "I testified truthfully and precisely, and I am ready at any time to testify before a representative of the government and if need be take an oath. I'm convinced that the current government in Poland will see justice done and will also get rid of its enemies."[51] Another one, recalling his return from a concentration camp in Germany, stated in a letter petitioning release from prison: "Even though I am of Mosaic faith, I hurried back to Poland not for *szaber* or gaining wealth, but because I consider myself a Polish citizen, and I know that this is my motherland, in order to build a true democratic Poland, to improve the fate of workers and peasants."[52] for which I fought in 1939 and where I got harmed while imprisoned as a POW until 1941."[53] Later on, he declared his desire not to emigrate, but to stay in Poland and "work for its might and wealth."[54] In a subsequent letter he wrote: " Even though I am of Mosaic faith, I always stood in defense of my Polish motherland."

This also meant avoiding fitting within the antisemitic narrative of Jewish vengeance. Such narratives and accusations arose during the proceedings and could cast Jewish witnesses as unreliable.[55] As a result Jewish witnesses claimed to be starting proceedings even in cases of those who murdered those the closest to them "not only because I was harmed by them, but also because if I was to conceal this crimes, I would feel co-responsible for it."[56]

Thus, postwar trials were far from being means of subversion of the structures of domination. The system of accountability that took shape in the practices of Polish state courts was neither long-lasting nor structural. This clearly demonstrates the extent to which the rules of the new government were a response also to the needs of the communities, which were, in fact, some of the main actors in state-building. In this case, the key fact was that the majority of murders against Jews took place in the countryside. As Michael J. Braddick and John Walter noted: "The legitimation of power, the creation of a public transcript, both empowers and constrains."[57] Inhabitants of rural areas, next to workers, became the bastion of the new Communists and the new government could not afford to lose their support.[58]

3 Jewish Civic Court in Poland

In September 1948 Marian Frauenglass, a lawyer, was accused of collaborating with the chairman of Judenrat in Zbaraż to guard Jews gathered for transports to forced labour and to beat those attempting to escape. Among those he had been accused of beating were Bronisława Bauer and her son Leon, who later died. The accusation was brought by a member of the Polish Workers Party in Kraków, based on information obtained from Bronisława Bauer. The accuser had also attempted to take over Frauenglass's apartment.[1] Following this denunciation, Frauenglass was tried by the Polish court on the basis of the August decree and cleared of any accusations. Interestingly, as its justification, the Polish court pointed to inaccuracies in Brauer's testimony and claimed that had she really been convinced of Frauenglass's involvement in her son's death, she would have "much earlier told everyone she met on her way about it." "As an intelligent person" she should have known that despite the high position of the accused, one should not be afraid of any repercussions when addressing the state legal system.[2]

Yet, as the case was still ongoing, in June 1948, Frauenglass addressed the Jewish Civic Court by the Central Committee of Jews in Poland to additionally clear his name among members of the Jewish community. As he stated, "the Central Committee of Jews in Poland, which I address regarding help in this just matter, having insight into Jewish issues during the occupation, will be able to pass an objective judgment in this case and will undoubtedly find a way to end this lawlessness and *drejfussjada* (Dreyfuss-like case)."[3] Among those ready to testify in his defense Frauenglass mentioned "20 to 30 witnesses," including such illustrious members of the community as the actress and director of the State Jewish Theatre in Warsaw, Ida Kamińska, and the rabbi of the Polish Army, Dawid Kahane.

Frauenglass presented the civic court with numerous depositions clearly testifying to his unblemished behaviour during the war and the fact that he was a regular employee of a train station where forced labourers were gathered, and rather than cooperating with the chairman of the Judenrat, he was actively persecuted by him. "Zbaraż is a small town, and it would be impossible to hide such situations," explained one of those testifying in favour of Frauenglass.[4] Finally, the civic court dismissed the case, showing, however, more understanding towards Frauenglass's accuser, Brauer, than the Polish state court. The court noted that "Brauerowa's testimony, while true in the subjective sense, was false in objective sense and can be explained by understandable oversensitivity of a mother who, after losing a son, attributes this loss to a person, at whose house her son worked and who probably had some type of conflict with him."[5] The court was, therefore, taking the experiences of the Holocaust not only in case of those accused of "collaboration" but also those spreading unsubstantiated rumours about them.

Jewish Civic Court (known in Polish mainly as *sąd obywatelski* or *sąd społeczny*, in Yiddish as *folks-gerikht*) operated from October 1946 to early 1950 by the Central Committee of Jews in Poland (*Centralny Komitet Żydów w Polsce*) – the central representative body of Polish Jewry.[6] While it is not explicitly stated here, other documents produced by Jewish historical commissions clearly state that this sense of duty to bear witness was caused above all by a perceived obligation to the dead. It can be claimed, therefore, that this effort to document atrocities and pursue those responsible for them was another way to mourn and commemorate those who died during the Holocaust.

The mission of the court, in its own words, was to "cleanse Jewish society of people who in one way or another cooperated with the Nazi authorities during the occupation, unmasking those traitors of the Jewish people who have tens and hundreds of thousands of victims on their conscience. Those traitors consider themselves or want to be considered as decent people and want to try to play a role in the life of our society."[7] The civic court of the Central Committee of Jews in Poland ruled in its first session that "holding any position of power during the occupation, such as belonging to the Judenrat, Ordnungsdienst and others, disqualifies a Jew. Jews who, during the occupation, held the above-mentioned positions can seek rehabilitation in front of the court if they prove that they took on their positions under force and did not cause harm to the Jewish community."[8]

The court investigated about 150 cases of those suspected of what was then perceived to be "collaboration." Men and women found guilty were punished with a rebuke, a reprimand, ostracism, suspension of the rights of a Jewish community member, and exclusion from the Jewish community. The punishments that the civic courts could issue were also limited to the community. The Polish Jewish civic court's charter lists a formal rebuke, a three-year suspension of communal rights, including rights to financial aid, with exclusion from the Jewish community as the harshest measure. In cases of particular gravity, the court turned those found guilty to the Polish state court system.[9]

The case of Bronisław Frauenglass was not unique. While the Jewish civic court had no authority to force suspected collaborators to stand before them, appealing only to their "sense of social duty,"[10] many of those who stood previously in front of Polish courts, either state jurisdiction or ones set up by political parties and professional organizations, still submitted later to trial by the civic court. Why was being cleared by the civic court so important for Holocaust survivors? Why were verdicts issued by the Polish state system not sufficient?

Jewish civic courts began their work in earnest in late 1946, just as the purges and local wartime trials around Europe were largely winding down. A progressing amnesty process in Western Europe led to local perpetrators gradually being integrated back into the society, rather than being brought to justice. The year 1947 brought with it the fall of the anti-fascist consensus and the beginning of the Cold War. The construction of the Iron Curtain naturally led to problems with the extradition of war crimes suspects from Germany and limited the possibility of trying them in Eastern Europe. Thus, the Jewish trials start, when others end in the world, where wartime atrocities of one's own community seemed normalized and forgotten. Setting up of these court was, thus, also (and maybe primarily) a response to the societal failure to recognize the Jewish dimension of the Second World War. The Jewish community had its own memory of atrocity that it had it deal with on its own.

Jewish civic courts were bodies that the survivors could trust, and that would enable them to deal with internal community matters without resorting to non-Jewish authorities. It was widely perceived that only a Jewish court could fully understand the specificity of their experiences and pass judgment on their behaviour in camps and ghettos. Those addressing it were also to some extent influenced by the Talmudic tradition of not turning one's own over to non-Jewish authorities. As an author of an article in the Displaced Persons press noted: "Such situations should be handled by us, and not by strangers."[11] There was also, as we can suspect, a common feeling of distrust of Polish authorities, which was why some survivors also turned to the Jewish committees when not only Jewish but also non-Jewish perpetrators of crimes against Jews were identified.[12] It can be asked if intruding trauma and unaddressed grievances into the public sphere did not incite more violence and hostility against former collaborators.

There was also an important aspect of sorting out such issues within the community: that of not feeding into growing antisemitic sentiment in the country in the immediate postwar period, which culminated with the July 1946 Kielce Pogrom.[13] A survivor recalled returning to his hometown of Koło:

> When I entered the building, my blood froze, as among three people there, I recognized a Jewish henchman. Not sure who this man with a murderous face was, I listened for a few moments to his boasting about his time spent in different camps and what his name really is. I ran to find my friend from Koło, who was at those camps at the same time and told him that today, by coincidence, I met a murderer of the Jews. [...] My friend told me that he would have handed him over into the hands of the justice by UB, but he is ashamed to hand over a Jew in Koło. At the same time, he said you were the worst murderer, worse than the most dangerous Gestapoman, and the worst policeman in our camp.[14]

Instead, the author of this testimony turned to the Jewish civic court in Warsaw.

When handing over a suspected collaborator to the Jewish civic court, members of the Jewish community could be certain that the judging panel understood choices made in the Holocaust, which might have been imperceptible to outsiders. Their judgment, through their symbolically charged punishments of various degrees of removal from the Jewish community, generated opportunities for moral restitution for individuals and repair and reconciliation for the community.

The scope of the court's functioning clearly shows that individual Jews and Jewish communities in the immediate postwar period were not yet ready to forgive those among them who they perceived to be traitors. In the shared narrative framework, these collaborators were worse, their betrayal was more painful, than the actions of the Nazi perpetrators. In the justification of the first verdict issued in the case of a former policeman from the Kraków ghetto, the Jewish civic court clearly stressed the moral aspect of the trial.

> The blow inflicted by a Jew against an abused Jew was more painful than the blow of a German, because he inflicted moral pain. [...] An individual who in the most tragic Jewish nation of that period when condemned to total extermination and when its best sons fought not for life, but for

> death worthy of man, this individual commits national treason and joins the enemy, and in this position abuses his own brothers, [and] should be considered outside the Jewish community.[15]

As historians Laura Jockusch and Gabriel Finder explained: "Because so little time had passed for reflection, the atmosphere was still so charged, and the wound was still so raw, many Jews were unable to make a distinction between the actual perpetrators (the Nazi Germans and their non-Jewish accomplices) and the few Jewish victims who aided them for whatever reason, between those with power and the Jewish powerless."[16] Justice, as carried out by the civic court, thus played a key part not only in establishing the truth, but also in constraining public anger and the need for revenge.

Jewish Civic Court in Poland as a Site of Revenge and Retribution

The aim of the civic court was not to punish; it was to bring back to a constructive place in society those who lost their place through their wartime actions. In this sense, it was by all means an instrument of transitional justice, where, to quote Michael Rothberg: "On the one hand, the drive for justice demands an account of subjects as implicated in histories of injustice and traumatic violence. On the other hand, the desire for social peace and progress diverts such a drive and seeks to create citizens for the dispensation who are disembodied from past histories."[17]

Many of those who stood in front of the civic court were previously attacked in private and public spaces; in some instances, they were saved from lynching by police or representatives of Jewish organizations and handed over to the court.[18] Immediately after the liberation of Sambor a group of Jews from Turek n/Stryjem came to the flat of Aleksander Berger in order to carry out a lynching. Berger missed death only by jumping out of the first-floor window. According to witnesses Berger showed exceptional ruthlessness, sadism, and torture of Jewish girls: he had promised freedom (in return for sex). He was also believed to have contributed to the death of his parents.[19]

The immediate reaction to this outbreak of vigilante justice was the setting up of Jewish honour courts, among them also the Jewish civic court. This was to a large degree an answer to this need for revenge, but also an attempt to stop individual attempts at carrying it out. As historians Gabriel Finder and Laura Jockusch wrote:

> The creation of the honour courts was largely a conscious effort on the part of postwar Jewish leaders to counteract tendencies to engage in vigilante justice and to parlay the desire for vengeance into a quasi-judicial, institutional forum for the expression of this sentiment. And to their credit, the honour courts – and for that matter, the Israeli courts in trials authorized by the 1950 law – made it their business to exact retribution when the facts of an individual case warranted it while eschewing revenge.[20]

Postwar trials were very much visible in Jewish shared communicative spaces, and for Polish Jews all around the world the civic court in Poland became a key site of getting retribution. The belief in the Jewish court system meant that people were ready to cross borders just to seek justice in the Jewish court rather than in the local justice system. Throughout its existence it was addressed directly by Jews residing at that point all over the world, testifying to rumours and stories regarding wartime actions of survivors following their migration from Poland and their functioning in various networks of Holocaust survivors. As a result, while employees of the court travelled extensively through Poland, its reach extended far outside of it. The extreme measures to which the courts went to capture those suspected of collaboration and to secure witness statements show how serious they were about the trust placed in them, as well as how much importance the community placed in rebuilding itself by first dealing with the past.

In May 1948 the Polish Ministry of Justice set up its own unit for investigating cases of collaboration in occupied Poland, which also began looking into wartime actions of members of the Judenrat and the Jewish Police. The Jewish Social Court saw it as a clear sign that the Ministry did not see them as sufficiently fulfilling their role, in particular not trying people before they managed to leave Poland.[21]

Denunciations and the Postwar Sense of Justice: Motives for Denunciations

"I am not a denouncer, nor have I ever been one," wrote Samuel Silberstein from Vienna in 1946 to the Provincial Jewish Committee in Łódź.[22] He had just heard that Stanisław Rowiński, manager of the Braun and Rowiński knitwear workshop in the Warsaw ghetto, had survived the Second World War and was participating actively in postwar Jewish communal life in Poland. Of course, in his letter Silberstein did exactly what he purported not to do: he denounced a fellow Jew. "I cannot come to Poland to personally settle my scores," he explained, "but my conscience does not allow me not to write to you…. I believe this to be my sacred duty."[23] Silberstein's letter became part of Rowiński's case file in the civic court of the Central Committee of Jews in Poland. The postwar quest by Jewish survivors of the Holocaust to seek justice from – and wreak revenge on – suspected Jewish collaborators with Nazi rule is refracted in large measure through the prism of such denunciatory letters. Addressed to Jewish communal bodies, political parties, or newspapers, the missives describe chance meetings with former kapos on the streets or in communal kitchens, rumours of the return of a former Jewish policeman to his pre-war hometown, or, most alarmingly, publish a putative Jewish collaborator's face in the newspaper among leaders of the postwar Jewish community or advise about his career in Polish state structures.[24] "Dr. Hercberg is currently a captain in the Polish Army, where he is enlisted as Gorodecki. He also claims to be Polish in his apartment building, even though the janitor knows him since he was a child," wrote one of the denouncers about a member of the Judenrat in Opatów.[25]

This was not a uniquely Jewish phenomenon, but a much wider occurrence. Polish courts were at that point swarmed with an "avalanche of denunciations" dealing with all types of wartime and postwar behaviours.[26] Written statements that fit this definition (though directed to the Jewish leadership rather than the state per se) can be found in the archives of Polish and DP courts, ranging from spur-of-the-moment notes scribbled on scraps of paper to multipage typed letters that elaborately describe the wartime behaviour of alleged collaborators and provide extensive lists of witnesses or even quotes from academic works. Most of these denounce the wartime behaviour of former members of the Judenrat, the Jewish order service, or prisoner functionaries in forced labour and concentration camps. Such denunciations came mainly from direct witnesses of the crimes, from victims who "survived it, and saw it, and felt the blows on my own back,"[27] or from their family members who sought justice for their suffering. Not all of those who desired to denounce an alleged collaborator thought that their voices would be heard, and thus some addressed the court through an intermediary with higher authority, such as a rabbi or a representative of a local Jewish organization who could write letters on their behalf.[28] Others felt a moral obligation to write a denunciation from their positions of achievement during wartime or their postwar life or, on the other hand, saw themselves as the voice of the street, that is, as representatives for Jews more socially or politically powerless than they who could not bear to see crimes go unpunished. Therefore, whereas one author of a denunciation introduced himself as "the father of a soldier of the Haganah who fought in the old town in Jerusalem [and] a brave worker at the Giv'ot Zaid [kibbutz in northern Israel]"[29] in an effort to establish credibility, another author with the same aim wrote, "My name means nothing, I am not a member of a party but a regular Jew."[30] Regardless of the means chosen, almost all writers of denunciations signed them clearly with their name and address, generally also providing contact information of individuals who could corroborate their stories.

Although denunciations focused primarily on shedding light on the wartime role of a suspected collaborator and urged the court to take a stance regarding alleged crimes, in many cases they took the form of elaborate descriptions of the criminals and their resort to cruelty. Such narratives often used emotionally charged language, with alleged collaborators usually referred to as "gangsters" or "thugs." They were "outcasts,"[31] "traitors,"[32] or, in the case of one former policeman in Ostrów, one of "Hitler's dogs" who bathed in "Jewish sufferings and torments."[33] As one denounced member of the Judenrat complained, "expressions such as 'the enemy of the Jewish nation,' 'enemy of the humanity,' 'selfish men' [are] terms which are meant to besmirch me in front of the civic court. Even though I do care deeply about the judges' good opinion of me, I do not think that my personal characteristics should be the subject of their interest."[34] To strengthen their accusations, the denouncers emphasized particular aspects of the alleged collaborators' crimes, such as instances of sexual violence or cruelty toward children. Those denounced often had evidently acted of their own volition. Additional details seen as incriminating by the denouncers ranged from physical attributes, such as a "murderous face,"[35] to earlier inclinations to criminal behaviour, with one Jewish policeman in Plaszow camp described as "having the opinion of a quarrelsome boy"[36] since childhood. Others mentioned collaborators' postwar criminal activity, such as involvement in the black market,[37] as proof of their bad character. Authors of denunciations often asserted that an alleged collaborator was hated or feared by the whole Jewish local community or camp population to buttress their claims.

Denunciations clearly demonstrate that the line between obtaining justice and serving revenge was very unclear. Those who addressed the courts often saw the aim of the courts as "serving justice and punishing rascals" and called for alleged collaborators "to be placed at the whipping post and handed over to the court."[38] This pursuit of revenge was most evident in the cases pressed by relatives and friends of victims who perished. A woman denouncing an alleged collaborator, whose presence in Bergen-Belsen displaced-persons camp she heard about from her sister-in-law, wrote to the civic court:

> It has been a few days as I was attempting to address you with this matter, but memories of this horrible tragedy lead me to despair. I am not able to speak about it. I would never rest in peace if I would not take revenge on this man, the perpetrator of my young husband's death, the father of my unfortunate son. Please forgive me the excited state in which I am writing this letter… The blood of my husband calls for revenge. Maybe this, at least in some way, will give me calm.[39]

Another denouncer requested revenge for a suspected collaborator "in the name of Jews who were harmed by his murderous hands."[40] In accordance with the sentiments prevalent in many such letters, one author wrote, "Providence saved us not only to remain alive but also to take revenge for our own torment and suffering and for that of those who no longer can take revenge."[41]

In most cases denouncers appeared to lack familiarity with the practices of the courts and consequently rarely gave indications of which form of punishment they saw as appropriate; conversely, some denouncers demanded punishments that were outside the scope of the courts' authority. For example, some denouncers described "gallows as the only fitting punishment for those human-animals."[42]

This call for revenge can be seen as reflecting the general attitude in the postwar Jewish community, rather than being limited to those likely to write denunciations. Rulings of the civic courts often stimulated ferocious discussion, mainly because they were considered too lenient. Individuals who gathered in the courtrooms raised such protests, as did the Jewish press, demanding punishment proportional to the crimes committed by those sentenced.[43] An author of the letter to a popular Jewish newspaper, *Folks Sztyme*, complained: "Will the sentence serve as a 'compensation' to their direct or indirect Jewish victims, who cannot take postwar revenge on them on their own? Are the accused not going to laugh at their sentence?"[44]

The courts' proceedings were seen as unjust in general, but they were particularly at odds with the moral vision of Judaism, at least insofar as the survivors perceived it. An author of an article lamented the "lack of discipline of our masses, truly laughable actions of our security and legal bodies [and] … a cowardly behaviour of our judges" and complained about the leniency of the sentences. "According to what codex do those gentleman work? Maybe according to the Jewish torah? But there are points there such as 'an eye for an eye' guaranteeing that everyone will get a deserved sentence."[45] Those who judged them had comparable dilemmas and had to make similar choices. They also had deeper understanding of the conditions under which such choices were taking place.

Many of the sentences bitterly referred to the limited punitive powers of the courts. Considering the magnitude of the crimes they dealt with, it is unsurprising that in numerous cases courts simultaneously issued the supreme penalties at their disposal and lamented their inadequacy in relation to the crimes committed. In one case, for example, the sentence explained, "Spilled Jewish blood must be avenged, even if only to the extent allowed by the statute of the rehabilitation committee."[46]

At the same time dismissing the claims in the denunciations as caused by revenge was one of the most productive ways of defense in the civic court. They claimed that denouncers had gotten carried away with the communal rush to take revenge and, "excited to the brink with the proceedings taking place, also wanted to take part in them."[47] A former Łódź ghetto official, denounced by a group of sanatorium patients, evocatively described his accusers' supporters as "sick people, seeking any sensation, who rarely have any visits from the outside, spending months or even years in an empty town, located 5 km from the nearest railway station, and for whom the only spiritual nourishments are conversations conducted during long hours of rest, creating an air where even the wildest gossips strike a chord."[48]

In many cases those at risk of standing trial attempted to discredit their accusers by resorting to rhetoric that portrayed Holocaust survivors as obsessed with revenge, ridden with mental disorders, and incapable of functioning in an ordered society in the absence of outside control and guidance. For example, the attorney for Regina Kupiec, who was later sentenced for crimes as a prisoner functionary in Birkenau, stated, "There is no doubt that difficult experiences and the horror of sufferings in the camp led to changes in the psyche of the witnesses, making them unable to organize events according to time, place, person, etc."[49] Although official court statements do not question the reliability of witnesses, leading social activists from among the Jewish displaced persons also discussed the effect of Holocaust trauma on early testimonies.[50] One activist wrote in a letter that was used in the Polish trial of an alleged collaborator: "The experiences of people were so awful, tragedies so horrible, that often unintentionally, the unfortunates, those hurt, search for culprits among people who, according to their subjective belief, are the perpetrators. We reached the opinion that judgment of crimes linked to one's behaviour in those times can be made only on the basis of concrete, objective proof."[51] This rhetoric was often linked to the portrayal of a denunciation as residual of wartime demoralization. One witness for a defense elaborated, "I was wondering what motives there are for those various denunciations. This is not only the urge to immediately find those guilty of their misfortune, the will to achieve satisfaction in finding the scapegoat, but very often also jealousy, that someone else survived. These are the results of general moral demoralization. Unfortunately, the best ones perished."[52] In a similar manner it was suggested during the trials that those who denounced others after the war were already known denouncers or had even been collaborators themselves during the occupation.[53]

The next step for defendants was to dispute the charges as personal in intent and motivated by malice, "ill will, hatred, jealousy, and personal accounts."[54] The defense also cited wartime conflict resulting from the privileged position of the defendant during the occupation as a factor in groundless postwar accusations for the sake of revenge.

The second, and probably more important, reason for the desire of their accusers to seek revenge was defendants' privileged position after liberation.[55] As was the case with wartime conflicts, such denunciations often came from individuals whose requests to the defendants for assistance had gone unanswered. One defendant attributed the denunciation of his accuser to a grievance that arose from the fact that "after his [accuser's] return [to Poland] from the Soviet Union, acting in the capacity of a member of the commission of social aid by the local Jewish committee, I refused his request for rations, as the warehouse was empty. While still in the building of the committee, he threatened that he would 'teach me.'"[56]

Aside from discrediting the authors of denunciations, defendants attempted to question the credibility of witnesses for the prosecution by revealing reasons that might have influenced them to testify at trial. For example, one alleged collaborator before the civic court in Warsaw uncovered a network of family links between those who had accused him. He wrote: "The persecutors, with a large dose of ill will, attempt to create an impression as if there were more of them. In reality, this whole scandal takes place strictly within one family … My own sense of justice does not allow me to present witnesses of whom there would be even the slightest suspicion that they are driven by factors other than the truth."[57]

As a last resort, the accused questioned the right of the courts to judge them and proceeded to seek justice outside the courts.[58] As already shown, civic courts were only one part of the tapestry of formal and informal methods of dealing with suspected collaborators. Some involved in trials also turned to other methods, such as social ostracism and beatings of defendants, to make their point outside court and ultimately to prevail in court.[59] During the rehabilitation proceedings of one former policeman in Poland, his denouncer, accompanied by Public Security Office functionaries (the Polish Communist secret police), paid him a visit and beat him up.[60] Others chose to forward their cases to non-Jewish courts, with known cases of false denouncers being tried by either Polish courts or the U.S. Army Counter Intelligence Corps in Germany and Austria.[61]

Debate on the practices, functions, and discourses of denunciation usually focuses on the negative aspects of this practice. Indeed, in many cases denunciation used as a weapon in the quest for personal revenge turned victims into victimizers. Justice in the Warsaw civic court, as in other courts in that period, was undoubtedly buried deep beneath piles of fraudulent testimonies and the settling of personal scores.

Denunciations did, however, play an important part in rebuilding the postwar Jewish community. With the establishment of the civic court, for example, Jews who encountered their former tormentors on the street found themselves, for the first time, in the presence of a body that would listen to them, irrespective of their social or political standing. Civic court served as a symbol of approachable leadership that was prepared to act on the information received. The act of writing a denunciation was also empowering; it elevated the author from a position of victimhood to one in which he or she could shape and decide the fate of the community. The fact that those who sought justice did not shy away from putting their names on their letters, even when they referred to those in positions of power, indicates that they viewed courts as just bodies, truly representative of the Jewish community, rather than fearing that courts were ruled by those in the position of privilege. Denunciations should not be studied, as is typically done, only in terms of the postwar quest for revenge or as a sign of the fragmentation of the Jewish society, but just as much as a symptom of its trust in the newly created Jewish community. In the process of coming forward and presenting denunciations, individuals allowed their voices to be heard and expressed their trust in their courts, a first step in rebuilding their communities.

Rehabilitation Requests

In an article written during the war, entitled "*Nasi bratobojcy*" [Our brothers' killers] Henryk Schachter mentioned the cruelty of the Judenrat and the Jewsh police and the call for their removal from society: "My eyes saw that picture. My eyes saw the sons produced by our nation and then I swore to myself. If I survive, there won't be a place for them among us. They will be punished. Punished as traitors of the nation. Punished as bandits and robbers. [...] Let this be a warning for [those] to whom this article is addressed. They should refrain from the positions they hold and await the time of God's trial, human trial for rehabilitation."[62]

While the primary way through which the civic court initiated its proceedings were denunciations, those who during the war held various positions of authority in camps and ghettos also addressed the court out of their own free will, asking for rehabilitation in the eyes of the community as they considered themselves unjustly punished by public opinion. Rehabilitation requests consisted of oral or written statements documenting the efforts of some condemned individuals to clear themselves from these indirect accusations. In the requests, survivors addressed the court by providing both their own version of events and deconstructing the gossip surrounding them, explaining who and why the rumours had been spread. Many of them did so just before emigration from Poland, wishing to start new life abroad without the shadow of "collaboration" following them. Others were previously beaten up, publicly insulted, or ostracized in another way, which included removal from communal buildings, kitchens, or synagogues.[63] In one instance, the court suspended a case after it turned out that a commandant of a Jewish transit camp, against whom they received a denunciation was, following liberation, lynched to death near Flossenburg by fellow prisoners.[64]

There were also those who were already cleared by the Polish state prosecutor's office, yet saw clearing their name in the eyes of the community as that of prime importance. Because those who addressed the courts usually did so as a last resort, haunted by gossips and hearsay, their rehabilitation requests were testimonies both to their wartime suffering and to that which they endured after the war. In those requests they had to prove that instead of (or addition to) holding wartime positions of authority, they also belonged to the community of pain and suffering. They, too, were martyrs, and wanted the court, and thus the community, to see them as such. As Sibylle Schmidt wrote: "In the discourse on survivor testimony, the ethical implications of accreditation have been widely discussed: listening to the victims' voices and acknowledging their authority has been conceived as an act of recognition, which can help heal individual trauma. As long as we, as audience, are listening to victims of political violence, we seem to be on the morally right side."[65] Unlike the wider community, the court treated those accused of collaboration as victims and, through that, fully validated their voices in the courtroom. In one such case, which illustrates this point, asking for rehabilitation after she was attacked by other survivors in a hostel, the former prisoner functionary Masza Engel wrote to the Jewish District Committee in Warsaw: "I am writing to the secretary of the district committee, as I would to my parents, you will understand me, I am a mother of a one-year-old child, I am pregnant with the second, I want to build the future of the Jewish nation."[66] While the civic court found her guilty of "the fact that in 1944, while at the Auschwitz (Oświęcim) camp, … she exercised the function of a kapo, and there were cases in which she beat her fellow prisoners," taking into account "the level of the social development of the accused," which was "not too high," and the fact that she was the mother of two children and expecting her third, the court deemed it sufficient to impose a reprimand.

It is undoubtedly a testament to the proliferation of false or mistaken denunciations that the court attempted to maintain a neutral standpoint towards rehabilitation requests, even when they were coming from people who admitted to holding positions of authority in the ghetto. This sympathetic stance went against popular feeling, which leaned strongly against both suspected collaborators and those associated with them, including family members.

In the absence of official documentation, the postwar search for justice among the surviving Jewish community, whether carried out by national jurisdiction, honour courts, citizens' tribunals, or rehabilitation commissions, was dominated by stories told by individual witnesses, defendants, and accusers. These stories were written down, shared, sometimes silenced, sometimes exaggerated, and followed Polish Jewish Holocaust survivors as they tried to continue their life in Poland, settled in Israel, or emigrated elsewhere. Thus, those who addressed the courts usually did it as a last resort, haunted by gossip and hearsay.

"I address you due to gossip circulating in Lublin regarding my role as a collaborator of the Judenrat," wrote survivor Majer Pinchas, who worked for the Jewish council as a bookkeeper.[67] In the course of the court investigation, it turned out that Pinchas was not only accused by members of the community of working with the Judenrat but, much more seriously, of being a Gestapo collaborator.[68] Pinchas, like many others, saw resorting to the civic court as the last step. He accused his accusers of being motivated by postwar grievances and jealousy, caused among others by his position of prominence in the local Jewish committee in Lublin after the war.[69] In his letter to the court, Pinchas underlined that due to accusations he lost his job with the committee and was facing a very difficult financial situation; he claimed that he could not afford to provide adequate medical care for his seven-month-old baby. His only sources of sustenance were parcels that he received from former fellow ghetto inmates who emigrated abroad.[70] The court, again, dismissed the case.

As was clear from Pinchas's case, such gossips and rumours could not only have serious emotional effects on those suspected by the community of collaboration but also could substantially impact their everyday lives. A teacher, Chawa Szmit, went to the civic court after an article published in popular Jewish newspaper, *Folks Sztyme*, referred to her as a cruel prisoner functionary, leading to Szmit losing her teaching position in a Jewish school in Łódź.[71] The court found that while Szmit was indeed a prisoner functionary, she took up that role unwillingly and acted in an exemplary way, using it to help fellow prisoners. In another instance, Adam Mazurek appealed to the court that he was "feeling innocent and at the same time emotionally overwhelmed" by accusations that as a member of the Judenrat or a Jewish policeman he had denounced a Jew in Kraków. As he stated, during the war he was neither in the Judenrat nor in the Jewish police. "Since the accusation [...] put me in a difficult situation in my workplace and as until clearing out of this case I will not have internal peace, I ask the court to resolve it as quickly as possible."[72] Another person, Marian Rotkoph, addressed the court after his name was mentioned as a Gestapo collaborator in a book commemorating the third anniversary of the liquidation of a ghetto in Kraków.[73] Importantly, Marian Rotkoph was indeed a member of the Ordnungsdienst, even if, as one of those testifying on his behalf stated, "He accepted this position crying, because it did not appeal to him in any way."[74] Rotkoph himself explained that people blamed him for being a relative of another high-level policeman, rather than for his own deeds.[75]

The most extreme cases were those of survivors who faced physical violence, such as being beaten after being "uncovered" by other survivors. In one case, the civic court suspended the case after it turned out that a commandant of a Jewish transit camp, against whom they received a denunciation, was lynched to death following liberation, near Flossenburg by fellow prisoners.[76] The court files show, however, a whole spectrum of potential substantial harassment linked to their wartime conduct. Such was the case of Karol Hertz, an employee of the Gdańsk Civic Militia, and during the war a member of the administration of the Ordnungsdienst in Łódź ghetto. Immediately after the war, in June 1945, Hertz was anonymously denounced and arrested by the Urząd Bezpieczeństwa in Łódź. He was released after a couple of days, having given his deposition and presenting witnesses who spoke on his behalf.[77] Even though Hertz was an employee of the civic militia, which vouchsafed for his integrity, the court conducted an in-depth investigation into his case, finally clearing his name in September 1948, a year after Hertz addressed it. Through that time, as we can gather from other cases, he was most likely boycotted by his community. It is not unlikely that, as again was the case with others, the stigma of a "collaborator" remained with him even after the passing of the verdict.

The Jewish civic court did not consider the responsibility of the Jewish Order Service or Judenrat as an institution; each defendant was individually tried, in each case to determine if he or she was responsible for the deeds committed. In the same vein, the civic court did not condemn surviving members of families of Jewish "collaborators," even though they might have been shunned by their community.[78] As Ewa Koźmińska-Frejlak has written in her study of the topic: "Accusations of collaboration against women were worded in a much more general way [than against men]. To initiate an investigation of a woman, it often sufficed to accuse her of consorting with a 'dubious character,' for example, a man whose function in the German organized apparatus of violence made him suspicious by default."[79]

Explaining why this should not be the case, Franciszka Brzezińska, the wife of a particularly infamous member of the Jewish Order Service in the Warsaw Ghetto, went to great lengths, in her letter asking for rehabilitation, to persuade the court that she did not partake in the crimes of her husband nor benefited from them in any way. She explained to the civic court: "At the beginning of the deportation action and as my husband was forced to undertake actions which were not fitting with my worldview, I began to press him to give up those actions. I attempted to persuade him day in and day out, and in those horrible times I did not benefit from benefits for policemen families. Like everyone else I hid like everyone else in cellars and basements and worked as a worker in a factory. Since my persuasions failed, I took my child and left."[80] The court dismissed her case, explaining that wives of policemen are not responsible for the actions of their husbands.

Specific cases included those where widows addressed the court to posthumously rehabilitate their husbands. Such was the case of Naumi Szenderowicz.[81] The court was in the process of proceeding with the case of her husband, a chairman of the Judenrat in Radom, when it learned about his suicide. The case was automatically suspended. Another case began after a rehabilitation request was filed by a mother regarding her son, residing in Buenos Aires, who was accused by fellow emigrants of collaboration.[82]

The question of staying in Poland or leaving was undoubtedly a key issue in the civic court proceedings, and one that still requires further analysis. The possibility of leaving was brought up by Rita Knyszyńska, a former overseer in a camp in Volkovysk, who interestingly brought up in her defense that she still resided in Poland.: "Please take into consideration that had I really been such a despicable and vile person [...] I would not now be in Poland but would have long [ago] been somewhere abroad, under a foreign name, and I would have not addressed you to investigate the case and carry out social proceedings, which I await with impatience."[83] She also stated that while she crossed the border into Germany a few times, she could not stay there "as there was a stain on me, which I had to wash off at all costs." Yet, as it turned out leaving did not guarantee safety from revenge.

In the four years of the court's functioning, against the backdrop of the turbulent social landscape of postwar Poland, mass migrations, antisemitic violence, and abandoned attempts at rebuilding Jewish life in Poland, it was, thus, victims or their relatives denouncing alleged collaborators to the court or alleged collaborators addressing the same court to clear their names (even absenting an official third-party denunciation against them). The court became a place where their stories met in three very different type of documents: rehabilitation requests, denunciations, and court rulings. These sources testify equally to the complexity of each victim's experience of the Holocaust and the emotional turmoil of immediate postwar life. These stories were raw, very private, and simultaneously animated by the communal dynamics in the aftermath of the Second World War. They spoke of the crimes committed, using the internal vocabulary of camps and ghettos, inaccessible to the outsiders but shared by the audience – the witnesses and the judging panel. This settling of accounts was personal and intimate, as intimate and personal as the violence that had been carried out by such "collaborators."

4 Polish Jews and Germany as the Site of Revenge

In the aftermath of the unconditional surrender of Germany on May 9, 1945, the country was divided into four occupational zones: northwest Germany under British control, the south under American, the east under Soviet, and the southwest under French. Berlin, which was in the Soviet zone, was further divided. West Berlin was occupied by the Western powers, and East Berlin was under Soviet control. Following liberation, the Allied Control Commission, the supreme authority of the allied government in Germany, faced many daunting challenges. One of these was resolving the fate of about nine million displaced persons (DPs) – foreign forced labourers and concentration camp inmates who found themselves in Germany at the end of the war. Repatriation of all DPs to their country of origin was estimated to take about six months and, indeed, between May and September 1945 about six million DPs left Germany. Nonetheless, two million DPs, including 50,000 Jews, refused to return to their former homeland. This group began to grow from September, as the first groups of Jews fleeing Poland began illegally entering the American Zone of Germany. By mid-1947, the Jewish DP population had reached about 250,000 people housed in hundreds of DP camps and urban centres, with about 185,000 of them in Germany, 45,000 in Austria, and 20,000 in Italy.

While awaiting emigration permits, DPs were housed in displaced-persons camps, administered by UNRRA (the United Nations Relief and Rehabilitation Administration) and later its successor agency, the International Refugee Organization; IRO. Together with aid agencies, in particular the JDC (Joint Distribution Committee), these organizations helped survivors organize their everyday lives anew. They provided medical assistance, aided in tracing missing relatives, established schools, helped with religious practice, and set up various cultural and social activities. They became centres of grassroot activities, initiated by the survivors themselves, who used this interim time in Germany to work on rebuilding their shattered communal life. As part of that effort, survivors organized political activities and parties, published newspapers, organized Yiddish language cultural life, and above all became involved in various forms of commemoration of both their loved ones and their destroyed communities, using the past as a foundation stone for their new, shared future.

For many Polish Jews, the camps were a liminal space: suspended between pre-war communal Jewish life in Poland, to which there was no return, and an uncertain future after emigration. Memories of Poland and still existing links to Poland were played out in the context of the strong Zionist impulse taking place in the camps, in particular, not only as imposed from the outside by representatives of the Yishuv, but to a large degree, as Avinoam J. Patt wrote, as "a unique, home-grown conclusion to wartime and postwar experiences, thereby revealing the tremendous agency of the DPs themselves in reconstructing political and cultural life in the aftermath of the destruction."[1] An important part in this was played by the need to deal with memories of what was referred to as collaboration and with the presence of collaborators among those building the new postwar community.

A Case Study: The Trial of Regina Kupiec

In 1948 one of the newspapers published in the Jewish displaced-persons camps of Germany reported a scene not uncommon in the first post-liberation years in Europe:

> On a bright sunny afternoon in May 1946 several thousand fans were enjoying a soccer game on the improvised sports field near Neu Freimann Siedlung. People of all ages, mainly from the nearby camps and Munich, as well as a small contingent of rooters from the opposition, ringed the field. The play was brisk, as was [to be] expected from two of the leading teams of the Soccer League, and to the satisfaction of the majority, the Neu Freimann team was ahead by a safe margin of two goals in the second quarter. As some fancy passing absorbed the onlookers, what appeared to be a fracas common among sports enthusiasts broke out on the south side of the field. An UNRRA official quietly disappeared from the judges' stand and before the crowds could be turned from the game, peace appeared to be restored.[2]

The official mentioned was H.J. Wachtel, director of the Neu Freimann UNRRA camp. A report he wrote provides crucial details about the brawl that took place during the football match. On intervening to break it up, he discovered that the cause of the commotion was a pregnant woman sitting among the spectators. She was the wife of the chairman of the Jewish Committee in a nearby camp. Wachtel reported: "People gathered around and started to scream 'kapo' and threatened this woman's life. […] The next day, at her own request, I turned this woman over to the Central Committee in order for them to clear her name."[3]

Regina Kupiec, born in 1916 in Warsaw, was a prisoner in the Warsaw Ghetto from 1940. During the Warsaw Ghetto Uprising in April 1943, she was transferred to Majdanek, then to Auschwitz three months later. While in Auschwitz, Kupiec was a prisoner functionary, first in Children's Block 25a and later in Women's Block 44 at Birkenau. She was liberated in May 1945 in the Sudetenland, where she had been transferred due to the *protekcja* (favouritism) she received. Kupiec later admitted that favouritism led to her transfer from Auschwitz. A year later, she was living in the Traustein camp, near Munich, where she was recognized by several former Birkenau prisoners at a football match.

The trial, held in front of a Munich court, focused on Kupiec's role as a functionary at Birkenau. Kupiec stated that her duties were limited to transporting food provisions from the warehouse to the inmates' block, and she claimed that she was "very good to everyone and even saved some people's lives."[4] However, witnesses at the trial presented a starkly different picture, uniformly testifying that she held a much more powerful position and that she abused her power by directing violence at the prisoners in the barracks. The most serious accusation was that she directly contributed to the deaths of other Jews by participating in drafting lists for the gas chambers.

The issue that was most emphasized, however, was that the victims of Kupiec's actions were those who could not defend themselves, especially children. One witness stated, "She stole the children's bread. After cutting pieces off the bread rations, she divided them among her friends."[5] Another claimed, "She stole the children's rations to obtain cosmetics for herself and other kapos."[6] Yet another maintained that "she stole the children's food to get powder and rouge for herself."[7] These accusations regarding children were underscored in the English translation of the trial proceedings, which was prepared for the American administration. This suggests that the prosecution considered them particularly grave allegations.

The defense witnesses summoned by Kupiec confirmed her image of being a "good" camp functionary and attempted to prove that her behaviour had caused no harm to anyone – she even went out of her way to help others. The person responsible for the crimes, it was suggested, might have been another prisoner functionary in the camp, a relative of the accused. One of those testifying in Kupiec's defense described her need to give testimony as "her human duty," asserting that the time when Kupiec was senior functionary in the block was the most difficult of the times at Auschwitz, the time when it was hardest to survive. Yet Kupiec did nothing to ensure her own survival at the cost of others. She concluded: "It is impossible that a person would, in a short period of time, change so much, that she would cause as much evil as she is accused of."[8] Though it was rare for the court to question witnesses' testimony, in this case it did reject statements in Kupiec's favour from prisoners who had been employed in "Kanada," classing them as unreliable. "Kanada" was a large warehouse where the belongings of those brought to Auschwitz-Birkenau were sorted, and the inmates employed there were considered to be in a privileged position.[9]

The final verdict must have been easy to reach. It was very rare to have so many witnesses confirm a suspect's behaviour in a court that had little access to official documentation and had to seek out testimonies from a population in constant flux. While the court dismissed the charge of participation in the selections, the extreme cruelty Kupiec had exhibited was sufficient reason to brand her a traitor to the Jewish people. This was the harshest verdict that was in the court's power to give. In the words of the survivors themselves, it meant that "[a collaborator] must be cut off from the Jewish community, so that wherever he goes or turns, in every land he will find people ready to impose the sentence of banishment, of not being able to be counted as one our people."[10] The court justified its decision in the following way:

> [Kupiec] behaved in a beastly manner to her fellow prisoners – Jewish children and women. Daily treatment of her fellow prisoners consisted of beating at every opportunity, use of various, malicious chicanery aimed at tormenting the remnants of human existence, destroying part of meal rations intended for the children and women, and at the same time brutally punishing those who asked for another spoonful of food, or who, without her knowledge, cooked some potatoes for themselves. The physical inflictions were constantly accompanied by such remarks as: "You'll end up in the crematorium, anyway"; "You'll leave the KZ only by the way of the oven"; and others. In contrast to the fellow prisoners whom she starved and with the aid of their stolen portions, she lived comfortably in the society of kapos and several Poles and carried on bartering for living essentials. Constant epithets which she hurled at Jewish women included "scurvy Jewess," "murderous Jewess."[11]

Kupiec was thus deemed unfit to remain part of the Jewish nation, especially because of the brutality of the crimes she had committed against fellow Jews. It was implied that, even by German standards, her behaviour had been inexcusable and that it was as a direct result of her actions that she was moved by camp administrators from the children's to the women's block in the barracks. In most cases it dealt with, the court would attempt to establish whether an accused person had had any chance of opting out of a compromising position and what the consequences would have been had they decided to do so.[12] However, it took a different line in the more drastic cases it heard: serious offenders could be held accountable for their deeds and subjected to the most severe punishment, even when they were only following orders. No exemption was given to Kupiec. She was sentenced as a traitor to the Jewish people, not only because of her exceptional sadism in beating up fellow prisoners and introducing a reign of terror into the camp but, above all, because she had done so on her own initiative. The presence of Germans had seldom been mentioned in the testimonies concerning her actions.

On closer reading of the verdict, we can see clearly that it depicts Kupiec as someone who *chose* to move outside the Jewish community. The key aim of the court was to show not only that wartime collaborators did not deserve to be part of the community of survivors but that, through their actions, they left it of their own volition.

Kupiec appealed the court's verdict. Her attorney pointed out several procedural errors and eventually questioned the legitimacy of the court's decision-making process. He claimed that it was "based on non-existent procedures" and an "archaic situation, unknown even at the time of the Inquisition courts."[13] However, these arguments were rejected and her appeal was rejected. The court explained that the Rehabilitation Commission followed prescribed procedures based on European examples, which were also unwritten in many countries.[14] The court did not address the attorney's other complaint, in which he questioned the ability of witnesses to recall traumatic events in the concentration camps. He claimed that the witnesses resorted to rhetoric similar to that found in stereotypical depictions of DPs as broken individuals with mental disorders, unable to function in society without outside control and guidance. He argued that "the difficult experiences and horror of suffering in the camp led to changes in the witnesses' psyche, making them unable to organize events according to time, place, person, etc."[15]

Thus, according to the judgment of the appeal court, Regina Kupiec remained a traitor to the Jewish people. The court ordered that the verdict be published in the Jewish press circulating in Germany's American Zone and sent to the Jewish Agency in Palestine, Joint, HIAS, and the Federation of Polish Jews, partly to prevent Kupiec from emigrating. However, she managed to leave Germany and emigrate to the United States six months after her trial in December 1948.[16] It is unclear what happened to her in her new country.

System of Justice in DP Camps

As Regina Kupiec's case clearly demonstrates, among the Jewish displaced persons, gathered and awaiting emigration in temporary camps in postwar Germany, Austria, and Italy, everything was revenge. Photographs from theatre plays depicted scenes of Hitler's humiliation,[17] and children in DP camps were considered by the DP leadership to be "the carriers of our revenge."[18] As the first issue of *Undzer Weg* [Our Way], the most influential and widely circulated Jewish newspaper in occupied Germany, proclaimed on its first page:

A Yiddish newspaper on this earth soaked in Jewish blood and sweat,

> Dreamed revenge came true, that I craved.
> Today storm is my song, each word a sword.[19]

At the same time, against the backdrop of lynch law, accusations, rumours, and anonymous denunciations, major national groups gathered in temporary centres in Germany, Austria, and Italy and began organizing their system of justice. As was the case across liberated Europe, the displaced persons' fight against wartime collaborators was a quest for justice and personal and communal revenge. For all of them, creating their own honour courts was a crucial part of their community-building process, so they could be judged by their own people, without the intermediary of the occupational army administration, international relief organizations, or, in particular, the German juridical system.

Yet, in the Jewish community, the responsibility towards remembrance as displayed in the practices of honour courts had a particular function. Its aim was to create a new future in Eretz Israel. Those who stood in front of the Jewish honour courts in DP camps – former kapos, Jewish policeman and members of the Judenrat – attempted to prove that they too deserved to be part of this future.

The system of Jewish DP courts formed part of a larger system of DP courts existing in all large displaced-persons camps in Italy and occupied Germany and Austria. Set up by survivors immediately after liberation, their primary aim was to deal with the everyday running of the camp. They were a necessary part of establishing normalcy and a step towards the rehabilitation of its inhabitants.[20] The collaboration trials, which will be the focus of this chapter, were only a fraction of the work undertaken by honour courts, as well as only a part of the tapestry of formal and informal methods of dealing with suspected collaborators in displaced-persons camps. In the immediate post-liberation period, prior to the establishment of the courts and in the early stages of their functioning, suspected collaborators were most often dealt with through less formal means: social ostracism, beatings, or murder, referred to in memoirs as "clearing out the kapos."[21] Estera Rauch-Kwiatkowska, born in 1921, who survived as a non-Jewish Pole in forced labour in Germany, recalled being constantly blackmailed by a couple of other forced labourers who knew of her identity. After liberation, instead of going to a Jewish displaced-persons camp, she decided to keep her "Aryan" papers and go to the Polish one – as she recalled, mainly because she wanted to get revenge on her tormentors. In the end she failed: one of them was stabbed to death earlier by other Poles, and the other escaped to Poland.[22] Another Holocaust survivor, Ruth Kluger, remembered visiting one of the DP camps with Ben Gurion: "We arrived in Munich … We sat in a room … Suddenly there was a deafening noise. It was horrible … someone had apprehended a kapo-there were people like that, and began to beat him until he was bloody. And Ben-Gurion just sat there … and I got up and ran outside … and they caught another kapo and started meting out justice to him as well. It was an awful thing."[23]

The DP press and surviving court documentation clearly show that the shadow of collaboration was always present in the life of Jewish displaced persons. In November 1945 the *Landsberg Lager Cajtung*, published in the large Landsberg DP Camp, described "many instances of [Landsberg DP] Centre residents attacking people designated as kapos by individuals and seriously injuring them."[24] Passionate exchanges on survival, resistance, and victimhood penetrated the camps. Screams of "kapo" or "odeman" in the early postwar days commonly preceded brawls and fights, and complaints of slander or false accusations of not only collaboration with the Germans, but also the NKVD[25] or the UPA[26] gradually became a staple of court proceedings throughout the new Jewish communities cropping up in Austria, Germany, and Italy. This was not a uniquely Jewish phenomenon, but more of a sign of the times, with *zniesławienie* [slander] being also the reason for the majority of cases tried by Polish DP honour courts.[27]

In one documented case, which took place in the Bad Ischl DP Camp in Austria, the president of the local Jewish table tennis club faced the honour court for referring to the behaviour of a DP camps policeman who knocked over a table tennis table as "odeman behaviour, which has its place in concentration camps or German torture chambers." Another in the same camp was tried for referring to the camp police commandant as a "concentration camp murderer" and for publicly stating that "a decent man would never become a camp policeman."[28] Documentation from other camps shows that such cases were swiftly punished by courts, usually with hefty financial fines.[29]

There is no doubt that the creation of courts was a response to this situation. When writing about setting up of the courts, another key DP newspaper, *Undzer Hofenung* [Our Hope] wrote:

> Man is by nature a social animal; since time immemorial he has strived towards a communal life and not towards isolation. In communal cohabitation, mankind can satisfy its material, moral, ethical, and other needs. Collective cohabitation limits man's freedom.
>
> In isolation, he creates forms of ethics and justice for his own benefit and adjusts to them himself. The moment he decides to live in society he falls under certain restrictions, which oblige everyone. Without an organised group, whether it be family, society, or a state, man cannot be in contradiction to the general laws or live in opposition to them according to his own judgment; he must submit to the generally accepted norms for the good of the group.[30]

While the allied occupational powers appreciated the role that courts played in regulating internal life of camps, which would have not otherwise been achieved without resorting to violence or employing military police, it does not mean that they accepted them unquestionably. On the contrary, they were unwilling to invest them with the full authority of law. The main reason for such a situation seems to have been a lack of regulation concerning the functioning of camp courts, in particular in the area of their jurisdiction and their competence in terms of imposing punishment. In the American zone of Germany, for example, for the functioning of courts for which we have ample documentation, the actual assignment of punishment was the responsibility of the Assembly Centre Director. The camp court was to function only as his advisory board, and even that was only allowed reluctantly, as qualms concerning the DPs "mental capacity"[31] or even moral right to sit on the tribunal were brought up by both members of the military and workers of relief agencies.[32] Such accusations were also brought up against Jewish witnesses testifying against Nazi criminals who abused them, with their testimonies sometimes seen as unreliable.[33]

As a result, the camp courts' power was legally limited to judging delinquencies committed within the confines of the camp, and in its judgments it could impose only administrative punishments, such as restrictions on movement, limitations on camp privileges, assignment of extra work and duties, and similar measures, stopping short of fines and imprisonment. Any more serious cases were to be referred to military courts of the allied occupational authorities, which had various punishments at their disposal ranging from fines, through to imprisonment, and even the death penalty. Such circumscribed authority allowed the allied powers to hold control over matters that camp courts may have not been particularly interested in curtailing, such as the black market or possession of arms. It also enabled them to be in command of who received entry visas to their countries and, through that, ensured the support of domestic public opinion and the press.[34] As a result the courts also tried Jews who were accused of crimes as prisoner functionaries or members of the Ordnungsdienst.[35]

One survivor recalled how he became the victim of the British administration:

> We were starving. I remembered I went into a village nearby. The people weren't home, they must have run away. I found some potatoes left over in a pot. I ate all the potatoes in the pot. I was drinking syrup; I couldn't help myself. We were about 5 guys and walked to another house. We saw people serving at a table. I asked them in German, can we sit down and join you. They said, "Get out of here." One of our guys got so mad he pushed the tablecloth. A little girl saw this through the window and got the police. English soldiers came and took the five of us and put us in jail for three days, for "plundering." This was in an English jail when we were supposed to be liberated!! I was so sick and miserable.[36]

Another one, located at the American zone of Germany, testified:

> On the way we got some sticks, we started to beat up some Germans on their shoulders and heads, they were riding on bicycles. It came up in a report in the police station, these people were beating up Germans, killing Germans. So, they changed the plans and they put us in another prison camp. The Americans were guarding this time.[37]

Fear of a lack of understanding on the part of those outside the survivor community, in particular non-Jews, was grounded in reality. Throughout their stay in postwar Germany, DPs were subject to military government law and directives. From the moment the DP camp system was set up as the war was ending, DPs of all nationalities lived under the threat of allied court martial.[38] Even after the end of military action in Germany, the Jewish survivor community was repeatedly informed by their press of cases where survivors standing in front of military courts were mistreated,[39] particularly when accused of offences that violated military government law: illegal possession of arms or illegal crossing of borders, and, most frequently, "black market" trading. Such was the case of 20-year-old Chaim K., a former inmate of Buchenwald, who was sentenced to 15 years in prison by a British military court for illegal possession of arms. During the trial, K., who did not speak English or German, the two languages in which the trial was conducted, did not receive any help from the Polish liaison officer, assistance to which he was entitled.[40] It was only because his case was reported to London by representatives of Jewish aid organizations, and thus reached the international public, that he was acquitted. Such instances reinforced survivors' determination to deal with criminal issues on their own.

Thus, the courts remained under the constant threat of closure as the allied administration monitored their activities, and in many cases did not refrain from intervening, in particular when they felt that the courts usurped jurisdiction and authority from the War Crimes Commission.[41] However, as their archives attest, this did not stop them from operating and in numerous cases passing sentences that clearly breached their limited powers. This fact was in many cases also acknowledged by some of the allied authorities, who recognized in correspondence that "the Jewish camps offenders will not be turned over to the Military Government Courts [...] and furthermore that [Jewish] witnesses will not appear against a member of the camp in the Military Government Courts."[42]

Trials of Suspected Collaborators

Despite the mounting number of problems concerning everyday camp life, from their first days of existence Jewish camp courts devoted time and energy to conducting investigations and later trials of suspected collaborators.[43] Already in the first trial held in front of Landsberg camp court in the American zone of Germany, on October 2, 1946, Majer Rubin, a policeman in the Skarżysko Kamienna forced labour camp, was sentenced to four months of imprisonment and life-long banishment from the Jewish community for beating up his fellow prisoners. This punishment was described as the harshest punishment envisaged by law.[44] Three weeks later, on October 29, the court in Landsberg sentenced Dovid Klejnman to the same punishment. As a policeman in the

Kraków Ghetto he had participated in deportations and later displayed brutality as a kapo in the Plaszow concentration camp.[45]

With growing difficulties around their functioning and lack of power in terms of penalizing offenders, the most important collaboration cases were, thus, with time, increasingly referred directly to central courts of honour: the briefly operational Court of Honour in Belsen,[46] the Court of Honour and Rehabilitation of the Union of Liberated Jews in the American Zone in Germany located in Munich, the Court of Honour at the Central Organization of Survivors in Italy (Merkaz Irgun Hapletaim Be'Italia) in Rome, and the Court of Honour in Linz, in Austria. From the summer of 1946, local camp courts in the American zone of Germany, where the vast majority of cases took place, were supervised by the Central Jewish honour court in Munich, set up by the Central Committee of Liberated Jews, with members of the central court elected by the delegates attending the US zone survivor congresses. A year later the committee set up a new body, the Rehabilitation Commission, which focused solely on cases of alleged collaboration with the Nazis. Starting in 1948, the Rehabilitation Commission in Munich took over all cases relating to accusations of collaboration. The rationale was that this body was more proficient than individual camp courts at locating evidence and providing witnesses. Additionally, because it functioned under the supervision of the Central Committee, which was approved by the US Military Government, it was, therefore, more appropriately authorized to carry out high-stakes trials. The commission also served as the court of appeal for those who thought they had been wrongly judged by camp courts and dealt with rehabilitation requests. This was particularly important as denunciations of camp inhabitants accused of collaboration were not always legitimate or filed in good faith. As archival documentation clearly shows, many (and indeed sometimes overzealous) motivations were at play, including acts of personal revenge or jealousy. Denunciations could be used to address tensions related to unsettled pre- or postwar scores, somebody's elevated position in the DP society, or their luck in obtaining emigration visas.

While in Poland, Jews were requested to file rehabilitation requests solely on the basis of their previous participation in the Jewish police or the Judenrat, but DPs could do so if they felt they were unfairly accused of criminal behaviour during the occupation.[47] Participation in the police or the Judenrat was not seen as an act of collaboration or as a reason for persecution and did not mean that the former functionary had to undergo a rehabilitation trial.

As the Rehabilitation Commission stated:

> Generally speaking, the police did not enjoy a good reputation. Generalizing, however, and transferring this view to all members of the police without addressing their cases individually can lead to hurtful injustice. In any case, without any ruling in the statute or any decision from a higher legal institution, which would unequivocally state that the activity of the police or other institutions in the ghetto was criminal, the Rehabilitation Commission treats this case equally to others, according to the general rules of the legal system and basing its judgment on individual proof of guilt or innocence.[48]

As was the case with the Jewish civic court in Poland, the rehabilitation commissions had a very limited scope of penalties at its disposal, yet ones that had much more powerful symbolic meaning. These varied from exclusion from the Jewish community, prohibition from holding any position in the organizations and institutions of the displaced persons, loosing entitlement to material assistance by any Jewish relief organization, or the right to emigration with the help of the Jewish Agency for Palestine or HIAS and, finally, being branded as a traitor of the Jewish nation. Henryk Frydman, a kapo from the Mielec labour camp, was sentenced as a traitor of the Jewish people not only due to his particular sadism in beating up fellow prisoners and the rule of terror that he introduced in the camp but above all because he did so "from his own initiative and rarely in the presence of any German."[49]

While in most cases the court attempted to establish whether the accused had a chance of opting out of their position and what the consequences would have been had they decided to do so,[50] in the most drastic cases, one could still be held accountable for their deeds and subjected to the most severe punishment, even when only following orders. Such was the case of Mieczysław Czapnicki, block leader of the concentration camp in Budzyń. Discussing his case, the court stated:

> [Czapnicki] hit a sick Jewish inmate on the head with a log of wood. When thereupon the inmate fell down in a hole specially prepared for him, the defendant took from the ground a big stone of about 10 kg, placed himself over the Jew and threw the stone twice against the head of the Jew smashing his head. [...] The standpoint of the court is that an order by a higher authority does not free anybody of guilt and punishment, and this is the same opinion of the state courts.[51]

In cases of particular gravity, the commission decided to refer those sentenced to the Military Courts. To underline the weight of this decision, once in front of the allied courts, the collaborators lost all help from the Jewish community as those tried for "denunciations by or of Jewish people" were not even entitled to free legal aid provided by the American Jewish Joint Distribution Committee.[52] One of the most notorious cases was that of Norbert Jolles, a camp senior in the ammunition factory of the Hasag concentration camp in Czestochowa. He was unequivocally described by former camp prisoners as a sadist who singlehandedly ruled the camp and had the right to beat not only the Jewish prisoners but even some of the German overseers. Testimonies suggested that he had influence on the contents of deportation lists and could thus ensure the death of all those who held incriminating evidence against him. As one person testified: "Jolles was kind of a spectre throughout the camps, and everybody was in great fear of him. If anybody wanted to threaten us, menace was clad in the words: Jolles will come to see you."[53] Jolles's culpability was magnified by the fact that he could have used his power in the camp or the ghetto to help other prisoners,[54] with witnesses claiming that "had he only been willing to act in our favour, everything would have become easier for us" and that he "was able to spare people's lives if he only intended to do so."[55] On that basis, the honour court in Munich not only sentenced him as a traitor of the Jewish People and referred him to the American Military Court but also simultaneously addressed the Polish Military Mission in Berlin to lodge a motion to extradite him to Poland. According to Jolles's file in the Instytut Pamięci Narodowej in Warsaw, his extradition was discussed by the Polish authorities in 1950 yet was never carried out due to lack of adequate proof of his guilt.[56]

Importantly, acting against Jewish people could also take place after the war. In late 1947 the honour court in Heidenheim Volt-Siedlung tried a case against Izaak Szwalbe, who was accused by members of the camp Jewish committee of "undermining the authority of Jewish self-government" by giving false information to the members of IRO and the German administration in the town where the camp was located. Szwalbe was found guilty, and the court addressed the camp's rabbinic authority to remove him from the "community of Israel" and to publish that information in the Jewish press. It also asked all surrounding Jewish camps and communities not to allow Szwalbe to settle there. The sentence was to be published in major Jewish DP newspapers in the area.[57] In the case of Nikolaj Lewinstein, accused of particular cruelty as the bloc elder in KZ Dachau, the honour court in the Federation of Lithuanian Jews stated that "since the sanctions which can be applied by the court are too lenient in comparison to his actions, he has by his own actions excluded himself from the community of Israel." The court then handed over the case to Philip Auerbach,[58] state commissioner of the Bavarian provincial government for religious, political, and racial victims of the Nazis.

While there were individual cases of defendants who contested the honour courts' procedures,[59] the courts' sentences were binding and recognized by the camp committees and the Jewish relief organizations. However, just like decisions of the camp courts, they often awoke ferocious discussion, mainly as a result of the leniency of their rulings.[60] This was protested against by those gathered in the court rooms, and also in the DP press, with both demanding punishment equivalent to the crimes committed by those sentenced. The courts' proceedings were seen as unjust in general, but in particular against the moral vision of Judaism. A DP newspaper contributor lamented the "lack of discipline of our masses, truly laughable actions of our security and legal bodies [and] [...] the cowardly behaviour of our judges." He complained about the leniency of sentences: "According to what codex do those gentleman work? Maybe according to the Jewish Torah? But there are points there such as 'an eye for an eye' guaranteeing that everyone will get a deserved sentence."[61]

There is no doubt that notwithstanding the judges' intentions, this leniency was partially forced by the court's limited punitive powers, which were often bitterly referred to in its sentences. Considering the magnitude of the crimes it dealt with, it is unsurprising that in numerous cases the court was pronouncing the supreme penalty at its disposal, while simultaneously underlining its inadequacy in relation to crimes committed. One such case was that of Arnold Einhorn, from Kattowitz, who, between August 1944 and April 1945, was the block elder in Melk, a sub-camp of Mauthausen concentration camp. During his rehabilitation trial, which took place in Munich in 1949, he was accused of beating fellow prisoners to death "while proving to the SS-man that he is an efficient kapo." Explaining the grounds for judgment, the court stated that "the fine is a result of an opinion that Jewish spilled blood must be revenged, even if only in the small extent of the statute of the rehabilitation committee."[62]

What has to be taken into consideration when assessing the severity of the courts' sentences is that because Jews already envisaged building a new country in Israel on the basis of the displaced-persons community, their camp justice system was to go far beyond keeping order in the camp and upholding their good image in the eyes of the allied administration. It was to be a crucial tool in creating a new future. To quote a 1946 article in *A Haim*:

> All of us here come from countries where a whip ruled, where various laws were imposed on us, which may not have been just but useful for the governments of those countries. We blindly fulfilled the orders of more or less important offices and thanked God that they do not bother us. Now, when we are temporarily located here, when we live together in one group, we go through spiritual and physical preparation to go to Eretz Israel as the healthy element, good citizens.[63]

DP courts were thus to play an extremely important role: that of educating the Jewish community, to "show how to behave in a moral and decent way, to guide towards the right path."[64]

This restorative rather than retributive character of DP justice was particularly crucial in the case of young people, for those who had received all their life education in ghettos and concentration camps and who might have erred through lack of guidance rather than through the fault of their character.[65] This educational aspect was clearly displayed in the court sentences, which focused not only on punishment but also on the lessons that the accused had to learn so that, enriched by them, they could return to become valuable members of the community. Such was the case of Jakov Flayshker, an attendant in the steam baths in Skarżysko Kamienna forced labour camp. On September 6, 1946, standing in front of the court of Camp Herzog in Hessisch-Lichtenau in Germany, Flayshker was sentenced for brutally abusing inmates, particularly women, by beating them on their faces and bodies, confiscating valuables, and "other brutal deeds." He was sentenced to three months imprisonment and deportation from the camp. As a DP newspaper reporting on the case stated, "the accused was given the opportunity of returning to the community after a year of the sentence; his misdemeanour should be forgiven if, during this year, he proves that he acted for the good of the Jewish community and deserves to become a rightful citizen."[66] In a similar case, concerning an OD-man in a kitchen in the Kaufering sub-camp of the Dachau concentration camp, "it was proved beyond doubt that the accused beat furiously and without pity those who wanted to receive soup," including knocking out the teeth of some prisoners. He was described as deserving lenient treatment to allow him to return to the Jewish community as "a type of an average policeman and not some murderer."[67] Such a stance was strongly promoted by Samuel Gringaus, a Kovno ghetto survivor,[68] and twice elected president of the Council of the Liberated Jews in Bavaria. Gringaus. the author of the first articles on the organizational aspect of life in the ghetto, including the sociology of power structures, was a firm believer in the positive rebuilding of the community, stating that the only way towards "inner purification and moral recovery" was not through blind revenge but through productive work and education.[69]

This view of the role of the court meant that handling justice in DP camps had to be restricted to those who understood the past experiences of camp and ghetto survivors. This of course ruled out any non-Jews, but also, in the opinion of many, those Jews who did not have direct experience of the Holocaust. "Those gentlemen from Russia," as one of the ghetto survivors bitterly wrote in a letter testifying in a collaboration trial, "speak loudly of heroism, but only we know that the true heroes remain silent today."[70] The relative leniency of the sentences can thus also be explained by the fact that their passage was entrusted to people who not only held public trust and were experienced lawyers but who also had personal experience of life in camps and ghettos. One of the key figures in the Munich Court of Honour, lawyer and social activist Władysław Freidheim, who survived the war first in the Warsaw ghetto and later as a kapo in a camp in Budzyń, voiced this attitude when writing:

> It is impossible for those who did not themselves go through the hell of the camp that they could understand how low 90 per cent of camp inhabitants fell. People became animals in the full meaning of this word. The saying "*homo homini lupus est*" took its full shape there. Great egoism reigned. Animalistic life instinct led to people reaching for all means to remain alive. Those means were not always clean. It happened that people occupied themselves with denunciations, believing that this way they can remain alive. Sometimes, at night, one stole a piece of bread from under another's head or some objects which were later sold for a piece of bread or a plate of soup. Unfortunately, this was happening every day. And it concerned people who would not even dream of anything like that before the war.[71]

Defense Strategies in Honour Courts

A cross-section of the Jewish postwar community stood in front of the displaced-persons honour courts, ranging from former kapos of small camps who struggled to compose a short defense statement, to educated members of the Judenrate who presented the praesidium with files of support letters from the highest echelons of society. Some of them had at that point already spent years trying to prove their innocence in front of subsequent courts and tribunals, constantly facing denunciations, rumours, and finger pointing, which chased them on their journeys through postwar Europe. Some found themselves in Germany exactly because they were trying to escape tribunals.[72] For others a court order brought them back to events that they thought were already buried in the ruins of Jewish life in occupied Poland. What they all shared was that with no documentation available, their only way of defense was putting their word against that of their accusers. As one former prisoner of Kaufering stated when testifying against a particularly brutal kapo: "Tens of people died from his hand. The whole camp knew about it, but unfortunately few of us survived, and above all nobody was in a state of mind to document his crimes."[73]

Displaced-persons camps are often seen as communities of memories; memories of pre-war life and of persecution, memories that were to serve as a warning and reminder of a new life that had to be fought for. Yet in a community created by memory, it could also become the toughest weapon in the fight for justice and revenge. For the defendants their ability to remember not only what happened during the war but also to recall those they encountered during and after the war who could help or hurt their case became their greatest and only asset when facing the tribunal. While the courts pulled all the strings to locate as many witnesses as possible, they were significantly aided in the endeavour by both the defendant and the prosecution who were eager to secure favourable court statements.[74] The files of the courts as well as the personal collections of the defendants contained evidence showing that in many cases gathering such testimony was a pre-emptive gesture of those who felt that due to their war time activities they could have been in danger of facing accusations later.

The first step of those who stood in front of the tribunal was to establish who they were; to prove that they shared the identity of She'erith Hapletah and, as such, deserved to remain part of the community; and to demonstrate that they did not fit the communal memory of the crime.

To prove their "Yiddish hertz" the defendants often composed their statements for the court in Yiddish, even if very faulty, rather than in Polish.[75] In these statements, as in those of the witnesses for the defense, they appear as "sons of decent middle class Jewish families,"[76] or even the "old Zionist family."[77] Almost uniformly, the defendants displayed from early youth strong links with the Jewish national cause, with one former policeman bringing up in his defense the case of his brother who was killed in Eretz Israel in 1938.[78] Crucially, such links were to continue during the occupation, with the defendants extending help towards Zionist activists in ghettos and camps, thus proving their "loyalty towards Jewish interests."[79] At least two defendants claimed that they were assigned to work in the Jewish police by the Zionist underground, and in the case of one of them, the court accepted this as a valid argument.[80] This was similar to the stance held by Polish state courts, where in the trials of Polish prisoner functionaries it was often assumed that a Polish patriot could not be at the same time a war criminal.[81]

In other instances, overusing the argument of pre-war Jewish association could prove dangerous. When found guilty, the fact that someone was a pre-war social activist could serve as a reason to judge his collaboration during the war more severely than those who had no links to the community before the war. And so in the Munich trial of Józef Hoch, a member of Lviv Judenrat, an important part of the sentence rested on the fact that he was found to have played a key part in the organization of deportations from the ghetto, and that "as a long-term social activist he did not behave honestly during the occupation."[82]

Stories of Zionist affiliations sometimes offered the only detailed information concerning a defendant's wartime experiences. While they usually denied all wrongdoing, or only admitted to it in a very limited degree, they did not divulge their duties as kapo or policeman, telling only stories of externalities, without revealing personal experiences. "I only had a thin stick, and I've never beaten anyone to death," stated one of the kapos, who according to all testimonies displayed particular brutality in a camp.[83] However, those who were not liberated in camps or during death marches often discussed in great details their fate in hiding or immediately after their liberation. They may have been in a better position in the ghetto, these testimonies seem to suggest, but they suffered just as much when hiding in the countryside or in the forests. They too belonged to the persecuted group, the community of sufferers. The reason why they would be put in front of the tribunal was the same in the vast majority of testimonies: it was personal revenge.

It is rare that the accused or their supporters spoke openly about who was interested in harming them, even though they often shared such information in private.[84] Instead, they usually referred to an anonymous person or group. "All accusations presented against me in a letter are despicable lies and come, I suppose, from a person or people who have some private resentment towards me or were mislead by a third party."[85] These are the words of Roman Merin, an official in *Zentrale der Judischen Altestenrate in Oberschlesien* (Central Office of the Jewish Councils of Elders in Upper Silesia) and a relative of its chairman, Moishe Merin. Witnesses in the trial of a Lviv Judenrat member, Ludwik Jaffe, spoke of a whole "campaign of defamation" directed against him by "people who on the basis of gossip and groundless rumours throw accusations at him and take upon themselves a horrible responsibility towards their conscience and towards the truth."[86]

The reason for revenge resulting in what the defense saw as groundless postwar accusations was often claimed to be a wartime conflict resulting from the privileged position of a defendant during the occupation. For example, Ludwik Jaffe, the head of the accommodation department in the Lviv ghetto, was to make enemies among people for whom he could not find a living place. As one witness for the defense stated: "It is clear that he was not able to fulfill the requests and demands of thousands of people gathered at that time in the Jewish centre in Lvov; it is also clear that helping the thousands was not possible."[87] Jaffe himself stated in his defense that when he was saving some people, "others muttered: why not us."[88] A similar issue was brought up in the case of David Gertler, head of the Sonderabteilung [Special Department] in the Jewish Order Service, and following the September 1942 mass deportations the most powerful man in the Litzmanstadt ghetto. When Gertler took over the provisioning of the ghetto, living standards did indeed improve, and despite his contacts with the Gestapo he was hailed by many survivors as saviour who managed to prolong the life of many. His supporters blamed those who criticized him: "If some suffered needlessly in those years, it was rather because of the impossible situation than through the intent or neglect of Gertler's direction."[89]

As the last resort, those facing the court defended themselves by questioning the witnesses' ability to recall the traumatic events from the occupation, resorting to rhetoric not dissimilar from that employed in stereotypical depictions of the DPs as a community ridden with mental disorders, unable to function as an ordered society without outside control and guidance. While there is no such questioning of the witnesses' reliability in the official court statements, the effect of the Holocaust trauma on early testimonies was also discussed at the time by leading activists in the camps' social life.[90]

The second, probably more important, alleged reason for revenge was the privileged position of the defendant after liberation. For many defendants their postwar activities served as the main defense argument, their moral authority stemming from their public role post-liberation. While the fact that someone "vanished after liberation" could be taken as proof that they were attempting to escape revenge,[91] remaining visible among the community signified a clear conscience. One of those who successfully employed this argument was Władysław Freidheim, the chairman of the Society of Jews from Poland, and a member of the Praesidium of the Committee of Liberated Jews, who was accused in

1948 of brutal behaviour as a kapo in Budzyń concentration camp. In his statement presented to the honour court in Munich, Freidheim wrote:

> All conferences took place under my leadership. Hundreds, and maybe thousands of Jews participated in them, among them a great number of those who were in camps with me and were liberated with me. None of them accused me of anything.
>
> From the first day after liberation until today I live in Munich. During my work I visited many camps where I met people who were with me in camps; none of them accused me of anything. [...] If I felt guilty of anything I would not have held the above-mentioned offices, and under no circumstances would I put myself in the lead of social work.[92]

Despite the part he played for three years in the Jewish Community, gossip about his collaboration, which forced him to file a rehabilitation request, began circulating only in 1948, when Freidheim was on the brink of emigrating. As he continued in his defense statement:

> In recent times some people (their names are not known to me) are spreading rumours that I have not behaved decently in the ghetto or camp. Those rumours place a shadow on my good name, which I have worked for over 25 years in social work [to establish] [...] I want to emigrate. The central Aliyah Commission organized certificates for me and my wife. I will not leave Germany leaving behind me even the slightest trace of suspicion on my person.

Accusations regarding the wartime activities of people in positions of power were to be, if we believe their defense, primarily a result of internal conflicts within camps. This was particularly underlined in the case of people who openly associated with political groups or organizations that were in conflict with the DP leadership. In by far the best known collaboration case which took place in front of the Central Court of Honour in Italy, Ludwik Jaffe argued that he was accused as a combined result of his affiliations with the Bund[93] and his position as the director of ORT in Italy. The sentence, which found that Jaffe had acted as a go-between for the Gestapo and the Judenrat and had participated in organizing deportations from the Sobieski school (the March action), was based on only a few testimonies, none of them coming from a direct witness of his actions. He was forbidden from taking public positions in the Jewish community and from benefiting from aid from Jewish organizations. In another case, a former policeman requested that his case should be tried in the central court in Munich, rather than in the appropriate camp court as he felt that the latter were ruled by party interests and could be negatively disposed towards those of different political outlooks.[94]

The first secretary of the Central Committee, Benisz Tkacz, also believed that his accusers had a political motive. He stood in front of the Rehabilitation Commission in March 1948, following accusations that he had abused his position as a secretary of the Jewish police in the Kovno ghetto. These accusations were presented to the election commission as he put forward his name to be elected for the third congress of Sherit Hapleitah.[95] In the last sentence of his statement Tkacz urged the commission to resolve the issue for both his sake and the sake of its image.[96] The commission agreed with his position and treated the case as one of particular importance.[97] In the case of both Tkacz and Freidheim, the final decision was that participating in the Jewish Police or being a kapo alone were not strong enough reasons to remove someone from the postwar Jewish communal life. It was only in cases of particular brutality where their position in the camp was to be suspended. Such was the case of Juliusz Zeigel, director of a DP camp in Italy and, during the occupation, a former councilman in Będzin ghetto and head of its labour department. The case was tried in front of the court of honour in Milan and the verdict announced on July 19, 1946, and despite the fact that Zeigel "expressed severe remorse," he was nonetheless sentenced for displaying particular cruelty and forbidden to hold any position in the public life of the Jews.[98] The honour court in Munich, on the other hand, removed individuals from their public positions, such as Chaim Aleksandrowicz, a policeman from the Kovno police, block elder in Kaufering camp, and representative of the Poalei Zion-Hitahdut Party.[99]

Even though the honour courts did not expect those who held positions of power in the camps to automatically undergo rehabilitation trials, many DPs held a strong conviction that people who collaborated should not hold any position in the postwar community. This topic was passionately discussed in the DP press and in personal conversations.[100] "You probably remember 'our friend' Mandelbaum from Wieliczka and his tricks in the camp," wrote one survivor to his former fellow camp inmate in September 1947. "This Mandelbaum today plays an important part in the social life, even though he is as much of a thief as he used to be." The author of the letter encouraged his reader to send his testimony in accusation of the said Mandelbaum, and his case indeed was taken to court.[101]

In many other cases, the court noted that the accusations were directed against instances of kapos in position of power rather than individuals standing trial. In the case of Benisz Tkacz, for example, the court, deciding in his favour, found that witnesses testifying in his case "did not show particular bitterness caused by his behaviour [in the ghetto] but saw it as inappropriate that a former policeman would hold an eminent position in Jewish society."[102] Similarly, in the case of Ludwik Jaffe, one of the witnesses who based his testimony on hearsay of Jaffe's behaviour saw making his statement as a "duty towards the society, because a man so discredited as Dr Jaffe, due to his cooperation with the Germans, does not need to participate in public life or take on communal posts."[103]

While the court also noted revenge to be a principal reason for persecution and underlined cases where witnesses spoke "with tears but no feeling of revenge,"[104] it was also aware of the defense strategies of those who stood trial. It was clear that the choice of witnesses for the defense reflected the pre-war and postwar social circles of the defendants and those who profited from their work during the war, rather than those who could testify to their actual conduct during the occupation. Moreover, much of the testimony came from those who used the trial to clear their own name too.[105] In many cases, for example, people who themselves had been tried for collaboration would volunteer to testify in favour of or against former fellow policemen from the same ghetto or camp.

As a result, the tribunal sometimes rejected testimony from certain witnesses automatically, including "prisoners who, thanks to their work, had privileged positions in the camp."[106] During the trial of Regina Kupiec, the honour court rejected as unreliable testimonies of fellow prisoners employed in "Kanada."[107] Similarly, during the trial of Leon Mercel, the court, although not rejecting the positive statements of his collaborators, nonetheless did not take them into consideration while passing sentence, stating: "Even if individual prisoners chosen by the accused benefited from his actions, this does not make him less guilty."[108] In another case, the court stated in its conclusion that "the commission sentenced the accused not because he treated the witnesses of the defense well but because he was beating up the witnesses of the prosecution."[109] The court also usually rejected statements from witnesses who were only called in by the defense to state that they had not heard of or seen any criminal actions of the accused.[110] Sometimes, testimonies were rejected for much more subjective reasons. For Daniel Neufeld, a member of the Litzmannstadt Cripo who was cleared of accusations, the denunciation of his roommate from Belsen camp was seen as questionable as its author "boasted of what he had done during the war and from his manner of talking he seemed to be an unreliable man."[111] The court also reacted strongly to any suspected cases of the witnesses of the opposite side being bribed or of testimony being falsified, which happened at least once.[112]

DP honour courts, like other Jewish DP institutions, were only a temporary measure. With the establishment of the State of Israel and introduction of the American Displaced Persons Acts of 1948 and 1950 in the United States, DP camps gradually closed down and most of their inhabitants left Europe. Almost all the DP camps were closed by the end of 1952 after around 136,000 emigrated to Israel, over 80,000 Jewish DPs went to the United States, and another 20,000 moved to other parts of North and South America, Australia, and Western Europe. The unprecedented discussion of the complexity of Jewish responses to the persecution that took place in front of honour courts died out as the survivors focused on rebuilding lives in their new homes.

Yet for such a short-lived phenomenon, DP honour courts played an astonishingly important role in the reconstruction of a community shattered by the Holocaust. As Rivka Brot writes, by setting up the courts Jews "fought to be recognized as a distinct national community with political, cultural, and legal autonomy to whatever extent possible under the existing circumstances."[113]

If there was justice in displaced-persons camps, then it was undoubtedly buried deep underneath piles of anonymous denunciations, fraudulent testimonies, and the settling of personal scores. Some of those who should have been sentenced were set free while others received sentences they did not deserve. For many, the very fact that they stood in front of the tribunal marked them for the rest of their lives. Irrespective of the sentence, the label of kapo or Jewish policeman stuck for years, whether they left for Israel, America, or Western Europe. Some were tried again, by other bodies, and again presented their carefully preserved testimony from decades back. The trials in themselves also did not change the society. The open, public, and unprecedented discussion in collaboration that could be witnessed in displaced-persons newspapers died out once the DPs reached their home countries. The topic of collaboration, if breached at all, was again relegated to hushed exchanges and meaningful looks behind someone's back. The crucial fact, however, is that this discussion did take place, even if only for a brief time. Unlike in Poland, where the central committee limited the amount of information on Jewish collaboration published in the Polish-Jewish press, lest it should feed antisemitic sentiment in the country, the DP press openly and very passionately discussed these aspects of the Jewish Holocaust experience, as articles on collaboration, published detailed reports from the trials and court proceedings, or public searches for suspected collaborators were omnipresent in their press. This alone can be seen as proof that the displaced-persons in Germany managed to create a true community in an astonishingly short period of time, and the search for justice played a key part in this.

5 Justice and Migrations

In her memoir on displaced-persons camps, an UNRRA director of Wildflecken camp described the following phenomenon happening among Polish DPs:

> Presently we were aware that a new indoor sport had been born among the waiting DPs – the sinister game of denunciation. There had always been a little of this, an occasional denunciation of a DP by a DP, sent to the investigating agents to pay off an old grudge cheaply or to get even for some fancied slight which, in their years of living so closely together, had built itself up from nothing to a towering injustice. Now we saw the mean blight spreading…
>
> Like a grey web spun out of their own suspense-strained bodies, denunciation of those who got through by those who had not yet caught hundreds of DPs in their final flight.[1]

Previous chapters have shown that the key moment when people were caught by those looking to get revenge or retribution against them happened in transit: on ships, trains, when receiving visas to go abroad. This was often considered the last moment before they could become anonymous, beginning life abroad, anew, sometimes under a changed name. A trial in front of the honour court ensured that their crimes were not wiped out from communal memory.

Probably the most infamous case of those who were caught when already on their way out of Germany was that of David Gertler, the omni-powerful head of the Litzmannstadt ghetto's Sonderabteilung. It seems that despite denunciations that kept reaching the Jewish DP leadership, Gertler, universally considered to be a Gestapo collaborator, was residing untroubled in Munich, even participating in the activities of the Łódź landsmanshaft.[2] This changed when Gertler began looking into emigrating from Germany to join his family in the United States. In November 1948, the Central Committee of Liberated Jews received a letter from a World Jewish Congress employee who was informed by former DPs sailing on a ship from Germany to South America of Gertler's presence in Munich. The letter in which he delivered this information stated quite clearly that the World Jewish Congress expected the Jewish leadership in Munich to undertake decisive steps in this matter. Yet, contrary to the expectations, taking into account Gertler's notoriety in Łódź, the DP honour court investigating his case was flooded with testimonies in his defense. Several of them came from the same localities and can be considered to be part of an organized defense attempt. Based on overwhelmingly positive evidence, and after consulting about the matter with the Jewish Historical Institute, the Central Court of Honour declared Gertler innocent.[3] What his case undoubtedly demonstrated was the extraordinary scope of exchange of information between Jewish communities around the world, with news, as well as gossip, clearly following the migration paths of Polish Jews. His accusers, however, succeeded, Gertler never managed to emigrate and remained until the end of his life in Munich.

This exchange of information between both survivors and various Jewish courts and tribunals was not unique. Almost immediately after it was set up, the Jewish civic court in Warsaw was sending attorneys to consult on cases with honour courts in Munich and Paris and remained in close working contract with Jewish tribunals investigating collaborators' and perpetrators' cases in South America, especially Argentina and Bolivia.[4] In February 1948 the court decided explicitly to "establish contact with civic courts around the world, or with Jewish organizations which fulfill the duties of courts."[5]

While the correspondence with the potential witnesses was robust, travelling in the times of the falling of the Iron Curtain and the growing isolation of Eastern Europe could prove to be very difficult. Despite willingness of the witnesses to testify, the political and economic context in which the court was functioning forced it to go to great lengths to secure witness statements. There were also practical difficulties associated with investigating and prosecuting large numbers of suspects. As time went by, it became more difficult to collect evidence and depose witnesses. In the court's documentation we find numerous references to negotiations with the Ministry of Foreign Affairs about entry visas to Poland for witnesses who escaped Poland, so that they could testify in trials.[6] Just as importantly, those who came back to Poland to testify had also to be assured that they also would be allowed to leave it.

The overall success of the court in locating testimonies was made possible by the extreme willingness of witnesses to testify, a testament to the intensity of their need for justice and revenge. They were not only willing to provide depositions in their new location, but even considered going back to Poland (which they had recently left) to testify. One of them, residing in Stuttgart, accused a member of Radom Judenrat of sending his wife to death because she would not have sexual relations with him. He wrote to Warsaw civic court: "I am ready to confirm the above testimony in person, if it's not too late and if it is possible for me to come to Poland and then go back [i.e., if he can get entry visa to Poland and then be allowed to return to Germany]. I am ready to pay for the journey myself, irrespective of the cost. I hope that the Civic Court takes my statement into account and judge the henchmen and former master of the ghetto."[7]

This extreme willingness to testify has to be put in context of the fact that even witnesses located in Poland, despite their best intentions, often had problems getting to court. Taking into account widespread poverty and problems with transport in postwar Poland, the court travelled extensively, both to collect testimony and to hold trials.[8] When it comes to taking depositions from those living abroad, as travel became close to impossible, the court asked for help from other judicial institutions, but also Jewish political organizations and individuals.[9] It also relied on the network of Jews who already left Poland. The duties of those involved in investigations of Jewish "collaborators" did not stop after they emigrated. When attorney Ludwik Gutmacher, the court chairman, emigrated to France in August 1948, he was given permission to undertake actions, in agreement with the organizations of Polish Jews in France, which would lead to "clearing the Jewish community from elements who, during the occupation, blemished themselves with collaboration on the territory of Poland."[10]

Simultaneously, the Polish court was flooded with messages from abroad. Those who addressed the courts usually did so as the last resort, hunted by gossips and hearsay. These requests show very clearly how the everyday lives of individuals could be haunted by the power of rumours, even those circulating in newly established Jewish communities very distant from their pre-war homes. In the spring of 1947 a certain Berek Finger, a tailor originally from Tyszowice near Lublin, at that point residing in Łódź, addressed Warsaw civic court to clear his name, following rumours about his wartime association with the Judenrat or the Jewish police, which were spread among members of the landsmanshaft of Tyszowice and its environs in Buenos Aires.[11] Finger explained in his deposition that even though he was offered a place in the Judenrat, he never accepted it. Instead, he spent the war first carrying out forced labour, and then, after the liquidation of the Tyszowice ghetto, hiding in local villages and forests and finally ending up in a number of camps, including Auschwitz. Following the end of the war, he served as a chairman of the local Jewish committee in Hrubieszów. To prove his story Finger secured depositions from other wartime inhabitants of Tyszowice, among them the wartime mayor of the town, who all confirmed that they had no knowledge of Finger's collaboration with the Germans. The civic court published a call for witnesses in Jewish newspapers to testify to Finger's actions as a collaborator, but to no avail. The case was thus dismissed in April 1948. Thus, even such a clear-cut case took approximately a year to resolve.

Another survivor, residing in Gothenburg in Sweden, addressed the civic court to provide proof of his innocence against rumours regarding his cooperation with the German Criminal Police (Kripo) in Łódź ghetto, which were spread among other Łódź ghetto survivors in Sweden.[12] He couldn't anymore, as he wrote to the civic court, live with the stigma of a traitor of a nation.[13]

A former Jewish policeman from the ghetto of Bełżyce complained, reflecting the desperation of those who were aware that the window of opportunity to leave Poland was soon closing: "In the autumn of 1946 I filed a request with the court by the Leadership of Polish Jews [civic court], asking for a rehabilitation. Two months ago, I filed two requests to speed up the process in the Jewish Committee in Lublin. I stood in full disposition of the Central Leadership in Warsaw, and despite that the case is proceeding at snail pace and as I want to emigrate from Poland as soon as possible, I kindly ask you to speed it up. Witnesses on my side are also planning on leaving Poland soon."[14] Another addressed the court for rehabilitation after having already been cleared by the Polish state prosecutor's office of crimes committed as a Jewish policeman in a ghetto of Kozowa in the Tarnopol region. In October 1948, he addressed the civic court as follows: "I am a Jew and my aim is to settle with my family on our land of Israel. I want, however, to go to our country with my head held high, I want to be able to look my fellow citizens straight in their eyes. I want to prove that in the period of my life spent under the occupation there was not any shade of suspicion that I had in any form or in any way disrespected the dignity of a Jew."[15]

Rehabilitation requests were, thus, to a large degree motivated by the realization of the transnational aspect of the civic court's functioning. Those addressing the court usually already had plans and hopes for the future and realized that only clearing their name could guarantee it.

The authority of the civic court extended far beyond Poland, and this was acknowledged by both Jewish institutions and individual Jews. Escaping Poland or leaving a DP camp did not mean getting away from revenge. As authors of those letters were fully aware, leaving Poland did not guarantee safety from those seeking retribution.

The "Shoah Echoes in Buczacz" section of the memorial book,[16] published in 1956 in Tel Aviv by Holocaust survivors from Buchach in today's Ukraine, describes the following story, which took place in Paris in early January 1947:

> A young Jewish man from Buchach, Adek W., who is currently visiting Paris, was strolling through the Place de la République on a Saturday. He saw a well-built figure approaching him from a distance. He immediately recognized him as his townsman and childhood friend, who during the Nazi occupation had been the head of the Jewish "*Ordnung-Schutz*" [Ordnungsdienst, the Jewish Order Service] and served as a representative of the Nazi Gestapo leader, sending hundreds and thousands of Jews to their deaths. He shouted to him in Polish: "Are you the murderer of the Jews of Buchach and the murderer of my family?"
>
> The other young man froze in his place, stunned by the sudden cry. Then he replied: "Yes, it is me. What do you want me to do?" Adek W. replied simply: "Come with me." The two went to Adek's hotel. When the door closed behind them and they were both in the room, Adek asked the murderer: "Have you reflected about what you did? Did you know you were executing innocent people, your own people? Tell me, murderer, why did you do it?"[17]

The above story ends with Adek brutally beating up the former policeman on two consecutive days and attempting to tattoo the word "Ordnungsdienst" on his forehead.[18] In the end, Adek decided to turn him in to the authorities:

> They went to the nearest French police station. There, Adek W. reported the case and demanded that the murderer be arrested. The police officer tried to evade the demand and said that it was not within his jurisdiction, and that he should address the higher authorities. Adek W. went to the Polish consul in Paris. After the Polish consul intervened, the French police agreed to arrest the murderer. When the next shipment of criminals to Poland leaves, the murderer of the Jews of Buchach will also be sent and will stand trial there and surely be punished.[19]

This story takes us on a journey from Buchach in occupied Poland to Paris and Venezuela, where the Jewish policeman had planned to emigrate. It then leads us to postwar Poland, where Adek's faith in Polish state justice remained strong despite his decision to leave the country. Finally, the story concludes in Tel Aviv, where it was published in the *Haaretz* newspaper and later included in the memorial book. Throughout this journey, the quest for justice and revenge involved transnational actors, movements, and exchanges.

It is one of numerous postwar testimonies demonstrating the transnational aspect of the individual search for revenge, understood by those carrying it out as a form of justice.

"Souls of 6 million victims were present during the trial taking place in the landsmanshaft of Ostrowiec Jews in Buenos Aires," reported *Forward* in early 1947 – a Yiddish language newspaper published in New York City. About 1,000 Polish Jewish residents in Buenos Aires, representatives of Jewish organizations, and major landsmashaftn as well as the local Jewish press were present on January 12, 1947, in the city's Great Synagogue at Tenente Possolo street to witness a religious trial of Abram and Lajbisz Zajfman, who were tried by the Jewish Community in Buenos Aires.

As *Forward* reported, "waves of hatred" went through the crowds, and one woman fainted as the ten witnesses called were giving their evidence. Further statements were read out from letters that arrived from elsewhere in Brazil and from Poland, Canada, the United States, Italy, Austria, Germany, Argentina, and France. Finally, the court agreed on a resolution calling the Polish government to ask for extradition of the two men, so that they could stand trial in a place where they committed their crimes. This decision was a clear reference to extradition by virtue of the 1943 Moscow Declaration, which stated that war criminals were to be judged in the countries in which they had committed their crimes. This was also the basis on which Nazi criminals were standing trial in Poland. The fact that this step was taken by the Jewish community against its members is a clear proof that their crimes were seen as deserving similar judgment as that of Nazi perpetrators.[20]

The Zajfman brothers were accused of participating in the deaths of several Jewish inhabitants in Ostrowiec and profiting financially from their deaths, likely by seizing their belongings. These accusations were primarily based on the brothers' roles as ghetto policemen, and later Abram Zajfman's position as a commandant of a forced labour camp in Ostrowiec. As the commandant, Abram Zajfman oversaw the final liquidation of the camp and the deportation of the remaining labourers to Auschwitz. The claims were greatly exaggerated; Zajfman, as the Jewish commandant of the camp, could not make any decisions on his own and could not be held solely responsible for the death of camp inhabitants.[21]

The return to Poland never happened, and the accusations never ended. Despite their insistence on innocence, the Zajfman brothers were unable to return to Poland and clear their names. In the late 1950s, Lejbusz Zajfman's wife wrote to Warsaw seeking confirmation of her husband's innocence, but the Jewish Historical Institute refused to provide the requested support. The Institute's reasoning was partly based on the brothers' failure to avail themselves of the opportunity to be cleared by the Polish honour court before leaving for Brazil.[22]

The community then turned to the Polish Ministry of Justice via the Polish embassy in Rio de Janeiro.[23] The Federation of Polish Jews in Brazil explicitly stated that "Chaskiel Rosenberg was a 100% traitor of the Polish Nation, tool of the Gestapo, criminal who should be tried equally to the Nazi criminals." The letter underlined the universal aspect of Rosenberg's crimes by appealing "to the consciousness of the Polish Consul" in the name of humanity.

In the same vein, showing the disparity between the will of the community and the needs of the rule of law, the civic court did not condemn surviving members of families of Jewish "collaborators," even though they might have been shunned by their community.[24] The extent to which this was often happening, can be seen in the example of a case, later investigated by the civic court, that took place in La Paz in Bolivia. A female survivor, Runa Fakler, underwent a public confrontation (a de facto public trial), for profiting from the suffering of others during the Holocaust as a wife of a kapo in the Plaszow concentration camp (she herself did not hold any position of prominence).[25] According to the documentation passed on from La Paz to the civic court in Warsaw, Fakler was boycotted by her community and (while visibly pregnant) beaten up on the street by a victim of her late husband's maltreatment. Such survivors, who did not directly "collaborate," addressed the court asking for rehabilitation and thus clearing their names in the eyes of their community. As was the case with Fakler, the issue of blame placed on survivors for the deeds of their family members was especially visible in case of women, who were accused of profiting from the crimes of their husbands or partners and, thus, held responsible for their actions. Ewa Koźmińska-Frejlak wrote in her study of the topic that "accusations of collaboration against women were worded in a much more general way [than against men]. To initiate an investigation of a woman, it often sufficed to accuse her of consorting with a "'dubious character,' for example, with a man whose function in the German organized apparatus of violence made him suspicious by default."[26]

Survivors who left Poland were not tried by various types of civic courts, but also under traditional rabbinic authority. Maks Szczęśliwy, former head of the Łódź ghetto provisioning department, who together with his family left Poland after the Kielce pogrom, was tried by the Rabbinic Court set up by the Jewish community in Helsinki.[27] The court consisted of three judges, as required by religious law, among them, the chief rabbi. The charge, adapted from the Nuremberg trials, was of "crimes against human rights." In 1950, a *beth din* [rabbinical court] was set up in New York to try Majer Mittlemen, who was recognized on the street in Brooklyn and accused by another survivor of displaying brutality as a prisoner functionary in the Muhldorf concentration camp.[28] Specifically, he was accused of beating to death the brother of the man who recognized him. In this case the beit din was therefore looking at a straightforward case of homicide, which would normally be investigated by the state's legal system. As was often the case, here too, lacking jurisdiction over the original crime, which took place in wartime Poland, the local state authorities refused to act. The Jewish court was the only option available to the survivors. When the trial took place, it was watched by about 40 people, half of whom were concentration camp survivors.

Unsurprisingly, a key scene of seeking revenge against collaborators became Mandate Palestine and then the state of Israel. In the first two years of the state of Israel's existence, 220,000 immigrants arrived from Europe, and in some instances encounters between survivors and their overseers in the ghettos and camps resulted in harsh exchanges, including lynching and attempted lynching. Before about 40 so-called kapo trials took place in Israel between 1950 and 1972,[29] newspapers from Mandatory Palestine spoke of a wealth of cases of former prisoner functionaries being recognized there on the streets, on public transport, or even among the soldiers of Yishuv.[30]

This need was not only limited to Holocaust survivors: retribution was carried out not only by those who were directly affected by alleged collaborators but also by people who had arrived in Mandatory Palestine before the war and had not suffered in Europe. Many residents of Tel Aviv and the rest of Mandatory Palestine had family members who had perished in Europe, and they sought to avenge the dead.[31] Thus, for those perceived to be collaborators, neither being away from the site of the trauma nor being in the "Jewish" space provided safety. As historian Dan Porat noted: "The Yishuv also grappled with the questions of how, given that it lacked any official police or judicial authority, to 'institutionalize' the examination and judgment of those suspected of collaboration. Furthermore, like the rest of the world, it had no experience in, and no moral and legal categories and language for, considering and judging the actions of people who had participated in an unprecedented mass murder machine."[32]

Newspapers published at the time speak of numerous instances of suspected collaborators being attacked. At midday on December 7, 1945, a middle-aged man was identified on a bus in central Tel Aviv, at the corner of Dizengoff and King George's streets. He was suddenly approached by a fellow passenger who asked if his name was Chaim Molczycki. The denouncer shouted at him and then passed out. A group of people who had gathered around the scene violently attacked the suspected collaborator. Subsequently, he was taken to the police station where he admitted that his name was indeed Chaim Molczycki and that he had served as the head of the Judenrat in Będzin ghetto in Upper Silesia. However, he tried to defend himself by claiming that he had taken the position under pressure. Eventually, he was released as no one pressed charges against him.[33]

Around the same time, in the same city a crowd beat up a suspected Jewish policeman from Ostrowiec Świętokrzyski. The man denied the accusations and disappeared before he could be formally charged.[34] In June 1946, in Yarkon Park, also in Tel Aviv, a group of new immigrants to Palestine attacked Sonia Baumgarten, a former prisoner functionary in the forced labour camp in Gleiwitz. The attackers claimed that Sonia acted with particular cruelty, torturing and exploiting the camp prisoners. It was even alleged that she had requested the transfer of some prisoners to the Auschwitz concentration camp. The immigrants also reported that Baumgarten had left Poland for Palestine out of fear of retaliation from other survivors.[35]

A month later, on the beach in Tel Aviv, a recent immigrant began to swear at and beat a Jewish soldier, whom he accused of being a particularly cruel prisoner functionary in a concentration camp. Again, the accused denied all charges and disappeared before he could be questioned by the police.[36]

This situation demanded a response from the legislature, which could redirect these socially tense encounters from the public space to socially accepted venues such as the courtroom. It was finally in 1950 that the Knesset passed the NNCL [Nazis and Nazi Collaborators (Punishment) Law, 5710–1950]. As Dan Porat noted: "On August 1, 1950, the statute's declared purpose was practical: to establish a legal basis for the prosecution of Nazi criminals and their collaborators. Another no less important objective was educational and symbolic: to proclaim the State of Israel as the successor to, and the avenger of, those who had perished in the Holocaust."[37] Thus the aim of the law, in the eyes of its creators, was above all to avenge Jewish blood.

Only once these aims were achieved, even to the small extent allowed by judicial trials, those dead could be mourned and the memory of trauma can be transformed into a new narrative memory of the mass crime.[38] Trials held both in Poland and abroad were, thus, a way of externalizing collective trauma and creating a new narrative, which would fit the needs of the re-building community. As Blustein wrote: "Individuals and societies must mourn their losses if recovery is to be possible, and they must do so by replacing traumatic memories, which are decontextualized and de-historicized, with narrative memories, the elements of which can be seen to hang together, even if imperfectly, in a coherent, temporally extended whole."[39] Courts were thus a way of recovery from both individual and shared trauma. They were the means for healing both on individual and collective levels. They allowed for the integration of "collaboration" into their collective self-understanding. And they allowed the impulse for individual revenge to stop along with the political consequences of it. The court gave survivors a chance to discuss their experiences in a setting with people who shared their traumatic experiences. They demanded that traumatic events be returned to the collective memory and were concerned by any attempts to sweep it under the carpet.

Aside from its primary aim of establishing some semblance of justice, trials held around the world played an important role in building a community of survivors coming from different parts of Europe. Thus, while these various types of courts, operating on a smaller scale, were less explicitly border-crossing, relying to a greater extent on witnesses remaining in the same camp or in its vicinity, they were trans-territorial in a different sense, crossing borders in more symbolic ways. The trials might have been held in some geographically distant place, but they had an organic, intimate connection to the location, where the crimes happened.[40]

This phenomenon was directly addressed during the Landsberg DP camp trial of Joseph Barzion, from Thessaloniki, a prisoner functionary in Auschwitz. One of those sitting on the judging panel was Leo Schwarz, a director of the Joint Distribution Committee program in the American zone of Germany, who described it as follows in his memoirs from the camp:

> On November 23, 1945, in the Landsberg Jewish courtroom, sits a closely packed knot of the tiny remnant from the Salonika ghetto, which Barzion ruled by the grace of Hitler. […] in their agitated hearts the seed of

> national awareness is beginning to sprout; in their instinctive reaction beats the pulse of a Jewish will-to-be, which binds them to the German, Polish, Lithuanian, and American Jews in a single unified mass.
>
> Thus, when I inquire of the defendant where he will go when the road is opened, and he replies, "To Palestine!" a cry explodes, an outcry in many tongues but in one emotion, "We do not want you in *our* land."

Later he concluded: "On the twenty-third of November, in the Jewish courtroom of Landsberg, I saw the socially and nationally amorphous mass of Salonika Jews emerge out of the flames of the concentration camps into a Jewish national community. It was not the criminal Barzion that constituted the central point of that trial. The proceedings centred in the audience, which was the courtroom in its spontaneous unified reaction."[41]

What was, thus, a key issue when it came to justice delivered in Jewish honour courts was that, unlike the trials of Nazi perpetrators, these trials did not take place in a large hall or theatre room. They took place in a small space, among fellow survivors. You could see the face of those on trial. You could look them straight in the eyes. You could testify when looking at them, you could have other survivors back you up. These trials created a community by allowing for an intimate response to an intimate crime.[42]

Thus, in a symbolic way, retribution returned to where it began, to Poland. This was no longer Poland that was considered to be the home place of Jews; it was Poland as a hostile land that amounted to being rejected by the Jewish community. Yet a courtroom in Buenos Aires, a synagogue in New York, or a small town in southern Germany became a place where the Polish Jewish community continued its existence.

Conclusion

Throughout the first half of the twentieth century, following each of the many crises tearing through East-Central Europe, people who were wronged by their oppressors, neighbours, or private enemies began to search for justice. With the state apparatus absent or barely working, they often resorted to individual violence and private acts of revenge to settle accounts against their wrongdoers. Just as the decades of wars and conflicts in East-Central Europe can be seen as part of the *continuum of crisis*,[43] the killings, lynchings, and pogroms that followed can be called the *continuum of vindictive violence*. Understanding this continuum of vindictive violence sheds light on the complex nature of societal dynamics in East-Central Europe during this period. It underscores the breakdown of traditional mechanisms of justice and the profound impact of prolonged crises on the fabric of society. The discussion surrounding revenge in the postwar era raises complex questions about justice, morality, and the role of violence in society. While revenge may offer a sense of satisfaction or closure to some, it also carries inherent risks that challenge the ideals of a civilized society. As we reflect on this historical period, it is important to consider the complexities of human behaviour, the limitations of legal systems, and the long-lasting impact of violence in the pursuit of justice. They belonged innately to the social dynamics of the times of crisis.

While the experience of war and occupation was highly differentiated, postwar revenge – killings, violent attacks, and lynching – occurred in communities all over the world. War itself fueled revenge fantasies and allowed people to carry out previously unimaginable actions.[44] In Eastern Europe the age of retribution stretched across the entire twentieth century. While this area is usually associated with total war, defined by both broadening and radicalizing industrialized mass warfare, but also by the combatants' deliberate choice to erase the civilian/soldier distinction,[45] periods of fierce post-conflict brutality reappeared with bitter regularity. Thus, this geographic space, due to its ethnic complexities, provides a unique case study in which we can investigate universal mechanisms following the devastation of war, foreign occupation, and genocide.

The aim of this book was to demonstrate that Polish Jews, survivors of the Holocaust, were also part of this story. By studying individual responses to harm, this book aimed to unravel the emotional scripts and needs of postwar communities of Holocaust survivors, particularly the need to regain control and shape one's own narrative. It further delved into the complex dynamics of postwar revenge, highlighting individual experiences within a larger historical context, emphasizing the intertwining of personal and collective emotions, while shedding light on the diverse perspectives and challenges faced by Holocaust survivors, Polish Jews, and pre-war citizens of Poland in their search for justice. It is necessary to take into consideration the complexities of identity, geography, and the interplay between personal and collective responses if we are to understand the postwar search for justice in the aftermath of the Holocaust. It is also crucial to remember that not all survivors had the same kind of agency, which depended on his or her individual position within the space delineated by the state for individual action. The limits of one's agency changed as power constellations within that state-delineated space changed. A recognition of the fundamentally incoherent and fluctuating nature of agency also helps to avoid retroactively judging the protagonists according to present-day moral standards; they instead give us a better understanding of the many complex, overlapping factors that structured the identities and perceptions that determined how people acted in the situation of state void.

The story of the postwar search for retribution among Holocaust survivors is a story of accountability in troubled times. It is a story of joined spaces: physical and temporal. It joins the centre of the postwar story of the rebuilding of Jewish life with that of the margins, places where Jews only remained for a moment after the war. It is a story of rebuilding and regaining equilibrium, attempted from above, carried out by formal institutions and from below by individuals. It is also a story of continuity, of breaking down the barrier between pre-war, wartime, and postwar history. Studying revenge shows us how global, national, regional, and local agendas overlapped to make ordinary people reconfigure how they saw themselves and how they interpreted the world around them. The identities and perceptions that emerged from these interactions enhance our understanding of the multiple factors that determined people's actions post-conflict. It allows us to consider issues of local agency without anachronistically applying today's ethical standards and oversimplified binary categories to people who operated in drastically different historical contexts. Finally, it shows the degree to which informal and formal interactions were interconnected. In fact, the majority of court cases analyzed were linked to prior informal interactions, and the dynamics of getting justice played out mainly beyond the legal realm. It also shows to what extent official justice had to stand the test of popular expectations and remained in a constant state of negotiation with the community.

While settings differed, taken together these stories paint a complex and varied, yet unified, picture of searching for peace, both within oneself and in the community, in particular through extrajudicial methods of resolving conflicts, recognized as entirely legitimate by the societies that employed them, often involving violent action, including lynching and physical intimidation. It shows how, in the absence of state presence, communities self-regulate to ensure their continuity and how, in the twentieth century, Polish Jews attempted to articulate, reconstruct, and police their own individual and group boundaries.

Notes

Epigraph

1 Anonymous Warsaw Man, "A Reply," in *To Live with Honor and Die with Honor!... Selected Documents from the Warsaw Ghetto Underground Archives "O. S." ("Oneg Shabbath")*, ed. Joseph Kermish (Jerusalem: Yad Vashem, 1986).

Introduction

1 USHMM Archive, Oral History interview with Norman Salsitz, 06.07.1999: RG-50.549.02.0052
2 Mark Dvorjetsky, "Adjustment of Detainees to Camp and Ghetto Life and Their Subsequent Readjustment to Normal Society," *Yad Vashem Studies* vol. 5 (1963): 213–14. Quoted in Ewa Koźminska-Frejlak, "The Adaptation of Survivors to the Post-War Reality from 1944 to 1949," in *Jewish Presence in Absence: The Aftermath of the Holocaust in Poland, 1944–2010*, eds. F. Tych and M. Adamczyk-Garbowska (Jerusalem: Yad Vashem, 2014), 161.
3 Yitzhak Zuckerman, *A Surplus of Memory. Chronicle of the Warsaw Ghetto Uprising*, trans. B. Harshav (Los Angeles: University of California Press, 1993), 634.
4 On the validity of this definition see Kevin M. Carlsmith, Daniel T. Gilbert, and Timothy D. Wilson, "The Paradoxical Consequences of Revenge," *Journal of Personality and Social Psychology* vol. 95, no. 6 (2008): 1316.
5 Rachel Stein, *Vengeful Citizens, Violent States*, p. 2. Stein defines core values as "an essential psychological function by providing standards by which both the self and others can be judged, and actions can be selected and justified. For this reason, they are widely viewed as one of the basic building blocks of human behaviour" (quote from p. 24).

6 Karina Schumann and Michael Ross, "The Benefits, Costs, and Paradox of Revenge," *Social and Personality Psychology Compass* 4, no. 12 (2010): 1193–1205; here, 1194.

7 Kit R. Christensen, *Revenge and Social Conflict* (Cambridge: Cambridge University Press, 2016), 23.

8 Tony Judt, "The Past Is Another Country: Myth and Memory in Post-War Europe," in *Memory and Power in Post-War Europe: Studies in the Presence of the Past*, ed. Jan-Werner Müller (Cambridge: Cambridge University Press, 2009), 165; Ville Kivimäki and Petri Karonen, eds., *Continued Violence and Troublesome Pasts: Post-War Europe between the Victors after the Second World War* (Helsinki: Finnish Literature Society, 2017); Ota Konrád, Boris Barth, and Jaromír Mrňka, eds., *Collective Identities and Post-War Violence in Europe, 1944–48. Reshaping the Nation* (London: Palgrave Macmillan, 2022).

9 The only exceptions are group efforts at revenge. See Dina Porat, *Li Nakam Veshilem*: *HaYishuv, Hashoah, Vekvutzat Hanokmim Shel Abba Kovner* (Haifa: Pardes Publishing, Haifa University Press, 2015).

10 Berel Lang, "Holocaust Memory and Revenge: The Presence of the Past," *Jewish Social Studies* vol. 2, no. 2 (1996), 1–20. On the absence of revenge in Poland, see Julian Kwiek, *Nie chcemy Żydów u siebie. Przejawy wrogości wobec Żydów w latach 1944–1947* (Warszawa: Wydawnictwo Nieoczywiste, 2021), 12.

11 Naftali Kantorowich, "What Happened to Me When I Returned Home," trans. Jerrold Landau, in *Rozhinoy; sefer zikaron le-kehilat Rozhinoy ve-ha-seviva*, ed. M. Sokolowsky (Tel Aviv: Former residents of Rozhinoy in Israel, 1957), 172.

12 Christopher R. Browning, *Remembering Survival: Inside a Nazi Slave-Labor Camp* (New York: W.W. Norton, 2010), 52. On this, see among others Joan Tumblety, "Introduction: Working with Memory as Source and Subject," in *Memory and History. Understanding Memory as Source and Subject*, ed. Joan Tumblety (Abingdon: Routledge, 2013), 1–16.

13 For a discussion of revenge, see Gregory M. Reichberg , "Jus ad bellum," in *War: Essays in Political Philosophy*, ed. Larry May (Cambridge: Cambridge University Press, 2008), 24.

14 See Mark Roseman, "'No, Herr Führer!' Jewish Revenge after the Holocaust: Between Fantasy and Reality," in *Revenge, Retribution, Reconciliation: Justice and Emotions between Conflict and Mediation. A Cross-Disciplinary Anthology*, ed. Laura Jockusch, Andreas Kraft, and Kim Wünschmann (Jerusalem: The Hebrew University Magnes Press, 2015). On this concept, see also Jeffrey Herf, *The Jewish Enemy: Nazi Propaganda during World War II and the Holocaust* (Cambridge Mass.: Harvard University Press, 2006), 127. On Poland, see Joanna Tokarska-Bakir, *Pogrom Cries – Essays on Polish-Jewish History, 1939–1946* (Frankfurt am Main: Peter Lang, 2017), 210.

15 See Mark Roseman, "'... but of Revenge Not a Sign.' Germans' Fear of Jewish Revenge after World War II," in *Jahrbuch für Antisemitismusforschung*, Bd. 22. (2013), 82.

16 Karina Schumann and Michael Ross, "The Benefits, Costs, and Paradox of Revenge," *Social and Personality Psychology Compass* vol. 4, no. 12 (2010): 1195.

17 John Kerrigan, *Revenge Tragedy: Aeschylus to Armageddon* (Oxford: Clarendon Press, 1996), 1.

18 Magdalena Waligórska, Yechiel Weizman, Alexander Friedman, and Ina Sorkina, "Holocaust Survivors Returning to their Hometowns in the Polish-Belarusian-Ukrainian Borderlands, 1944–1948," *Journal of Holocaust Research* (forthcoming).

19 I took this concept from Elena Jakel, who explored it in the context of Ukrainian Jews. See Elena Jakel, "'Ukraine without Jews?' Nationality and Belonging in Soviet Ukraine, 1943–1948" (PhD Dissertation, University of Illinois at Urbana-Champaign, 2014).

20 Katie Barclay, "Space and Place," in *Early Modern Emotions. An Introduction*, ed. Susan Broomhall (London: Routledge, 2017), 21. I would like to thank Dr. Hannes Ziegler for pointing this book out to me and for generously allowing me to make use of his extraordinary book collection on the topic.

21 See Mark Roseman, "'... but of Revenge Not a Sign.' Germans' Fear of Jewish Revenge after World War II," in *Jahrbuch für Antisemitismusforschung*, Bd. 22. (2013), 82.

22 Mary Fulbrook, *A Small Town near Auschwitz: Ordinary Nazis and the Holocaust* (Oxford: Oxford University Press, 2013); Elżbieta Janicka, "Pamięć przyswojona. Koncepcja polskiego doświadczenia zagłady Żydów jako traumy zbiorowej w świetle rewizji kategorii świadka," *Studia Litteraria et Historica* no. 3/4 (2015): 148–226; see also Christina Morina and Krijn Thijs, eds., *Probing the Limits of Categorization: The Bystander in Holocaust History* (New York: Berghan Books, 2019).

23 Jan Grabowski, *Hunt for Jews: Betrayal and Murder in German-Occupied Poland* (Bloomington: Indiana University Press, 2013), 3–4.

24 Litman Mor, *The War for Life* (Tel Aviv: n.p., 2007), 207, quoted in Franziska Exeler, "Reckoning with Occupation: Soviet Power, Local Communities, and the Ghosts of Wartime Behavior in Post-1944 Belorussia," (PhD diss., Princeton University, 2013), 174. http://arks.princeton.edu/ark:/88435/dsp01gf06g2796.

25 On this see Martin C. Dean, *Collaboration in the Holocaust: Crimes of the Local Police in Belorussia and Ukraine, 1941–1944* (Basingstoke: Macmillan, 2000); Markus Eikel and Valentina Sivaieva, "City Mayors, Raion Chiefs, and Village Elders in Ukraine, 1941–4: How Local Administrators Co-operated

with the German Occupation Authorities," *Contemporary European History* 23, 3 (2014): 405–28.

26 There are multiple elements necessary to constitute the crime of meshorah, each of them containing essential terms or conditions that are subject to diverse understanding and, therefore, of divergent legal standards and communal practice. The definition of the crime is that: "If a Jew acted, voluntarily, in such a manner as to cause a fellow Jew to be subjected to the jurisdiction or power of an oppressive authority which would act in a disproportionally violent manner against this person or property of the victim, including the likelihood of escalation of violence to death of the victim; then he has violated the crime of Mesirah." Saul J. Berman, *Boundaries of Loyalty: Testimony against Fellow Jews in Non-Jewish Courts* (Cambridge: Cambridge University Press, 2016), 75.

27 Tuvia Friling, *A Jewish Kapo in Auschwitz: History, Memory, and the Politics of Survival*, transl. Haim Watzman (Waltham: Brandeis University Press, 2014), 228.

28 On this, see Yehuda Bauer, *The Death of the Shtetl* (New Haven: Yale University Press), 1. Moreover, we usually have only one side of the story: non-Jewish locals from rural Polish areas before 1939 were less likely to leave autobiographical materials than Jews from the area who later settled in North America and Israel.

29 Nancy Wood, *Vectors of Memory: Legacies of Trauma in Post-War Europe* (Oxford: Berg, 1999), 2.

30 In this book I use the term "liberation" when speaking about the Red Army's entry into occupied Polish lands as this is how it was perceived by survivors.

31 Laura Jockusch, *Collect and Record! Jewish Holocaust Documentation in Early Postwar Europe* (Oxford: Oxford University Press, 2012); Agnieszka Haska, "Dowody i zeznania. Świadectwa o Zagładzie w pierwszych latach powojennych," *Teksty drugie*, no 3 (2018): 361–72.

32 Monika Rice, *"What! Still Alive?!" Jewish Survivors in Poland and Israel Remember Homecoming* (Syracuse: Syracuse University Press, 2017), 57.

33 Rice, *"What! Still Alive?!"*, 55.

34 On defining the "final stage" of the Holocaust through survivor testimony, see Kobi Kabalek, "Edges of History and Memory: The 'Final Stage' of the Holocaust," *Dapim: Studies on the Holocaust* vol. 29, no. 3 (2015): 240–63.

35 According to Monika Adamczyk Garbowska and Adam Kopciowski, 540 memorial books talking about locations in pre-war Poland were published by 2005. See Monika Adamczyk Garbowska and Adam Kopciowski, "Memorial Books as a Remembrance of Collective Trauma," in *Jewish Presence in Absence. The Aftermath of the Holocaust in Poland, 1944–2010,*

Feliks Tych and Monika Adamczyk Garbowska, eds. (Jerusalem: Yad Vashem, 2014), 506.

36 Rebecca Kobrin, *Jewish Bialystok and Its Diaspora* (Bloomington: Indiana University Press, 2010), 9.

37 Monika Adamczyk-Garbowska, Adam Kopciowski, and Andrzej Trzciński, "Księgi Pamięci jako źródło wiedzy o historii, kulturze i zagładzie polskich Żydów," in *Tam był kiedyś mój dom. Księgi Pamięci Gmin Żydowskich*, ed. Monika Adamczyk-Garbowska, Adam Kopciowski, and Andrzej Trzciński (Lublin: Wydawnictwo UMCS, 2009), 23.

38 On the point of language, see Anette Wieviorka, "From Survivor to Witness: Voices from the Shoah," in *War and Remembering in the Twentieth Century*, ed. Jay Winter and Emmanuel Sivan (Cambridge: Cambridge University Press, 1999), 130.

39 L. Losh, ed., "Fighter of the Jewish War," in *Sefer zikaron le-kehilot Szczuczyn Wasiliszki Ostryna Nowy-Dwor Rozanka* (Tel Aviv: Former Residents of Szczuczyn Wasiliszki 1966), 92.

40 As Anita Shapira has noted: "It appears that from the first moment the reports were verified, the leaders made conscious efforts to direct the feelings of enmity and rage into constructive channels and to guide youth toward finding satisfaction in the military frameworks within the community. This was conceived as a substitute for revenge aimed at the Germans, a desire for vengeance that was beyond the realm of attainment. The Palestinian arena was meant to absorb the psychological energy generated by the information on the Holocaust and to direct it into the struggle for gaining Jewish sovereignty over Palestine. Anita Shapira, *Land and Power. The Zionist Resort to Force, 1881–1948*, trans. W. Templer (Stanford: Stanford University Press, 1992), 327.

41 Elie Wiesel's speech, "The Holocaust: Beginning or End?," quoted in Noah Shenker, *Reframing Holocaust Testimony* (Bloomington: Indiana University Press, 2015), 111.

42 On the approaches to the collection and dissemination of testimonies of the three institutions, see Shenker, *Reframing Holocaust Testimony*; Amit Pinchevski, "The Audiovisual Unconscious: Media and Trauma in the Video Archive for Holocaust Testimonies," *Critical Inquiry* vol. 39 (2012): 142–66.

43 Dawn Skorczewski, "'You Want Me to Sing?' Holocaust Testimonies in the Intersubjective Field," *Dapim: Studies on the Holocaust* 32, no. 2 (2018): 112–27; here: 127.

44 Rozmowa z Kazikiem Ratajzerem, in Grupińska, *Ciągle po kole*, 277.

45 Rozmowa z Kazikiem Ratajzerem, in Grupińska, *Ciągle po kole*, 278.

46 For a discussion of court testimonies of Jewish witnesses, see Anna Hájková, "'What Kind of Narrative Is Legal Testimony?' Terezín witnesses

before Czechoslovak, Austrian, and German Courts," in *Rethinking Holocaust Justice: Essays across Disciplines*, ed. Norman Goda (New York: Berghahn, 2017), 71–99.

47 Zuckerman, *A Surplus of Memory*, 634–5.

48 Jeffrey Blustein, "Traumatic Emotions," in *Emotions and Mass Atrocity. Philosophical and Theoretical Explorations*, eds. Thomas Brudholm and Johannes Lang (Cambridge: Cambridge University Press, 2018), 236. On revenge fantasy, see Judith Lewis Herman, *Trauma and Recovery: The Aftermath of Violence – From Domestic Abuse to Political Terror* (New York: Basic Books, 1992), 189.

49 Jan-Werner Müller, "Introduction: The Power of Memory, the Memory of Power and the Power over Memory," in *Memory and Power in Post-War Europe* (Cambridge: Cambridge University Press, 2002), 20.

50 Abraham Wein shows how in the Yiddish and Hebrew versions of the same text in one memorial book interpretation of a certain action as revenge appears only in the Hebrew version. See Abraham Wein, "'Memorial Books,' as a Source for Research into the History of Jewish Communities in Europe," in *Yad Vashem Studies on the European Catastrophe and Resistance* vol. 9 (1973): 260–1.

51 Adamczyk-Garbowska and Kopciowski, "Memorial Books as a Remembrance of Collective Trauma," in *Jewish Presence in Absence: The Aftermath of the Holocaust in Poland, 1944–2010.*, ed. Felikx Tych and Monika Adamczyk-Garbowska, trans. Grzegorz Dąbskowski and Jessica Taylor-Kucia. (Jerusalem: Yad Vashem, 2014), 527.

52 See Alan Rosen, *The Wonder of Their Voices: The 1946 Holocaust Interviews of David Boder* (Oxford: Oxford University Press, 2010), 202–26; Alan Rosen, *Sounds of Defiance. The Holocaust, Multilingualism and the Problem of English* (Lincoln and London: University of Nebraska Press, 2005).

53 Rosen, *The Wonder of Their Voices*.

54 Joanna Tokarska-Bakir, *Pogrom Cries – Essays on Polish-Jewish History, 1939–1946* (Frankfurt am Main: Peter Lang Publishing, 2017), 142.

1. "He Wept and We Didn't": Liberation, Revenge, and a Survivor's Return

1 Barbara Engelking, ed., "Dziennika Adama Kamiennego," in *Sny chociaż mamy wspaniałe… Okupacyjne dzienniki Żydów z okolic Mińska Mazowieckiego*, (Warszawa: Stowarzyszenie Centrum Badań nad Zagładą Żydów, 2016), 32.

2 Holocaust Survivors Film Project, Interview with Ewa L. (408).

3 USHMM, The Jeff and Toby Herr Oral History Archive, Interview with Esther Raab.

4 Emmanuel Ringelblum, *Notes from the Warsaw Ghetto*, ed. Jacob Sloan, (iBooks, 2006), 300; quoted in Zoe Waxman, *Writing the Holocaust: Identity, Testimony, Representation* (Oxford: Oxford University Press, 2005), 35.
5 Katarzyna Person, *Warsaw Ghetto Police: The Jewish Order Service during the Nazi Occupation*, trans. Z. Nowak Soliński (Ithaca: Cornell University Press, 2021), 140–2.
6 Rozmowa z Maszą Glajtman-Putermilch, in Anka Grupińska, *Ciągle po Kole. Rozmowy z żołnierzami warszawskiego getta* (Warszawa: wielka litera, 2022), 77. See Avinoam Patt, *The Jewish Heroes of Warsaw. The Aftermath of the Revolt* (Detroit: Wayne State University Press, 2021), 324.
7 "Opowieść Szmula Rona," in Grupińska, *Ciągle po kole*, 49.
8 B. Shefner, "Vladka- A Heroine of the Warsaw Ghetto" *Forverts*, June 1, 1946, quoted in Patt, *The Jewish Heroes of Warsaw*, 334.
9 On that, see Shai Lavi, "'The Jews Are Coming': Vengeance and Revenge in Post-Nazi Europe." *Law, Culture and the Humanities* vol. 1, no. 3 (October 2005): 282–301.
10 Anita Shapira, *Land and Power. The Zionist Resort to Force, 1881–1948*, trans. W. Templer (Stanford: Stanford University Press, 1992), 336.
11 Barbara Epstein, *The Minsk Ghetto 1941–1943. Jewish Resistance and Soviet Internationalism* (Berkeley: University of California Press, 2008), 189.
12 Evgeny Finkel, *Ordinary Jews: Choice and Survival During the Holocaust* (Princeton: Princeton University Press, 2017), 137.
13 Bogdan Musial, *Sowjetische Partisanen 1941–1944. Mythos und Wirklichkeit* (Munchen: Paderborn, 2009); Kenneth Slepyan, *Stalin's Guerrillas. Soviet Partisans in World War II* (Lawrence/KS: University Press of Kansas, 2006).
14 Alina Skibińska, "The Return of Jewish Holocaust Survivors and the Reaction of the Polish Population," in *Jewish Presence in Absence: The Aftermath of the Holocaust in Poland, 1944–2010*, ed. Feliks Tych and Monika Adamczyk-Garbowska (Jerusalem: Yad Vashem, 2014), 53. The number of Jews who survived as part of partisan units or in family camps did not exceed 15,000. Skibińska, 54. See JHIA 301/4009 for testimony of women who joined a Polish partisan unit as non-Jews but were denounced by fellow female partisans. See also JHIA 301/4673 (Karol Grebl) on Jews not allowed into Polish partisan units.
15 Franziska Exeler, "Reckoning with Occupation." 144.
16 Jeffrey Burds, "Sexual Violence in Europe in World War II, 1939–1945," *Politics and Society* vol. 37, no. 1 (2009), 58.
17 On this, see Magdalena Semczyszyn, "Żydzi w sowieckich oddziałach partyzanckich na północno-wschodnich terenach Drugiej RP 1941–1944 – zarys problematyki," *Zagłada Żydów. Studia i Materiały*, vol. 17 (2021): 139–71; here, p. 149.

18 Magdalena Semczyszyn, "Żydzi w sowieckich oddziałach partyzanckich," 161.

19 Dina Porat, *The Fall of the Sparrow. The Life and Times of Abba Kovner* (Stanford: Stanford University Press, 2009), 150. On the other side, see Leonid Smilovitsky, "Antisemitism in the Soviet Partisan Movement, 1941–1944: The Case of Belorussia," *Holocaust and Genocide Studies* vol. 20, no. 2 (2006): 207–34.

20 Avraham Eisenberg, "In the Forests and Reprisal Activities," trans. Ala Gamulka, in *Rokitno (Volin) ve-ha-seviva; sefer edut ve-zikaron*, ed. E. Leoni (Tel Aviv: Former residents of Rokitno in Israel, 1967), 342–46.

21 For Jews carrying out revenge during the war with the support of non-Jewish partisan groups, see, among others, JHIA 301/3327 (Alina Colle).

22 On Soviet partisans, see Bogdan Musial, *Sowjetische Partisanen 1941–1944: Mythos Und Wirklichkeit* (Paderborn: Ferdinand Schöningh Verlag, 2009), 255–61, 314, 321–2; Masha Cerovic, "'Au chien, une mort de chien.' Les partisans face aux 'traîtres à la Patrie,'" *Cahier du monde russe* 49, no. 2 (2008): 239–62.

23 Sara Mages, trans., "Partisans," in *Ayara shehayta Olkanik.* (Haifa: Hebrew Reali School in Haifa), 63.

24 Gitl Fialkov, "In Destruction and Anguish," trans. Kevin and Sara Allen, in *Ayaratenu Visotsk; sefer zikaron*, ed. Arie Fialkov (Haifa, Association of former residents of Visotsk in Israel, 1963), 119.

25 Asher Binder, "From Sheep to Slaughter – Punishment to Our Killers," trans. Ala Gamulka, in *Rokitno (Volin) ve-ha-seviva*, 340.

26 Boris Kozinitz, "A Partisan's Story," in *Sefer Dokshitz-Parafianov*, ed. David Stockfish, trans. Yariv Eldar, Daniella HarPaz Mechnikov (Tel Aviv: Association of Former Residents of Dokszyce-Parafianow in Israel, 1970), 219.

27 Jechiel Górny, "Dziennik," in *Archiwum Ringelbluma. Dzienniki z Getta Warszawskiego*, ed. K. Person, M. Trębacz, Z. Trębacz (Warszawa: ŻIH, 2015).

28 Interview Archive, "Forced Labor 1939–1945," Interview no. 581, Roma B.

29 Yaacov Lozowick, "Introduction," in *The Anguish of Liberation. Testimonies from 1945*, ed. Yehudit Kleinman and Nina Springer-Aharoni (Jerusalem: Yad Vashem, 1995), 8.

30 On liberation as a process, see Dan Stone, *The Liberation of the Camps. The End of the Holocaust and its Aftermath* (New Haven and London: Yale University Press, 2015), 2.

31 On Jewish policemen being "quietly done away with" in concentration camps, see JHIA, 301/5346. See also testimonies on policemen being murdered in trains, Zev Weisblum, on murders in Buchenwald YVA O.62/133. Testimony of Maksymilian Hollender.

32 Video Archive for Holocaust Testimonies at Yale, Interview with Eugene N., Interview no. 616894.
33 Tony Judt, "The Past Is Another Country: Myth and Memory in Post-War Europe," in *Memory and Power in Post-War Europe: Studies in the Presence of the Past*, ed. Jan-Werner Müller (Cambridge: Cambridge University Press, 2009), 165.
34 USC Shoah Foundation testimony of Pola Schek-Yogev (28857).
35 JHIA, 301/2842.
36 On this, see Stone, *The Liberation of the Camps*, 98.
37 YVA, O.3/7343, Testimony of Jakub Gutenbaum.
38 "Journal of Philip D. Vock, August 1945," in *Jewish Responses to Persecution: 1944–1946* vol. V, ed. Leah Wolfson (Lanham, MD: Alta Mira Press in association with the United States Holocaust Memorial Museum, 2015), 75.
39 Elie Wiesel, *Un di velt hot geshvign* (Buenos Aires: Tsentral-Farband fun Poylishe Yidn in Argentine, 1956); Naomi Seidman, "Elie Wiesel and the Scandal of Jewish Rage," *Jewish Social Studies: History, Culture, and Society* vol. 3, no. 1 (Fall 1996): 1–19. As Zoe Waxman notes: "That the motivation for revenge is suppressed in Night illustrates an important development in Wiesel's understanding of the position of the survivor-witness." Zoe Waxman, *Writing the Holocaust: Identity, Testimony, Representation* (Oxford: Oxford University Press, 2005), 110.
40 Atina Grossmann, *Jews, Germans, and Allies. Close Encounters in Occupied Germany* (Princeton: Princeton University Press, 2007), 89.
41 Larry Orbach and Vivien Orbach-Smith, *Soaring Underground: A Young Fugitive's Life in Nazi Berlin* (London: Andre Deutsch, 1996), 330–1. Quoted in Grossmann, *Jews, Germans, and Allies: Close Encounters in Occupied Germany*, 63. See also Konrad Charmatz, *Nightmares: Memoirs of the Years of Horror under Nazi Rule in Europe, 1939–1945*, trans. Miriam Dashkin Beckerman, ed. Matthew Kudelka (Syracuse: Syracuse University Press, 2003), 239–40.
42 British Video Archive for Holocaust Testimonies, R., Leon (3158)
43 Dvorjetsky, "Adjustment of Detainees to Camp and Ghetto Life and Their Subsequent Readjustment to Normal Society," 208.
44 Bela Braver, in *The Anguish of Liberation. Testimonies from 1945*, ed. Yehudit Kleinman and Nina Springer-Aharoni (Jerusalem: Yad Vashem, 1995), 19.
45 Shapira, *Land and Power. The Zionist Resort to Force, 1881–1948*, 23.
46 Fortunoff Video Archive for Holocaust Testimonies, Avraham B. (4611).
47 Fortunoff Video Archive for Holocaust Testimonies, Robert Mendler.
48 Fortunoff Video Archive for Holocaust Testimonies, Renata Skotnicka-Zajdman.

49 Some 300,000 to 500,000 Jews were drafted into the Red Army. See Harriet Murav and Gennady Estraikh, eds., *Soviet Jews in World War II: Fighting, Witnessing, Remembering* (Boston: Academic Studies Press, 2014).

50 *Words of Truth,* October 30, 1943, quoted in Gross, *Revolution from Abroad*, 249.

51 See Kenneth B. Moss, *An Unchosen People. Jewish Political Reckoning in Interwar Poland* (New Heaven: Harvard University Press, 2021), 18.

52 Hanebrink, *A Spectre Haunting Europe,* 166.

53 Jakow Egit. "'Cu a naj Leben' (Cwaj jor jidiszer jiszuw In Niderszlezje)," (Wrocław: Wyd. Niderszlezje, 1947), 19. Quoted in: Kamil Kijek, "Ostatnie polskie sztetł? Komunizm, zimna wojna, świat żydowski a społeczność żydowska Dzierzoniowa, 1945-1950" (in preparation),

54 Ethel Keitelgisser, "My Return Home," in *Sefer Radzyn*, ed. Yitzchak Zigelman (Tel Aviv: Radzyn (Podlaski) Immigrants Association in Israel, 1957), 293.

55 JHIA, 301/49 (Mendel Szczupak).

56 Avishai Dolinsky, "We Will Never Forget," in *Zabludow; dapim mi-tokh yisker-bukh*, 163.

57 Ephraim Farber, "Imprisoned by the Germans," in *Sefer zikaron le-kehilat Shebreshin*, ed. Dov Shuval (Haifa: Association of Former Inhabitants of Shebreshin in Israel and the Diaspora, 1984), 200.

58 Leona Toker, "The Holocaust in Russian Literature," in *Literature of the Holocaust*, ed. Alan Rosen (Cambridge: Cambridge University Press, 2013), 129. One of the first published collections of testimonies from the Holocaust was entitled *Dos blut ruft tsu nekome! Vos gelitene dertseyln vegn di fashistishe akhzaryes inem okupirtn poyln*, ed. L. Kvitko, Y. Nusinov, and Y. Katzenelson (Moscow, 1941). As Hannah Pollin Galay wrote: "In the introduction, JAFC member Shakhne Epshteyn offers instructions for how the reader should understand these witness narratives: What do these documents call for – in describing the tragedy not only of individuals but of millions? Not to *kines* or to *eykhe* [lamentations], not to tears or *takhnunim* [confessional prayers]. They call for hatred and revenge" (36). Hannah Pollin-Galay and Avrom Sutzkever, "Art of Testimony: Witnessing with the Poet in the Wartime Soviet Union," *Jewish Social Studies* vol. 21, no. 2 (Winter 2016): 1–34; here: 8.

59 Jeffrey Burds, "Sexual Violence in Europe in World War II, 1939–1945," 50.

60 The United States Holocaust Memorial Museum Oral History Branch, Interview with Leo and Zelda Lewis, RG- 50.477.1420.

61 Archiwum Akt Nowych, Ministerstwo Administracji Publicznej, Departament Polityczny, 1945, 3/403, Ministerstwo Administracji Publicznej, Departament Polityczny, Wydział narodowościowy, Raport, 2 stycznia 1945.

62 JHIA, 303/XVIII/16, 11, CKŻP do Ministerstwa Bezpieczeństwa Publicznego, 6 listopada 1946.

63 Hela Listapad-Izakowicz, "Life in the Ghetto and the Activity of the Partisans," trans. Jerrold Landau, in *Kehilat Sierpc; sefer zikaron*, ed. E. Talmi (Tel Aviv: The former residents of Sierpc in Israel and abroad, 1959), 451.

64 On surviving on the "Aryan" side, see Joanna Nalewajko-Kulikov, *Strategie przetrwania. Żydzi po "aryjskiej" stronie Warszawy* (Warsaw: Neriton, 2004).

65 Dariusz Stola, "Jewish Emigration from Communist Poland: the Decline of Polish Jewry in the Aftermath of the Holocaust," *East European Jewish Affairs* vol. 47, no. 2–3 (2017), 170.

66 See an important comparative study: Magdalena Waligórska, Yechiel Weizman, Alexander Friedman, and Ina Sorkina, "Holocaust Survivors Returning to Their Hometowns in the Polish-Belarusian-Ukrainian Borderlands, 1944–1948," *Journal of Holocaust Research* vol. 37, no. 2 (2023): 191–212.

67 Franziska Exeler, "Reckoning with Occupation," (Ph.D. diss., Princeton University, 2013), 153. For example, in early 1946, a little more than 6,000 Polish Jews returned to Lviv from the eastern territories of the Soviet Union. About 5,000 had attended the one synagogue that reopened after the war. Most of the original members of this first postwar Jewish community left Lviv for Poland before the end of 1946, frightened by blood libel rumours and a near-pogrom in Lviv in June 1945. A new Jewish population arrived from the eastern oblasts and, by 1949, 95 per cent of all Jews in Lviv were easterners. Tarak Cyril Amar, *The Paradox of Ukrainian Lvov: A Borderland City between Stalinists, Nazis and Nationalists* (Ithaca: Cornell University Press, 2015), 264.

68 Natalia Aleksiun, *Dokąd dalej? Ruch syjonistyczny w Polsce (1944–1950)* (Warszawa: Trio, 2002), 51–7; Dariusz Stola, "Jewish Emigration from Communist Poland: The Decline of Polish Jewry in the Aftermath of the Holocaust," *East European Jewish Affairs* 47, no. 2–3 (2007): 175–6; Albert Stankowski, "Nowe spojrzenie na statystyki dotyczące emigracji Żydów z Polski po 1944 roku," in *Studia z historii Żydów w Polsce po 1945 roku,* ed. Grzegorz Berendt, August Grabski, and Albert Stankowski (Warszawa: Żydowski Instytut Historyczny, 2000), 103–51.

69 See Leszek Olejnik, *Polityka narodowościowa Polski w latach 1944–1960* (Łódz: Wydawnictwo Uniwersytetu Łódziego, 2003).

70 Natalia Aleksiun, "Returning from the Land of the Dead: Jews in Eastern Galicia in the Immediate Aftermath of the Holocaust," *Kwartalnik Historii Żydów*, no. 2 (2013): 257–71, here, 258.

71 Yehoshua Yaffe, "People of Novogrudok after Liberation," trans. O. Delatycki, in *Pinkas Novogrudok*, ed. Eliezer Yerushalami, David Cohen, and Helen Cohn (New York: Jewishgen, 2013), 639.

72 On this, see Andreas Reckwitz, "Affective Spaces: A Praxeological Outlook," *Rethinking History. The Journal of Theory and Practice* vol. 16 (2012): 241–58.

73 Christopher Browning, "'Alleviation' and 'Compliance': The Survival Strategies of the Jewish Leadership in the Wierzbnik Ghetto and Starachowice Factory Slave Labor Camps," in *Gray Zones: Ambiguity and Compromise in the Holocaust and Its Aftermath*, ed. Jonathan Petropoulos and John K. Roth (London: Berghahn Books, 2012), 26–36.

74 Andrew Kornbluth, *The August Trials. The Holocaust and Post-War Justice in Poland* (Cambridge: Harvard University Press, 2021), 39.

75 Anna Cichopek-Gajraj, *Beyond Violence: Jewish Survivors in Poland and Slovakia, 1944–48* (Cambridge: Cambridge University Press, 2014), 233.

76 Susan Broomhall, "Introduction: Violence and Emotions in Early Modern Europe," in *Violence and Emotions in Early Modern Europe*, ed. S. Broomhall, S. Finn (London: Routledge, 2016), 3; Johan Huizinga, *The Waning of the Middle Ages: A Study of the Forms of Life, Thought and Art in France and the Netherlands in the XIVth and XVth Centuries* (England: E. Arnold, 1924), 1–21.

77 This includes looking out for people with what were considered by attackers as "Jewish" facial features, checking IDs, checking if men were circumcised.

78 Rykała, *W reakcji na powojenną przemoc antysemicką*, 47.

79 Rykała, *W reakcji na powojenną przemoc antysemicką*, 130.

80 Andrzej Rykała, *W reakcji na powojenną przemoc antysemicką. Samoobrona Żydów w Łodzi – uwarunkowania społeczno-polityczne i przestrzenne* (Łódź: Wydawnictwo Uniwersytetu Łódzkiego, 2020), 46. See also Kwiek for a list of murders of Jews committed in postwar Poland: Kwiek, *Nie chcemy Żydów u siebie*. See also Tokarska-Bakir, *Pogrom Cries*, 257.

81 Julian Kwiek, *Nie chcemy Żydów u siebie. Przejawy wrogości wobec Żydów w latach 1944–1947* (Warszawa: Wydawnictwo Nieoczywiste, 2021), 247.

82 Kwiek, *Nie chcemy Żydów u siebie*, 250.

83 Alina Skibińska, "Powiat Biłgorajski," in *Dalej jest noc*, 367.

84 Kenneth B. Moss, *An Unchosen People. Jewish Political Reckoning in Interwar Poland* (New Heaven: Harvard University Press, 2021), 26.

85 As Andrzej Rykała shows, the purely politically motivated murders formed only a small percentage of murders of Jews. The majority were caused by greed or traditional antisemitic. Rykała, *W reakcji na powojenną przemoc antysemicką*, 56.

86 Tokarska-Bakir, *Pogrom Cries*, 271.

87 On that see Tokarska-Bakir, *Pogrom Cries*, 210.

88 Adam Kopciowski, "Przemoc antyżydowska w powojennej Polsce w świetle ksiąg pamięci," *Zagłada Żydów. Studia i Materiały* (2018): 212–47. See also "Księgi pamięci jako źródło," 37–8, on rumours of ghosts of Jewish victims of local collaborators who were blamed on a series of fires in the locality.

89 Y. Dawidowicz, "Czyzewo- Today. On the Vestiges of a Disappeared Jewish Life," trans. Gloria Berkenstat Freund, in *Sefer Zikaron Czyzewo*, ed. Shimon Kanc (Tel Aviv: Former residents of Czyzewo in Israel and the USA, 1961), 1121.
90 Rykała, *W reakcji na powojenną przemoc antysemicką*, 2, 1.
91 On these, see Kamil Kijek, "Violence as Political Experience among Jewish Youth," in *From Europe's East to the Middle East*, 243–70.
92 JHIA, 303/XVIII/1 Projekt utworzenia Żydowskiej Straży Obywatelskiej; Skibińska, "Powroty ocalałych," in *Prowincja noc. Życie i zagłada Żydów w dystrykcie warszawskim* (Warszawa: Centrum Badań nad Zagładą Żydów, 2007), 575.
93 JHIA, 303/XVIII/38 p. 7, Sprawozdanie z pracy K.S. przy Wojewódzkim Komitecie Żydowskim w Krakowie za okres 1 VIII do 1 X 1946. In Kraków the unit was described as "very well prepared" after they underwent both shooting and street combat preparation courses.
94 AAN, 1214, 30/IV-23 t. 2, Redakcja czasopisma "Folkscajtung," Ogólnożydowski związek Robotniczy "Bund" w Polsce 1900–1948, Protokół zebrania robotników żydowskich miasta Wałbrzycha z dnia 6.8.1946.
95 Rykała, *W reakcji na powojenną przemoc antysemicką*, 140–52.
96 JHIA, 303/XVIII/38 p. 7, Sprawozdanie z pracy K.S. przy Wojewódzkim Komitecie Żydowskim w Krakowie za okres 1 VIII do 1 X 1946.
97 Natalia Aleksiun, "Intimate Violence: Jewish Testimonies on Victims and Perpetrators in Eastern Galicia," *Holocaust Studies. A Journal of Culture and History* vol. 23 (2017): 17–33.
98 Fortunoff Video Archive for Holocaust Testimonies, Interview with Allen S.
99 Pollin-Galay, *Ecologies of Witnessing*, 110.
100 See Engelking, "We Are Completely Dependent on Them …", 154.
101 M. Simion, "Following the Murderers," in *Sefer zikaron li-ḳehilat Horodoḳ (ʻa. y. Byalisṭoḳ)*, ed. Mosheh Simyon (Tel Aviv: ha-Irgunim shel yots'e Horodoḳ be-Yiśra'el uve-Argenṭinah, 1963), 115.
102 Anonymous Warsaw Poet, "And I Will Impart My Revenge upon Edom," in *Jewish Responses to Persecution: 1942–1943, vol. IV*, ed. Emil Kerenji (Lanham, MD: AltaMira Press in association with the United States Holocaust Memorial Museum, 2015).
103 "Remember That Which the Nazi Amalek Perpetrated against You," in *Sefer Kobylnik*, ed. Yitzhak Siegelman (Haifa: Committee of former residents of Kobylnik in Israel, 1967), 273.
104 Avishai Dolinsky, "We Will Never Forget," in *Zabludow; dapim mi-tokh yisker-bukh*, ed. Nechama Shmueli-Schmusch (Tel Aviv: Former Residents of Zabludow in Israel, 1987), 163.

105 USHMM Archive, Oral History interview with Norman Salsitz, 06.07.1999: RG-50.549.02.0052.
106 Rachel Alter-Borkowski, "On the Ruins," in *Sefer zikaron le-kehilat Kolno*, ed. Aizik Remba and Benjamin Halevy (Tel Aviv: Kolner Organization and Sifirat Poalim, 1971), 64.
107 Weizman, *Unsettled Heritage*, 34–5. Among examples brought by Weizman from Polish towns are grounds of the cemeteries used immediately after the war as a site of the municipal food market or barracks for the homeless.
108 Rachel Zaltshtein-Freter, "Radzyn After the Destruction," in *Sefer Radzyn*, ed. Y. Avi-Ara et al. (Tel Aviv: Radzyn Podlaski Society, 1957), 300.
109 L. Fursztenberg, "On the Ruins," in *Pinkas Sochaczew*, ed. A. Sh. Sztejn and G. Wejszman, (Jerusalem, Former residents of Sochaczew in Israel, 1962), 546.
110 Natalia Aleksiun, "Returning from the Land of the Dead: Jews in Eastern Galicia in the Immediate Aftermath of the Holocaust."
111 Weizman, *Unsettled Heritage*, 11.
112 Naftali Kantorowich, "What Happened to Me when I Returned Home," in *Rozhinoy; sefer zikaron le-kehilat Rozhinoy ve-ha-seviva*, ed. M. Sokolowsky (Tel Aviv, Former residents of Rozhinoy in Israel, 1957), 171.
113 On weeping as a feminine trait during postwar trials, see Sahron Geva, Female Witnesses at the Eichmann Trial, 143.
114 Mariasza Botwinik, "On the Roads of Destruction and Revenge," in *Ner tamid: yizkor le-Krevitsh*, ed. Matityahu Bar-Ratzon (Tel Aviv, Krivitsh Societies in Israel and the Diaspora, 1977), 666.
115 JHIA. 301/1526.
116 "Skazanie agenta gestapo w Legnicy," *Nowe Życie: trybuna Wojewódzkiego Komitetu Żydowskiego na Dolnym Śląsku* 7 (1947): s. 6
117 As these stories appear already in early testimonies collected by ŻIH, we can reflect to what extent this was helped by the fact that over a half of those collecting testimonies were women. See Jockusch, *Collect and Record*, 92.
118 Aleksiun, "Gender and Nostalgia: Images of Women in Early Yizker Bikher," 72.
119 Aleksiun, "Gender and Nostalgia: Images of Women in Early Yizker Bikher," 73.
120 Cichopek-Gajraj, *Beyond Violence*, 8.
121 Hebrew University, Kestenberg Archive, (257) 30–53, Interview with Teresa S.
122 Rykała, *W reakcji na powojenną przemoc antysemicką*, 40.
123 JHIA, 301/3351.
124 JHIA, 313/54.
125 JHIA, 301/2505.

126 M. Maltz, *Years of Horror*, 125, quoted in Aleksiun, "Returning from the Land of the Dead: Jews in Eastern Galicia in the Immediate Aftermath of the Holocaust," 268.
127 See Franziska Exeler, "The Ambivalent State: Determining Guilt in the Post-World War II Soviet Union," *Slavic Review, 75* (3) (2016): 616.
128 Alexander Statiev, *The Soviet Counterinsurgency in the Western Borderlands* (Cambridge: Cambridge University Press, 2010), 280.
129 Shmuel Kopelovitsh, "Taking Some More Vengeance," trans. Emma Karabelnik, in *Voronova; sefer zikaron le-kedoshei Voronova she-nispu be-shoat ha-natsim*, ed. H. Rabin (Voronova Societies in Israel and the United States, 1971).
130 "Shoah Foundation, 1222, Samuel Honigman, 27." Quoted in John-Paul Himka, "Ukrainian Nationalists and the Holocaust."
131 JHIA, 301/2530.
132 Sender Appelboim, "In the Forests and Villages with the People of Raflovka and Environs during the Years 1942–1944," trans. Esther Snyder, in *Sefer zikaron le-'ayarot Rafalowka ha-yeshenah, Rafalowka he-hadashah, Olizarka, Zoludzk veha-sevivah*, ed. Pinhas and Malkah Hagin (Tel Aviv: Tel-Aviv : Irgun yots'e Rafalovkah ha-yeshanah, Rafalovkah ha-hadashah, Olizarkah, Z'alutsk veha-sevivah, 1996), 48–53.
133 Oral History Interview, Mira Shelub.
134 Exeler, "Reckoning with Occupation: Soviet Power, Local Communities, and the Ghosts of Wartime Behavior in Post-1944 Belorussia."
135 Penter, "Local Collaborators on Trial," 343; Statiev, *The Soviet Counterinsurgency in the Western Borderlands*, 278.
136 Fortunoff Video Archive for Holocaust Testimonies, Interview with Rachel S.
137 Wendy Lower, *The Ravine. A Family, A Photograph, A Holocaust Massacre Revealed* (London: Head of Zeus, 2021); Juliette Cadiot and Tanja Penter. "Law and Justice in Wartime and Post-War Jahrbücher Für Stalinism." *Geschichte Osteuropas* vol. 61, no. 2 (2013): 161–71.
138 Snyder, "The Reconstruction of Nations," 178.
139 Pinhas Pantorin, "Remember What Amalek Did to Thee," trans. Ala Gamulka, *Kowel; sefer edut ve-zikaron le-kehilatenu she-ala aleha ha-koret*, ed. Eliezer Leoni-Zopperfin (Tel Aviv: 1957), 499,
140 Baruch Milch, *Testament* (Warszawa: Karta, 2001).
141 Penter, "Local Collaborators on Trial," 359.
142 USC Shoah Foundation Institute, Joe Kubryk.
143 Jan T. Gross, *Revolution from Abroad. The Soviet Conquest of Poland's Western Ukraine and Western Belorussia* (Princeton: Princeton University Press, 2002), 67.
144 Exeler, "Reckoning with Occupation: Soviet Power, Local Communities, and the Ghosts of Wartime Behavior in Post-1944 Belorussia," 285.

145 On this, see Aleksiun, "Intimate Violence: Jewish Testimonies on Victims and Perpetrators in Eastern Galicia."

146 Miriam Bergman, "How Pictures of the Martyrs Were Obtained from the N.K.V.D.," in *Sefer yizkor le-kehilat Sarny*, trans. Jacob Solomon Berger, ed. Y. Kariv (Tel Aviv: Former Residents of Sarny and Vicinity in Israel, 1961), 376.

147 Tzivia Nabozhny–Wildstein, "Through the Ponary Pit and Exile to Kolyma," 389–949, in *Sefer yizkor le-kehilat Sarny* for a story of a man who spent 11 years in Kolyma after attempting to get repatriation visas for children of Polish citizens from the orphanage which he managed.

148 JHIA, 303/XVIII/16, p. 11, CKŻP do Ministerstwa Bezpieczeństwa Publicznego, 6 listopada 1946. See also August Grabski, *Jews and Political Life in Poland*, 182; Cała, *Ochrona bezpieczeństwa fizycznego Żydów w Polsce powojennej*, 173–4, 208, 223.

149 Kornbluth, *The August Trials*, 113.

150 Kornbluth, *The August Trials*, 123.

151 AAN, Ministerstwo Administracji Publicznej, Departament Polityczny, 1945, 3/403, Motel Brukier, Zeznanie, 21.12.1944.

152 Kornbluth, *The August Trials*, 217.

153 Dariusz Libionka, Alina Skibińska, "'I Swear to Fight for a Free and Mighty Poland, Carry Out the Orders of My Superiors, So Help Me God.' Jews in the Home Army. An Episode from Ostrowiec Świętokrzyski," *Holocaust Studies and Materials* (2008), 247.

154 AAN, Ministerstwo Administracji Publicznej, Departament Polityczny, 1945, 3/403, Protokół sprawozdawczy z obecnej sytuacji Żydów w Irenie, 13.10.1945.

155 AAN, Ministerstwo Administracji Publicznej, Departament Polityczny, 1945, 3/403, Do wojewody białostockiego w Białymstoku [December 1944].

156 AAN, Ministerstwo Administracji Publicznej, Departament Polityczny, 1945, 3/403, Rozkaz nr 116 Komendanta Głównego Milicji Obywatelskiej z dnia 25 lipca 1945.

157 AAN, Ministerstwo Administracji Publicznej, Departament Polityczny, 1945, 3/403, Rozkaz nr 124 Komendanta Głównego Milicji Obywatelskiej z dnia 25 sierpnia 1945 r.

158 JHIA, 301/2802.

159 Rudawski, *Mój obcy kraj?*, 164–7. Quoted in Skibińska, „Powroty ocalałych," 573.

160 JHIA, CKŻP, Komisja Specjalna, 303/XVIII/43, k. 9, published in Cała, *Ochrona bezpieczeństwa fizycznego Żydów w Polsce powojennej*, 219.

161 JHIA, CKŻP, Wydział Organizacyjny, 303/IV, 30, k.11, published in Cała, *Ochrona bezpieczeństwa fizycznego Żydów w Polsce powojennej*, p. 169.

162 AAN, Ministerstwo Administracji Publicznej, Departament Polityczny, 1945, 3/403, Ministerstwo Administracji Publicznej, Departament polityczny, Wydział Narodowościowy, Sprawozdanie za okres od 15 stycznia do 10 marca 1945.

163 Magdalena Waligórska, Yechiel Weizman, Alexander Friedman, and Ina Sorkina, "Holocaust Survivors Returning to their Hometowns in the Polish-Belarusian-Ukrainian Borderlands, 1944–1948," 203.
164 Jan Snopko, "Początki działalności powiatowego urzędu bezpieczeństwa w Augustowie," *Studia Podlaskie* tom XV, 273–317; "Stosunek milicjantów powiatu radzyńskiego."
165 In his study of Jewish Communists in Poland, Jeff Schatz puts revenge on anti-Semites, anti-communists and collaborators as one of the key reasons why Jews would after the war join the security apparatus. Jaff Schatz, *The Generation. The Rise and Fall of the Jewish Communists of Poland* (Berkeley: University of California Press, 1991), 226.
166 JHIA 301/2532 (Józef Kapłański).
167 Kean College Oral Testimonies Project, Interview with Paul M.
168 IPN, Bi/0/52/970.
169 IPN, RZ-OO-80–44.
170 IPN, BU/0/193/3925; USC Morry Rolider (24352).
171 IPN, WR_0_57_91Blumstein.
172 IPN, BU/0/193/3925, See also USC Morry Rolider, (24352).
173 Tuvia Friedman, *Nazi Hunter*, trans. David C. Gross, (Haifa 2006), 134–5.
174 Tokarska-Bakir, *Pogrom Cries*, 170.
175 See also Hanebrink, *A Specter Haunting Europe*, 171.
176 Joanna Tokarska-Bakir, "The Polish Underground Organization Wolność i Niezawisłość and Anti-Jewish Pogroms, 1945–6," *Patterns of Prejudice* vol. 51, no. 2 (2017): 111–36; here: 114.
177 On fears of Judeo-bolshevism elsewhere in Eastern Europe, see Hanebrink, *A Specter Haunting Europe*, 163.
178 Zygmunt Woźniczka, "Obóz pracy w Świętochłowicach- Zgodzie i jego komendant," *Dzieje Najnowsze* no. 4 (1999): 17–35; Jerzy Kochanowski, *W polskiej niewoli. Niemieccy jeńcy wojenni w Polsce 1945–1950* (Warszawa: Wydawnictwo Neriton, 2001).
179 Anne Applebaum, *Iron Curtain: The Crushing of Eastern Europe, 1944–1956* (Knopf Doubleday Publishing Group, 2012).
180 Piotr Forecki, "Fantazmat Julii Brystiger," *Środkowoeuropejskie Studia Polityczne*, no. 1 (2017): 47–69.
181 Forecki, "Fantazmat Julii Brystiger," 56.

2. Holocaust Survivors and State Courts

1 Tadeusz Borowski, *Ludzie, którzy szli.*
2 Stathis N. Kalyvas, *The Logic of Violence in Civil War* (Cambridge: Cambridge UP, 2006), 389.
3 Gregory M. Reichberg , "Jus ad bellum," in *War: Essays in Political Philosophy*, ed. Larry May (Cambridge: Cambridge University Press, 2008), 2.

4 *Manifest Polskiego Komitetu Wyzwolenia Narodowego, Dz. U. z 1944 r. nr l, załącznik.*
5 Politics as a Vocation," in *From Max Weber: Essays in Sociology*, ed. H.H. Gerth and C. Wright Mills (New York: Taylor & Francis, 1946), 78.
6 Leszek Kubicki, *Zbrodnie wojenne w świetle prawa polskiego* (Warszawa: PWN, 1963), 180–1.
7 See Hanna Yablonka, "The Eichmann Trial: Was It the Jewish Nuremberg?," *The Loyola of Los Angeles International and Comparative Law Review* 301 (2012): 307.
8 Łukasz Starowieyski, Oprawcy na szafocie. Publiczne egzekucje w Polsce po II wojnie. https://dzieje.pl/wiadomosci/oprawcy-na-szafocie-publiczne-egzekucje-w-polsce-po-ii-wojnie
9 Marek Przybylski, "Publiczna egzekucja Arthura Greisera w poznańskiej prasie," in *Media wobec śmierci*, vol. 1, ed. K. Kwasik, J. Jaroszyński, G. Łęcicki (Warszawa: Elipsa, 2012).
10 "Szubienice w Stutthfie," PKF, nr specjalny 1946, in Marcin Owsiński, *Lagrowi ludzie. Śledztwo i pierwszy proces stutthofski (1945–1946). Opowieść o przemianie* (Łódź: Księży Młyn, 2022), 463.
11 "Jutro o godz. 7 rano Greiser zawiśnie na szubienicy. Wyrok wykonany będzie publicznie na stokach Cytadeli," *Głos Wielkopolski – dodatek nadzwyczajny*, July 20, 1946, quoted in Artur Pawlicki, *Procesy osób oskarżonych o popełnienie zbrodni niemieckich w Kraju Warty przed polskimi sądami specjalnymi w latach 1945–1946*, t. 1 (Poznań-Warszawa: Instytut Pamięci Narodowej, 2019), 253.
12 Pollin-Galay, *Ecologies of Witnessing*, 111. As Hannah Pollin-Galay writes: "This same forensic genre, which offers witnesses a wealth of resources when trying to name the local criminal and explain the damage of his betrayal, appears thinner when applied to more systematic forces of destruction."
13 Pollin-Galay, *Ecologies of Witnessing*, 123.
14 Daniel Blatman, *The Death Marches: The Final Phase of Nazi Genocide*, trans. Ch. Galai (Cambridge: Harvard University Press, 2011), 425.
15 IPN, RG-15.177M,0004, Specjalny Sąd Karny w Lublinie, Akta w sprawie Ernesta Fenckiego.
16 IPN, RG-15.177M,0005, Akta Prokuratora Specjalnego Sądu Karnego w Lublinie w sprawie Paula Hoffmana.
17 See IPN, RG-15.156M.00012, Sąd Okręgowy w Warszawie, Akta w sprawie karnej Fritza-Adolfa Fischera, Affidavit, Boruch Etam.
18 IPN, RG-15.156M.0004, Sąd Okręgowy w Warszawie, Akta w sprawie karnej Eustachego Prindyna, Antoniego Kollinga, Adama Hice, Augusta Wasserfuhra, and Karola Schopfla. For other cases of Nazi perpetrators recognized by displaced persons, see IPN RG.15.156M.0007, Sąd Okręgowy

w Warszawie, Akta w Sprawie Karnej Józea Gogola, IPN RG.15.157M.0007, Sąd Okręgowy w Warszawie, Akta w sprawie karnej Fryderyka Prussa.

19 See IPN, RG-15.156M.00012, Sąd Okręgowy w Warszawie, Akta w sprawie karnej Fritza-Adolfa Fischera.

20 "Revenge Is Sweet (How I Caught the Murderer and Liquidator of the Czenstochow Small Ghetto and Turned Him Over to the Hands of Justice)," in *Shenstokhover Yidn*, ed. R. Mahler, (NY: United Czestochower Relief Committee and Ladies Auxiliary, 1947), 245.

21 Jockush, *Collect and Record*, 106.

22 JHIA 301/4832 (Testimony of Salomon Hirschberg).

23 Donald Bloxham, "Prosecuting the Past in the Post-War Decade: Political Strategy and National Myth-Making," in *Holocaust and Justice: Representation and Historiography of the Holocaust in Post-War Trials*, ed. D. Bankier and D. Michman (Jerusalem: Yad Vashem; New York: Berghahn Books, 2010), 32–3.

24 Leszek Kubicki, *Zbrodnie wojenne w świetle prawa polskiego* (Warszawa: PWN, 1963), 180–1.

25 Quoted in Gabriel N. Finder and Alexander V. Prusin, *Justice Behind the Iron Curtain: Nazis on Trial in Communist Poland* (Toronto: University of Toronto Press, 2018), 19–20. The jurisdiction of the decree was expanded five times by 1949.

26 Owsiński, *Lagrowi ludzie*, 390.

27 See for example IPN, RG-15175M.0001.

28 Dziurok, "Skazani na karę śmierci przez Specjalny Sąd Karny w Katowicach," 149.

29 RG-15.176M.00016 Akta Prokuratora Specjalnego Sądu Karnego w Lublinie w sprawie Rudolfa Webera, Report of Preliminary Interrogation, 5.10.1945.

30 Around 300 members of the underground were sentenced based on the August Decree. See Wójcicka, *U kresu pewnej moralności*, 359.

31 IPN, Po 796/7, Akta Prokuratora Specjalnego Sądu Karnego w Poznaniu w sprawie Abrama Rozenbauma, Abram Rozenbaum, Prośba do Specjalnego Sądu Karnego w Poznaniu, 27. 8. 1946.

32 Kornbluth, *The August Trials*, 223.

33 Krzysztof Persak, "Jedwabne before the Court. Poland's Justice and the Jedwabne Massacre – Investigations and Court Proceedings, 1947–1974," *East European Politics and Societies* vol 25, issue 3 (2011): 410–32; here, 417.

34 Anna Bikont, "A young boy attacked us once and started shooting …" 277. This is one of the few cases that I came across of children contemplating carrying out revenge, rather than only thinking about it. This goes against the fear of aid workers and psychologists that "angry, forlorn children might act out or seek revenge." Lower, *The Ravine*, footnote 117. On a typical child's search for revenge, see "Letters from

Robert S. and Arno M., Limoges, France, November 11 and August 4, 1945," in *Jewish Responses to Persecution, 1945–1946, vol. VI*, 254.

35 Anna Bikont, "A young boy attacked us once and started shooting …," 278.

36 On the Polish penal system immediately after the war, see Andrzej Rzepliński, *Sądownictwo w PRL* (Londyn: Polonia, 1990); Zdzisław Albin Ziemba, *Prawo przeciwko społeczeństwu. Polskie prawo karne w latach 1945–1956* (Warszawa: Instytut Stosowanych Nauk Społecznych Uniwersytetu Warszawskiego, 1997); Antoni Lityński, "Ustawodawstwo karne w pierwszych latach Polski Ludowej," in *Wojna domowa czy nowa okupacja? Polska po roku 1944*, ed. Andrzej Ajnenkiel (Wrocław: Ossolineum, 1998), 120–40.

37 On this, see Gabriel N. Finder and Alexander V. Prusin, "Jewish Collaborators on Trial in Poland, 1944–1956," *Polin: Studies in Polish Jewry*, vol. 20, 122–48. This was not a unique phenomenon. For example, at least 52 members of Jewish councils and ghetto policemen from Transnistria were accused of collaboration and tried by Soviet Military Courts between 1944 and 1949. On that, see Wolfgang Schneider, "From the Ghetto to the Gulag, from the Ghetto to Israel: Soviet Collaboration Trials against the Shargorod Ghetto's Jewish Council," *Journal of Modern European History* vol. 17, issue 1 (2019): 83–97.

38 IPN Lu 315/226, Specjalny Sąd Karny w Lublinie, Akta w sprawie karnej przeciwko Maks Heimberg vel Szymon Falk, Protokół z przyjęcia ustnego zawiadomienia o przestępstwie, 11 April 1945.

39 IPN, Lu 315/292, Specjalny Sąd Karny w Lublinie, Akta w sprawie karnej przeciwko: Symech-Binem Smolarz, Protokół przesłuchania świadka, 15. 05. 1946.

40 IPN, Ld 498/545, Sąd Okręgowy w Łodzi, Akta w sprawie karnej przeciwko: Abram Glatzman.

41 IPN, Ld 498/545, Sąd Okręgowy w Łodzi, Akta w sprawie karnej przeciwko: Abram Glatzman, Sentencja wyroku.

42 IPN, Po 796/7, Akta Prokuratora Specjalnego Sądu Karnego w Poznaniu w sprawie Abrama Rozenbauma, Abram Rozenbaum do Specjalnego Sądu Karnego w Poznaniu, 27.8.1946.

43 IPN, Po 796/7, Akta Prokuratora Specjalnego Sądu Karnego w Poznaniu w sprawie Abrama Rozenbauma, Protokół rozprawy głównej, 6.03.1947.

44 IPN, Po 796/7, Akta Prokuratora Specjalnego Sądu Karnego w Poznaniu w sprawie Abrama Rozenbauma, Zeznanie z 26.05.1945.

45 IPN, Po 796/7, Akta Prokuratora Specjalnego Sądu Karnego w Poznaniu w sprawie Abrama Rozenbauma, Symcha Smolarz do Specjalnego Sądu Karnego, 9.09.1946.

46 Zofia Wóycicka, "U «kresu Pewnej moralności»: Dyskusje wokół procesów więźniów Funkcyjnych W Polsce 1945–1950," *Zagłada Żydów. Studia i Materiały*, no. 3 (2007): 355–85.

47 IPN, Ld 498/588, Akta Sądu okręgowego w Łodzi w sprawie Leona (Lajba) Krajna.
48 JHIA, 313/5, Sentencja Wyroku, 11 March 1948.
49 Tokarska-Bakir, *Pogrom Cries*, 43.
50 Cichopek-Gajraj, *Beyond Violence*, 235.
51 Libionka, Skibińska, '"I Swear to Fight for a Free and Mighty Poland," 247.
52 IPN, Po 796/7, Akta Prokuratora Specjalnego Sądu Karnego w Poznaniu w sprawie Abrama Rozenbauma, Abram Rozenbaum do Wojewódzkiego Komitetu PPR w Łodzi 18.11.1946.
53 IPN, Po 796/7, Akta Prokuratora Specjalnego Sądu Karnego w Poznaniu w sprawie Abrama Rozenbauma, Abram Rozenbaum do Specjalnego Sądu Karnego w Poznaniu, 27.8.46.
54 IPN, Po 796/7, Akta Prokuratora Specjalnego Sądu Karnego w Poznaniu w sprawie Abrama Rozenbauma, Abram Rozenbaum do Specjalnego Sądu Karnego w Poznaniu, 18.9.46.
55 See 303/XVI/153, 10, Wojewódzki Komitet Żydowski w Lublinie do Centralnego Komitetu Żydów, Wydział Prawny, 29 września 1947.
56 RG-15.179M.0005, Specjalny Sąd Karny w Krakowie, Akta w sprawie Anieli Adamik, Stefania Madej do Prokuratora Sadu Specjalnego w Krakowie, 10 lipca 1945.
57 Michael J. Braddick and John Walter, "Introduction. Grids of Power: Order, Hierarchy and Subordination in Early Modern Society," in *Negotiating Power in Early Modern Society Order, Hierarchy and Subordination in Britain and Ireland*, ed. Michael J. Braddick and John Walter (Cambridge: Cambridge University Press, 2010), 10.
58 Żbikowski, "The Postwar Wave of Pogroms and Killings," 91. Kornbluth, *The August Trials*, 88.

3. Jewish Civic Court in Poland

1 JHIA, 313/23 (Case of Marian Frauenglas), 4, Frauenglas, the Central Committee of Polish Jews, 9 June 1948.
2 JHIA, 313/23 (Case of Marian Frauenglas), 51, Sentence in the name of the Polish Republic, 2 September 1948.
3 JHIA, 313/23 (Case of Marian Frauenglas), 5 Frauenglas to the Central Committee of Polish Jews, 9 June 1948.
4 JHIA, 313/23 (Case of Marian Frauenglas), 19, Testimony of witness Eugeniusz Landsberg.
5 JHIA, 313/23 (Case of Marian Frauenglas), 5, speaker for the persecution to the Civic Court by the Central Committee of Jews in Poland, May 23, 1949.
6 For more on the Jewish Civic Court see David Engel, "Who Is a Collaborator? The Trials of Michał Weichert," in *The Jews in Poland*, vol. 2,

ed. Sławomir Kapralski (Kraków: Jagiellonian University, 1999), 339–70; Gabriel N. Finder, "'Sweep Out Evil from Your Midst': The Jewish People's Court in Post-War Poland," in *Beyond Camps and Forced Labour: Current International Research on Survivors of Nazi Persecution*, eds. Johannes-Dieter Steinert and Inge Weber-Newth, (Osnabrück: Secolo, 2005), 269–79; Gabriel N. Finder, "The Trial of Shepsl Rotholc and the Politics of Retribution in the Aftermath of the Holocaust," *Gal-Ed* 20 (2006): 63–89.

7 Quoted in Gabriel N. Finder, "Proces Szepsla Rotholca a polityka kary w następstwie Zagłady" *Zagłada Żydów. Studia i Materiały* issue 2 (2006) 225.

8 JHIA, Żydowska Agencja Prasowa, 116/226.

9 JHIA, 313/27 (Case of Wilhelm Gemeiner).

10 JHIA, 313/134 (Case of Roman Wachtel), 3: Letter of the Civic Court to Roman Wachtel, no date.

11 M. Tsukerfayn, "Undzer Lager Gericht," *Undzer Hofenung*, September 25, 1946, 7.

12 JHIA, 313/16 (Case of Rudy Cymermann); JHIA, 313/62 (Case of Aleksandra Kurowska).

13 On the trope of "Jewish collaboration" in postwar antisemitic discourse in Poland, see Katarzyna Person, *Policjanci. Wizerunek Żydowskiej Służby Porządkowej w getcie warszawskim* (Warszawa: Żydowski Instytut Historyczny, 2018).

14 JHIA, 313/50, List do Centralnego Komitetu Żydowskiego w Warszawie, 26.07.1948.

15 JHIA, 313/1 (Case of Aleksander Eintracht), 41: Verdict, 24 June 1949.

16 Jockusch and Finder, "Introduction," in *Jewish Honor Courts*, 11–12.

17 Michael Rothberg, *The Implicated Subject. Beyond Victims and Perpetrators* (Stanford: Stanford University Press, 2019), 95.

18 See Katarzyna Person, "Building a Community of Survivors in Post-War Jewish Courts: The Case of Regina Kupiec," in *Shoah: Ereignis und Erinnerung*, ed. A. Bothe, M. Schärtl, and S. Schüler-Springorum (Berlin: Hentrich&Hentrich, 2018), 171–84.

19 JHIA 301/2810 (Case of Aleksander Berger).

20 Laura Jockusch and Gabriel Finder, "Introduction," 5.

21 JHIA, 313/153, 48, Protokół posiedzenia Prezydium, May 26, 1948. There were, indeed, cases where the suspect could no longer be located after moving abroad JHIA, 313/19 (Case of Julek Fajner).

22 Parts of this sub-chapter appeared in Katarzyna Person, "Jews Denouncing Jews. Denunciations of Putative Collaborators and Reactions to Them in the Postwar Jewish Courts of Honor," in *Jewish Honor Courts: Revenge, Retribution, and Reconciliation in Europe and Israel after the Holocaust*, eds. G. Finder and L. Jockusch (Wayne State University Press, 2015), 225–46.

23 JHIA, 313/106, Samuel Silberstein, "Do Wojewódzkiego Komitetu Żydowskiego w Łodzi," December 24, 1946, 4.
24 For example, see JHIA, 301/4781 (Berek Finkelstein) on a member of the Judenrat in Miechów who after the war became an officer in the Polish army.
25 JHIA, 301/3328 (Henryk Hercberg).
26 Kornbluth, *The August Trials*, 115. For a denunciation addressed to the Jewish Historical Institute (addressed vaguely as "the authorities") see JHIA, 301/4100 (Bronisława Heinberg).
27 JHIA, 313/ 29, Statement of Eliahu Weinberg, 5.
28 For example, see JHIA, 313/97 for a letter written by the Jewish Committee in Olsztyn on behalf of the survivors from Świeciany and Vilnius passing through the city, "Wojewódzki Komitet Żydowski w Olsztynie to the Civic Court in Warsaw," January 21, 1947, 4.
29 JHIA, 313/128, "Maurycy Rubin do Prezydium Sądu Społecznego," January 26, 1949, 286.
30 JHIA, 313/53, "Do Wydziału Prawnego przy CKŻP," July 14, 1948, 6.
31 JHIA, 313/1, Henryk Mandel, "Do Sądu Obywatelskiego przy Centralnym Kom. Żydów w Polsce," July 3, 1948, 10.
32 JHIA, 313/118, Statement of Abram Rymarz, July 22, 1942, 7.
33 JHIA, 313/107, Majer Goldberg, "Nieczyści," Unzer Veg, n.d., 7.
34 JHIA, 313/144, 117.
35 JHIA, 313/50, Letter to the Central Jewish Committee in Warsaw, July 26, 1948, 4.
36 JHIA, 313/1, "Protokół," January 14, 1948, 9.
37 JHIA, 313/98, Decision of the Prosecution, August 26, 1949, 5.
38 JHIA, 313/43, "Do sądu społecznego przy C.K.Ż.P.," n.d., 4.
39 JHIA, 313/82, "Drodzy Przyjaciele," n.d., 11.
40 JHIA, 313/50, Letter to the Central Jewish Committee in Warsaw, July 26, 1948, 4.
41 JHIA, 313/107, "Nieczyści," *Unzer Veg*, n.d., 8.
42 JHIA, 313/107, "Nieczyści," 7.
43 For a protest in a courtroom, see "Harbere sztrofn far kapos!" *Landsberg Lager Cajtung* (November 12, 1945): 6.
44 Jakub Szymczak, *Ja łebków nie dawałem! Procesy przed Żydowskim Sądem Społecznym* (Warszawa: Czarne, 2022).
45 Ben Ami, "Wi zat bei undz der gerechtikajts-organ?" *A Heim* (June 4, 1946): 11.
46 See YVA, M 21.2, folder 77, "Baschluss in Angelegenheit nr. r. 65/48 c.," August 2, 1949.
47 JHIA, 313/1, Aleksander Eintracht, "Odwołanie," June 24, 1949, 57.
48 JHIA, 313/39, "Wyjaśnienie do zeznań złożonych w dniu 21 marca 1947," March 31, 1947, 30.

49 YIVO Archive, RG 294.2, MK 483, Microfilm reel 20, folder 222. "Adw. Dawid-Julian Holcman do Komisji Rehabilitacyjnej przy Centralnym Komitecie Żydowskim w Monachium," June 17, 1948."

50 See Samuel Gringauz, "Some Methodological Problems in the Study of the Ghetto," *Jewish Social Studies* 12.1 (1950): 65.

51 JHIA, 313/121, Henry Griffel, Letter to Henryk Gutmacher, February 18, 1947, 99.

52 JHIA, 313/121, Letter by N. Szenderowicz, April 18, 1946, 12.

53 JHIA, 313/20, "Zeznanie w sprawie Runy Kornblich," December 15, 1948, 109.

54 "Nieczyści," 9.

55 On defendants' privileged position after liberation, see Zeev W. Mankowitz, *Life Between Memory and Hope: The Survivors of the Holocaust in Occupied Germany* (Cambridge: Cambridge University Press, 2002), 204–5.

56 Pinchas, "Do Sądu Społecznego w Warszawie," 59.

57 JHIA 313/107, M. Rozenman, "Wyjaśnienie," January 17, 1948, 94.

58 See YIVO Archive, RG 294.2, MK 483, Microfilm reel 20, folder 222, "Adw. Dawid-Julian Holcman do Komisji Rehabilitacyjnej przy Centralnym Komitecie Żydowskim w Monachium, June 17, 1948," For a similar case, see YIVO Archive, RG 294.2, MK 483, Microfilm reel 14, folder 180, Józef Hoch, "Baszlus," October 29, 1947.

59 For assaults on former Jewish policemen after the war in Poland, see, for example, JHIA, 313/7, Aleksander Berger (Zamieński), "Protokół," January 29, 1947, 7.

60 JHIA, 313/71, Meyer Pinchas, "Do szefa wojewódzkiego Urzędu Bezpieczeństwa Publicznego w Lublinie," March 25, 1949, 43.

61 JHIA, 313/128, Dr. J. Bardach, "Do sądu obywatelskiego przy Centralnym Komitecie Ż.P.," November 2, 1947, 193.

62 JHIA 301/2809.

63 JHIA, 313/130, 17, Minutes.

64 JHIA 313/12 (Case of Lolek (Ignacy) Brandes).

65 Sibylle Schmidt, "Perpetrators' Knowledge: What and How Can We Learn from Perpetrator Testimony," *Journal of Perpetrator Research* vol. 1, no.1 (2017): 99.

66 JHIA, 313/18 (Case of Masza Engel), 2; Letter of Masza Engel to the Civic Court, 21 January 1947.

67 JHIA, 313/71 (Case of Pinchas Majer), Pinchas Majer to the Civic Court by the Central Committee of Jews in Poland, September 7, 1948.

68 JHIA, 313/71 (Case of Pinchas Majer), 5, Winberg to the Civic Court by the Central Committee of Jews in Poland, no date.

69 JHIA, 313/71 (Case of Pinchas Majer), 61, Pinchas Majer to the Civic Court in Warsaw, May 26, 1949.

70 JHIA, 313/71 (Case of Pinchas Majer), 63, Pinchas Majer to the Civic Court in Warsaw, May 26, 1949.
71 JHIA, 313/120 (Case of Chawa Szmit), Chawa Szmit to the Civic Court, February 8, 1949.
72 JHIA, 313/75, 4. Adam Mazurek, do Sądu Obywatelskiego przy Centralnym Komitecie Żydów w Polsce. 17.09.1948.
73 JHIA, 313/ 105, 6. Dawid Lamensdorf, Oświadczenie, 11.06.1946.
74 JHIA, 313/ 105, 10. Markus Anisfeld, Oświadczenie.
75 JHIA, 313/ 105, 168. Marian Rotkopf, do sądu społecznego przy centralnym komitecie żydów w Polsce, Wyjaśnienie.
76 JHIA, 313/12 (Case of Lolek (Ignacy) Brandes).
77 JHIA, 313/44 (Case of Karol Hertz), 5, Karol Hertz to the Central Committee of Jews in Poland in Warsaw, September 19, 1947.
78 JHIA, 313/13 (Case of Franciszka Brzezińska).
79 Ewa Koźmińska-Frejlak in "I'm Going to the Oven Because I Wouldn't Give Myself to Him," 256.
80 JHIA, 303/13 (Case of Franciszka Brzezińska), 3.
81 JHIA, 313/121 (Case of Szenderwoicz Naumi)
82 JHIA, 13/135 Nachym Fuks do Społecznego Sądu Obywatelskiego, 11.10.1948.
83 JHIA, 313/59 (Case of Rita Knyszyńska) 7; Rita Knyszyńska to the Central Committee of Jews in Poland – Legal Department in Warsaw.

4. Polish Jews and Germany as the Site of Revenge

1 Avinoam Patt, "Stateless Citizens of Israel. Jewish Displaced Persons and Zionism in Post-War Germany," in *The Disentanglement of Populations: Migration, Expulsion, and Displacement in Post-War Europe, 1944–49*, ed. Jessica Reinisch and Elizabeth White, (Palgrave Macmillan, 2011), 163.
2 YIVO Archive, RG 294.2, MK 483, Microfilm reel 20, folder 222, Anonymous article, "Court of Honor." Parts of this sub-chapter appeared in Katarzyna Person, "Building a Community of Survivors in Post-War Jewish Honor Courts: The Case of Regina Kupiec," in *Shoah: Ereignis und Erinnerung*, ed. A. Bothe, M. Schärtl and S. Schüler-Springorum (Berlin: Hentrich & Hentrich, 2018), 171–84.
3 YIVO Archive, RG 294.2, MK 483, Microfilm reel 20, folder 222, H. J. Wachtel, "Incident at Neu Freiman." May 1946.
4 YIVO Archive, RG 294.2, MK 483, Microfilm reel 20, folder 222, Testimony of Regina Kupiec.
5 YIVO Archive, RG 294.2, MK 483, Microfilm reel 20, folder 222, Testimony of Chawa Mangarten.

6 YIVO Archive, RG 294.2, MK 483, Microfilm reel 20, folder 222, Testimony of Estera Pikier.
7 YIVO Archive, RG 294.2, MK 483, Microfilm reel 20, folder 222, Testimony of Hanka Waksberg.
8 YIVO Archive, RG 294.2, MK 483, Microfilm reel 20, folder 222, Testimony of Dr. R. Zalcberg.
9 YIVO Archive, RG 294.2, MK 483, Microfilm reel 20, folder 222, Dawid Julian Holman, "Skarga o rewizję procesu." In many cases, people who were themselves tried for collaboration would volunteer to testify for or against fellow policemen or kapos who had been in the same ghetto or camp (see YVA, M.21.2, folder 58, Benisz Tkacz, "Erklarung"). Sometimes, because of this, the tribunal would automatically reject testimonies from certain witnesses. These included "prisoners who thanks to their work had a privileged position in the camp" (see YIVO Archive, RG 294.2, MK 483, Microfilm reel 21, folder 244, Dawid Honigman, "Baszlus"). Interestingly, this was the opposite of the stance of Polish state courts, where victims of privilege were considered to be more reliable, as they had a better understanding of the functioning of the camp. They were also considered more reliable as they were more likely to be recruited from among members of intelligentsia or those who had means or contacts to bribe their way into a position of privilege. Wójcicka, "U kresu pewnej moralności," 371.
10 Suhkolitsky, C., "Tsvei Problemen," *Undzer Vort* no. 4 (April 5, 1946); translated and quoted in Mankowitz, *Life between Memory and Hope*, 205 n72.
11 YIVO Archive, RG 294.2, MK 483, Microfilm reel 20, folder 222, Regina Kupiec, "Verdict."
12 YIVO Archive, RG 294.2, MK 483, Microfilm reel 44, folder 1595, Testimony of Moshe Zajdof.
13 YIVO Archive, RG 294.2, MK 483, Microfilm reel 20, folder 222, Dawid Julian Holcman, "Skarga o rewizję procesu."
14 YIVO Archive, RG 294.2, MK 483, Microfilm reel 20, folder 222, Rehabilitation Commission of Federation of Liberated Jews in U.S. Zone Germany, Resolve.
15 YIVO Archive, RG 294.2, MK 483, Microfilm reel 20, folder 222, "Adw. Dawid-Julian Holcman do Komisji Rehabilitacyjnej przy Centralnym Komitecie Żydowskim w Monachium. 17.06.1948."
16 Jockusch, "Rehabilitating the Past?" 73.
17 *Jewish Responses to Prosecution*, vol. 5, 192.
18 Grossmann, *Jews, Germans and Allies*, 231.
19 Schwarz, *The Redeemers*, 60.
20 For a comparison with Polish DP camp courts, see their documentation in the Piłsudski Institute Archive in New York. For example, files 24/243

[Przepisy, regulaminy i prawo sądowe], 24/244 [Sąd Obywatelski w Adelheide].

21 See the memoir of Kathryn Hume, a deputy director of UNRRA team in Wildfelcken, Kathryn Hulme, *The Wild Place* (Boston: Little, Brown [1953]), 14.

22 JHIA, 301/3330.

23 Quoted in Friling, *A Jewish Kapo in Auschwitz.*

24 See "Appeal to Residents of the Landsberg Center," in *Landsberg Lager Cajtung*, November 12, 1945, 6.

25 YIVO Archive, RG 294.2, MK 483, Microfilm reel 69, folder 987, "Erklejrung in injen Backenrot – Jakubowicz."

26 YIVO Archive, RG 294.2, MK 483, Microfilm reel 52, folder 703, *Föhrenwald*, "Urteil (kegn Ester Bojarska un Chaim Szwarc)."

27 Instytut Piłsudskiego w Nowym Jorku, Uchodźcy polscy w Niemczech po 1945 r. 244, Sąd Obywatelski w Allheide, Repetytorium na rok 1946.

28 YIVO Archive, RG 294.4, MK 492, Microfilm reel 14, folder 345. Komenda Policji Żydowskiej Bad Ischl, "Akt oskarżenia," no. 13/46 (August 3, 1946), 14/46 (September 20, 1946), and 15/46 (September 30, 1946). For other cases, see YIVO Archive, RG 294.4, MK 492, Microfilm reel 53, folder 714. Komenda "Protokol" for Berek Aved, policeman in Feldafing accused of "being a ghetto policeman and killing people with his own hands."

29 See YIVO Archives, RG 294.2, MK 483, Microfilm reel 51, folder 694, "Urteil" for a Fohrenwald camp inhabitant sentenced to 400 mark fine for claiming that a camp policeman "during the war threw living people into the oven."

30 Adv. M. Tsukerfayn, "Our Camp-Tribunal" *Undzer Hofnung* 25.09.1946, 3.

31 UNRRA Archive, S-0408-0020-10 303 – Protection – Internal Administration and Self-Government of Displaced Persons Camps UNRRA Divisional Liaison Officer HQ 52 L Div to UNRRA District director HQ MG 1 Corps District, subject: Camp Tribunals, December 27, 1945. See also YIVO Archives, RG 294.2, MK 483, Microfilm reel 53, folder 714, Camp Court Fohrenwald to the Legal Section of Jewish Central Committee, Munich. Report bearing upon the lawfulness of the activity of the Court in Camp Foehrenwald, November 4, 1946. On the functioning of camp courts, see UNRRA Archive, S-0437-0018-09 Displaced Persons – General – Camp Courts, especially R.W. Collins, Deputy Zone Director, Department of Field Operations to District Director, UNRRA District No.5, UNRRA, subject: Court Activities at Reinhardt-Kaserne, Neu Ulm, March 7, 1947.

32 Lucy Dawidowicz, *From That Place and Time: A Memoir, 1938–1947* (New York: W.W. Norton & Co Inc, 1998), 303.

33 Edith Raim, *Justiz zwischen Diktatur und Demokratie*, 1143.

34 On that, see Mark Wyman, *DP: Europe's Displaced Persons, 1945–1951* (London: Associated University Presses, c1989), 185.

35 Raim, *Justiz zwischen Diktatur und Demokratie*, 1032 and 1164.

36 Cy J. Holocaust Testimony (HVT-1666), Fortunoff Video Archive for Holocaust Testimonies, Yale University Library.

37 Living Memorial to the Holocaust-Museum of Jewish Heritage, Testimony of F., Leon.

38 In May 1945, Polish (at that point that also included Polish Jewish) DPs in Dortmund were threatened with court martial for not submitting to curfew rules, spending nights outside their barracks, or leaving the camp without a permit. See "Przepisy dla uczestników obozu Nr. 2, 2 maja 1945," *Głos Wyzwolenia. Pismo obozowe wyzwolonych z niewoli niemieckiej robotników przymusowych w Dortmundzie* no. 8, May 3, 1945, 4.

39 As Rivka Brot notes, the military government judiciary in the American zone included three courts: "a general court, the higher instance; an intermediate court; and a summary court, the lower instance by which most of the DPs were tried" (Brot, "Conflicting Jurisdictions." 177, *n*12). See also Oscar A. Mintzer, *In Defense of the Survivors: The Letters and Documents of Oscar A. Mintzer, AJDC Legal Advisor, Germany, 1945–46* (Berkeley: Judah L. Magnes Museum, 1999).

40 Control Office for Germany and Austria, Letter to Brian Robertson, March 11, 1946, The National Archives (NA), London, FO 1032/2257, Treatment of Jewish DPs and other irrepatriables: vol II.

41 For the most famous instance of authority conflict, see the case of the suspected kapo from Gorlitz, Salomon Schlusinger, in UNRRA Archive S-0425-0018-12 Legal Matters-Courts-Camps; and Margarete Myers Feinstein, *Holocaust Survivors in Post-War Germany, 1945–1957* (Cambridge: Cambridge University Press, 2010), 245–6.

42 UNRRA Archive, S-0425-0018-12, Legal Matters-Courts-Camps, Memorandum from Major General H. L. McBride Headquarters Ninth Inf. Div. to the Commanding General Third US Army, November 21, 1946.

43 For a discussion of the Föhrenwald court and police, see Angelika Königseder and Juliane Wetzel, *Waiting for Hope: Jewish Displaced Persons in Post-World War II Germany* (Evanston, Ill. : Northwestern University Press, 2001), 134–41; on the Belsen court and police see 199–201.

44 "Fun gerichts-zal," *Landsberger Lager Cajtung*, April 15, 1946, 2.

45 "Harbere sztrofn far kapos" *Landsberger Lager Cajtung*, November 12, 1945, 6.

46 On the honour court in Belsen, see Yad Vashem Archive (YVA) O-70/30 and documents in YIVO Archive, RG 294.2, MK 483, Microfilm reel 114, folder 1583.

47 Some Jews living in DP camps chose the Polish Social Court rather than honour courts to judge their rehabilitation cases. See for example JHIA,

313/128, Teichholtz Bronisław, head of provisioning in the Lwow Judenrat, living in Vienna. His case was suspended in August 1948 due to problems with bringing witnesses for the defense to attend the trial in Poland.

48 YIVO Archive ,RG 294.2, MK 483, Microfilm reel 20, folder 221, Benisz Tkacz, Baszlus.

49 YIVO Archive, RG 294.2, MK 483, Microfilm Reel 21, folder 224, "Baszlus."

50 YIVO Archive, RG 294.2, MK 483, Microfilm Reel 44, folder 1595, the trial of David Naufeld.

51 YIVO Archive, RG 294.2, MK 483, Microfilm Reel 21, folder 224, Mietek Czapnicki, Decision of October 5, 1949.

52 YIVO Archive, Leo Schwarz papers, Folder 451, Maurice Lipian, director, Military district no. 1 to all AJDC area team representatives and AJDC field personnel, subject: Legal aid procedure, November 6, 1947. On the attitude of DP representative bodies to the rulings of military courts, see "Der C.K. wegn urtejl in landsberger process," *A Heim*, June 4, 1946, 1. See also Rivka Brot, "Everyday Justice: Legal Aid for Jewish Displaced Persons, Germany, 1945–1950," *Holocaust and Genocide Studies* vol. 136, no. 2 (2022): 224–41.

53 Yad Vashem Archive, M.21.2, folder 4, Testimony of Leib Storch.

54 Yad Vashem Archive, M.21.2 file 79.

55 Yad Vashem Archive, M.21.2, folder 4, Testimonies of Chaim Fisz and Rola Klempner.

56 Instytut Pamięci Narodowej Archive, GK 164/1424, Norbert Jolles.

57 "Urtejl fun ern-gericht in Heidenheim," *Jidisze Cajtung*, 13.01. 1948: 5.

58 "Urtejl fun ern-gericht," *Jidisze Cajtung*, 16.03. 1948: 5.

59 See YIVO Archives, RG 294.2, MK 483, Microfilm reel 20, folder 222, Regina Kupiec.

60 On the discussion over the social court in Italy see A. Beker, "A par werter wegn flichts-gericht," *Il Cammino (Baderach)* 30 (39) 1946: 5.

61 See Ben Ami, "Wi zat bei undz der gerechtikajts-organ?" *A Heim* (June 4, 1946): 11.

62 See Yad Vashem Archive, M 21.2, file 77 (Aron Einhorn) Baschluss in Angelegenheit nr. R. 65/48 c. Einhorn Arnold.

63 Ben Ami, "Wi zat bei undz der gerechtikajts-organ?" *A Heim*, June 4, 1946: 11.

64 M. Cukerfajn, "Undzer Lager Gericht," *Undzer Hofenung* September 25, 1946: 7.

65 M. Cukerfajn, "Undzer Lager Gericht," *Undzer Hofenung*, September 25, 1946: 7.

66 "Urteil fun lager-gericht n. 146," *Undzer Hofenung* September 25, 1946: 7.

67 YIVO Archive RG 294.2, MK 483, Microfilm.21 folder 244 Dawid Honigman, Baszlus

68 Leo Baeck Institute, LBI Archives, AR 25385, Interview with Samuel Gringauz; see also "The Ghetto as an Experiment of Jewish Social

Organization (Three Years of Kovno Ghetto)," *Jewish Social Studies* 11 (1949): 3–20; "Some Methodological Problems in the Study of the Ghetto," *Jewish Social Studies* 12, No. 1 (Jan. 1950): 65–72. For a discussion of the role played by Gringauz in the DP camps, see Ze'ev Mankowitz, *Life between Memory and Hope: The Survivors of the Holocaust in Occupied Germany* (Cambridge: Cambridge University Press, 2002), 173–91.

69 Samuel Gringauz, "In cejchn fun martirertum, hofnung un arbet," *Landsberger lager-cajtung* no. 14, January 18, 1946, 1, quoted in: Mankowitz, *Life between Memory and Hope*, 187.

70 YIVO Archive, RG 294.3 MK 489, Microfilm reel17, folder 189, Abraham Steczer to Herman Altbauer, March 10, 1948.

71 YIVO Archive, RG 294.2, MK 483, Władysław Freidheim.

72 See JHIA, 313/48. Józef Hoch, member of Judenrat in Lviv, accused of forcing Judenrat employees to participate in deportation actions. Following the request of persecution, the matter was forwarded to the criminal court due to the character of the case. We do not know the result of this case, but Hoch most likely left Poland before it took place as he was tried again in Germany. Numerous others whose cases were brought before the Polish court managed to disappear in Germany more successfully, as there is no documentation referring to their subsequent trials. See for example JHIA 313/43- Helesiewicz Mendel, kapo in Krzepice camp.

73 YIVO Archive, RG 294.2, MK 483, Microfilm reel 114, folder 1586. Testimony of Chaim Posłuszny in the case of Alfons Kurz, 15 May 1946.

74 For example, in the case of Uszer Lokiec functionary from forced labor camp a sub-camp of Majdanek, which took place in Bergen Belsen, the court managed to find 13 survivors of Blizyn who were witnesses of his behaviour.

75 YIVO Archive, RG 294.3 MK 489, Microfilm reel 17, folder 189. Hermann Altbauer composed his defense statement in faulty Yiddish, although he conducted his personal correspondence in Polish, which was the language in which he was educated. See Testimony of Hermann Altbauer, February 10, 1942.

76 YIVO Archive, RG 294.3 MK 489, Microfilm reel 17 folder 189, Abraham Sterczer [?] do Sądu Honorowego Żydów w Milano, March 10, 1948.

77 YIVO Archive, RG 294.2, MK 483, Microfilm reel 20, folder 221, Testimony of Mordechaj Karnowsky.

78 YIVO Archive, RG 294.2, MK 483, Microfilm reel 20, folder 221, testimony of Mordechaj Karnowsky, see also Benisz Tkacz Cu der Rehabilitacje Komisje Munchen, March 25, 1948. and in the same folder testimony of Jicchok Batner for Tkacz's links to Zionism in his university years.

79 YIVO Archive RG 294.2, MK 483, Microfilm reel 20, folder 22, Testimony of Zelmar Finkel.

80 See YVA, M.21.2, folder 32 (Case file of Chaim Aleksandrowicz).
81 Wójcicka, "U kresu pewnej moralności," 374.
82 YIVO Archive, RG 294.2, MK 483, Microfilm reel 14, folder 180, Józef Hoch "Baszlus," October 29, 1947.
83 YIVO Archive, RG 294.2, MK 483, Microfilm reel 114, folder 1586, testimony of Adolf Katz.
84 YIVO Archive, RG 294.3 MK 489, Microfilm reel 17, folder 189, Testimony of Hermann Altbauer, February 10, 1942.
85 Yad Vashem Archive, M. 21/2 folder 126, Romek Merin, "Oświadczenie."
86 YIVO Archive, Bund Collection, Me 17–240, Jakub Labiner, "Oświadczenie."
87 YIVO Archive, Bund Collection, Me 17–240, Stefania Milwiw, "Zaświadczenie."
88 YIVO Archive, Bund Collection, Me 17–240, Ludwik Jaffe, "Deklarung."
89 Yad Vashem Archive, M. 21/2 folder 111, Testimony of Gustawa Beckerman, April 30, 1946.
90 See Gringauz, "Some Methodological Problems in the Study of the Ghetto."
91 Yad Vashem Archive, M 21.2, folder 77, "Baschluss in Angelegenheit nr. r. 65/48 c.," August 2, 1949.
92 YIVO Archive, RG 294.2, MK 483, Microfilm reel 18, folder 195. Władysław Freidheim, Cum Presidentum fun Central Komitet fun di befrajde idn in Us-Zone Dajczland, August 7, 1947.
93 On the Zionist critique of Bundism in DP camps, see Mankowitz, *Life between Memory and Hope*, 73–6. Ludwik Jaffe's case was widely reported in the displaced persons press in Italy. See, for example, "Prozes kegn Dir. L. Jafe in Gezelschaftl. Gericht," *Il Cammino* (August 27, 1948): 4.
94 See also YIVO Archive, RG 294.2, MK 483, Microfilm reel 18, folder 202. For an accusation of one of the members of the Boelcke Kaserne committee of collaboration and a request that the case be forwarded to the Munich honour court to guarantee an objective ruling, see also "M. Nochhauser do sądu honorowego w Boelcke Kaserne," April 19, 1948.
95 YIVO Archive, RG 294.2, MK 483, Microfilm reel 20, folder 221, Benisz Tkacz, Dringende wendung, March 19, 1948.
96 YIVO Archive, RG 294.2, MK 483, Microfilm reel 20, folder 221, Benisz Tkacz, Dringende wendung, March 19, 1948.
97 YIVO Archive, RG 294.2, MK 483, Microfilm reel 20, folder 221, Rehabilitacje komisje Cu der Centraler Wal- Komisje, March 21, 1948.
98 "2-ter Kolaborazie-Prozes in Gez. Gericht," *Il Cammino* 95.283 (September 3, 1948): 3. On the Juliusz Zeigel (Julius Siegel) case, see also Rivka Brot, "Julius Siegel: A 'Kapo' in Four (Judicial) Acts," *Dapim: Studies on the Shoah* 25 (2011): 65–127.

99 See Yad Vashem Archive, M.21.2, folder 32 (case file of Chaim Aleksandrowicz). In the case of Henryk Gliksman, a former policeman from Częstochowa, the court believed that he was working on orders from the Zionist underground. Yad Vashem Archive, M.21.2, folder 51 (Case file of Henryk Gliksman).

100 See B. Orenstein, "Wos iz azojns kapo?" *Jidysze Cajtung*, December 6, 1946, 6.

101 YIVO Archive, RG 294.2, MK 483, Microfilm reel 47, folder 639, A letter to Szpigler regarding Berysz Mandelbaum.

102 YIVO Archive, RG 294.2, MK 483, Microfilm reel 20, folder 221, Benisz Tkacz, Dringende wendung, March 19, 1948.

103 YIVO Archive, Bund Collection, Me 17–240, Erklärung von Dr Moises Landau.

104 YIVO Archive, RG 294.2, MK 483, Microfilm reel 21, folder 244, Dawid Honigman, Baszlus.

105 YIVO Archive, RG 294.2, MK 483, Microfilm reel 114, folder 1594. See for example a case of Chazciel Jungster, former kapo in numerous camps in which one of the witnesses openly stated that the witnesses for the defense had been bribed. The evidence of Hirsch Rotenberg.

106 YIVO Archive, RG 294.2, MK 483, Microfilm reel 21, folder 244. Dawid Honigman, "Baszlus," November 25, 1948. On the *rasha* (an evil-doer) as a witness, see Saul J. Berman, *Boundries of Loyalty*, p. 194.

107 YIVO Archive, RG 294.2, MK 483, Microfilm reel 20, folder 222.

108 YIVO Archive RG 294.2, MK 483, Microfilm reel 21, folder 22, Henryk Frydman, "Baszlus".

109 YIVO Archive, RG 294.2, MK 483, Microfilm reel 21, folder 244, Dawid Honigman, "Baszlus."

110 YIVO Archive RG 294.2, MK 483, Microfilm reel 21, folder 224, Henryk Frydman, "Baszlus."

111 YIVO Archive RG 294.2, MK 483, Microfilm reel 114, folder 1595, Comment on the testimony of Hirsh Vileski.

112 YIVO Archive RG 294.2, MK 483, Microfilm reel 21, folder 222, Regina Kupiec, Verdict, YVA M.21.2 file 79 Bericht-Akten-Notiz Betr. Anklage gegen Leon Mercel.

113 Brot, "Conflicting Jurisdictions," 193. See also Rivka Brot, *Be'eyzor haafor: hakapo hayehudi kemishpat* (Tel Aviv: The Open University Publishing House, the David Berg Institute for Law and History, 2019).

5. Justice and Migrations

1 Wyman, *DP: Europe's displaced persons*, 179.

2 IPN, GK 164/60 vol.1–2. Even though in 1947 an investigation into his case was initiated after receiving one of the denunciations by the Main

Commission for the Investigation of German Crimes in Poland, the matter was dropped for lack of incriminating evidence, and no extradition request was filed. See also JHIA, 313/64.

3 For another case of collaboration between the Jewish Historical Institute and social courts in Germany, see, for example, correspondence between the Institute and the Central Committee of Liberated Jews in the British Zone on Szlamo Munzberg, former policeman in the ghetto in Radom. The displaced-persons organization gathered testimony in camps against people who were tried in Poland. See JHIA, 313/96- for correspondence between the Jewish Historical Institute and Jewish Historical Documentation in Linz regarding Pilawski Józef, Bełek, German collaborator in Sobowice.

4 JHIA, 313/153, p. 23, Protokół posiedzenia Prezydium Sądu, no date; and 44, Protokół posiedzenia Prezydium, April 28, 1948.

5 JHIA, 313/153, p. 38, Protokół posiedzenia Prezydium, February 26, 1948.

6 JHIA, 313/153, p. 46, Protokół posiedzenia Prezydium, May 12, 1948.

7 JHIA, 313/144 (Case of Hersz-Henryk Zameczkowski), 121, Hersz London do Żydowskiego Instytutu Historycznego w Warszawie. Ewa Koźmińska-Frejlak in "'I'm Going to the Oven Because I Wouldn't Give Myself to Him': The Role of Gender in the Polish Jewish Civic Court," in *Jewish Honour Courts Revenge, Retribution and Reconciliation in Europe and Israel after the Holocaust*, 247–78.

8 JHIA, 313/100 (Case of Mojżesz Press Szoel), 35, Mojżesz Press Szoel to Centralny Komitet Żydowski w Warszawie, April 5, 1947.

9 In one case witnesses were located via Bund channels in Stockholm. See JHIA, 313/153, 46, Protokół posiedzenia Prezydium, May 12, 1948.

10 JHIA, 313/153, p. 50, Protokół posiedzenia Prezydium, August 19, 1948.

11 JHIA, 313/22 (Case of Berek Finger).

12 JHIA, 313/15 (Case of Abram Cybuch). For unknown reasons, this particular case was dismissed as the person filling in the request was located outside Poland, even though the court carried out many others.

13 JHIA, 313/15 (Case of Abram Cybuch), 6, Abram Cybuch to the Board of the Jewish Community in Łódź, August 2, 1947.

14 JHIA, 313/100 (Case of Mojżesz Press Szoel), 31, Mojżesz Press Szoel, Request to the Central Jewish Committee in Warsaw, March 26, 1947.

15 JHIA, 313/142 (Case of Nuchym Zahnstecher), 5, Nuchym Zahnstecher, Petition to the Civic Court by the Central Committee of Jews in Poland, October 11, 1948.

16 On yizkor books see, among others, *Memorial Books of Eastern European Jewry: Essays on the History and Meanings of Yizker Volumes*, ed. Rosemary Horowitz (Jefferson: McFarland, 2014).

17 *Sefer Buczacz: Matsevet Zikaron Le-kehila Kedosha*, ed. Yisrael Cohen (Tel Aviv: Am Oved, 1956), 298 [document transl. by Jessica Cohen].
18 For another story of a member of the Ordnungsdienst willingly subjecting himself to punishment, see Zuckerman, *A Surplus of Memory*, 636–7.
19 *Sefer Buczacz: Matsevet Zikaron Le-kehila Kedosha*, 298.
20 JHIA 313/143 (Case of Abram and Lejbuś Zajfman), 8, Ziomkostwo Ostrowskie w New-Yorku żąda Sądu nad dwoma zdrajcami.
21 Szymczak, *Ja łebków nie dawałem*.
22 Szymczak, *Ja łebków nie dawałem*.
23 This was, however, not an isolated case. On that, see Katarzyna Person, "Jewish Courts of Honor in the American Zone of Occupied Germany and the Allied Judiciary," in *Our Courage: Jews in Postwar Europe 1945–48*, ed. Kata Bohus, Atina Grossmann, Werner Hanak, and Mirjam Wenzel (Berlin: De Gruyter-Oldenburg, 2020), 258–73.
24 JHIA, 313/13 (Case of Franciszka Brzezińska).
25 JHIA, 313/120 (Case of Runa Fakler-Kornbluh). This case is discussed in depth by Ewa Koźmińska-Frejlak in "'I'm Going to the Oven Because I Wouldn't Give Myself to Him': The Role of Gender in the Polish Jewish Civic Court," in *Jewish Honour Courts Revenge, Retribution and Reconciliation in Europe and Israel after the Holocaust*, 247–78.
26 Ewa Koźmińska-Frejlak in "I'm Going to the Oven Because I Wouldn't Give Myself to Him," 256.
27 Simo Muir, "Rumkowski's Scapegoat? The Case of Łódź Ghetto Functionary Maks Szczęśliwy at a Rabbinic/Honor Court in Helsinki, 1949–1953," *Holocaust and Genocide Studies*.
28 Joel Silverman, "Krieger v. Mittelman and Jewish Perception of the Refugee in the Early Cold War," *Judaism* 55, no. 1 and 2 (2006): 40–54.
29 Porat, *Bitter Reckoning*
30 For a story of a soldier attacked on a beach in Tel Aviv, see *Haaretz* 15.07.1946. 4.
31 Porat, *Bitter Reckoning*, 42.
32 Porat, *Bitter Reckoning*, 228.
33 See "Letter to the editor," *Haaretz*, 8.12.1945 for a letter from Chaim M., in which he asks once again for an investigation into all the accusations against him.
34 *Haaretz* 06.01.1946.
35 *Al Hamishmar* 11.06.1946, *Haaretz* 01.09.1946.
36 *Haaretz* 15.06.1946.
37 Yehudit Dori Deston, Dan Porat, "A Prisoner, Legislator, and Jurist: Joseph Lamm's Legal Legacy in Relation to the Nazis and Nazi Collaborators (Punishment) Law, 1950," *Holocaust and Genocide Studies* vol. 37, issue 1 (2023): 74–89.

38 Blustein, "Traumatic Emotions," 240.

39 Blustein, "Traumatic Emotions," 261.

40 On this need, see Lawrence Douglas, "The Didactic Trial: Filtering History and Memory into the Courtroom," in *Holocaust and Justice: Representation and Historiography of the Holocaust in Post-War Trials*, ed. D. Bankier and D. Michman (Jerusalem; Yad Vashem, 2010), 19.

41 Leo W. Schwarz, *The Redeemers: A Saga of the Years 1945–1952* (New York; Farrar, Straus and Young, 1953), 68. While Schwarz's book was published a few years after the event, in 1953, this description matches perfectly the description of the trial published at a time in the DP newspaper *Landsberg Lager Cajtung* (see "Far Barcion Proces kegn dem merder fun saloniker geto farn jidiszn gericht in Landsberg," in *Landsberg Lager Cajtung* 2 December 1945), 7.

42 On intimate violence, see Natalia Aleksiun, "Intimate Violence: Jewish Testimonies on Victims and Perpetrators in Eastern Galicia," *Holocaust Studies* vol. 23, issue 1–2 (2017): 17–33.

43 Peter Holquist, *Making War. Forging Revolution. Russia's Continuum of Crisis, 1914–1921* (Cambridge: Harvard University Press, 2020).

44 Tomislav Dulić, *Utopias of Nation: Local Mass Killing in Bosnia and Herzegovina, 1941–1942* (Uppsala: Uppsala universitet, 2005); Vladimir Solonari, *Purifying the Nation: Population Exchange and Ethnic Cleansing in Nazi-Allied Romania* (Washington/Baltimore: Woodrow Wilson Center Press/Johns Hopkins University Press, 2009).

45 Franziska Exeler, *Ghosts of War: Nazi Occupation and Its Aftermath in Soviet Belarus* (Ithaca: Cornell University Press, 2022).

Bibliography

Adamczyk-Garbowska, Monkia, and Adam Kopciowski, "Memorial Books as a Remembrance of Collective Trauma." In *Jewish Presence in Absence: The Aftermath of the Holocaust in Poland, 1944–2010*, edited by Felikx Tych and Monika Adamczyk-Garbowska. Translated by Grzegorz Dąbskowski and Jessica Taylor-Kucia. Jerusalem: Yad Vashem, 2014.

Adamczyk-Garbowska, Monika, Adam Kopciowski, and Andrzej Trzciński, eds. *"Tam był kiedyś mój dom." Księgi Pamięci Gmin Żydowskich*. Lublin: Wydawnictwo UMCS, 2009.

Aleksiun, Natalia, introduction and annotation. "The Situation of the Jews in Poland as Seen by the Soviet Security Forces in 1945." *Jews in Eastern Europe* vol. 37, no. 3 (1998): 52–68.

Aleksiun, Natalia. *Dokąd dalej? Ruch syjonistyczny w Polsce (1944–1950)*. Warszawa: Trio, 2002.

– "Gender and Nostalgia: Images of Women in Early Yizker Bikher." *Jewish Culture and History* vol. 5, issue 1 (2002): 69–90.

– "Return from the Land of the Dead: Jews in Eastern Galicia in the Immediate Aftermath of the Holocaust." *Kwartalnik Historii Żydów* no. 2 (2013): 257–271

– "Intimate Violence: Jewish Testimonies on Victims and Perpetrators in Eastern Galicia." *Holocaust Studies* vol. 23, issue 1–2 (2017): 17–33.

Amar, Tarak Cyril. *The Paradox of Ukrainian Lvov: A Borderland City between Stalinists, Nazis and Nationalists*. Ithaca: Cornell University Press, 2015.

Applebaum, Anne. *Iron Curtain: The Crushing of Eastern Europe, 1944–1956*. New York: Knopf Doubleday Publishing Group, 2012.

Ayara shehayta Olkanik. Haifa: Hebrew Reali School in Haifa

Bankier, D., and D. Michman, eds. *Holocaust and Justice: Representation and Historiography of the Holocaust in Post-War Trials*. Jerusalem: Yad Vashem; New York: Berghahn Books, 2010.

Barclay, Katie. "Space and Place." In *Early Modern Emotions. An Introduction*, edited by Susan Broomhall. London: Routledge, 2017.

Bar-Ratzon, Matityahu, ed. *Ner tamid: yizkor le-Krevitsh*. Tel Aviv, Krivitsh Societies in Israel and the Diaspora, 1977.

Bauer, Yehuda. *The Death of the Shtetl*. New Haven: Yale University Press, 2010.

Berger, Jacob Solomon, trans., and Kariv, Y., ed. *Sefer yizkor le-kehilat Sarny*. Tel Aviv: Former Residents of Sarny and Vicinity in Israel, 1961.

Berman, Saul J. *Boundaries of Loyalty: Testimony against Fellow Jews in Non-Jewish Courts*. Cambridge: Cambridge University Press, 2016.

Bikont, Anna. "'A Young Boy Attacked Us Once and Started Shooting; We Didn't Even Run Any More.' Murders Committed on Jews from the Village of Strzegom by AK and BCh Members." *Holocaust. Studies and Materials* (2017): 163–280.

Blatman, Daniel. "The Encounter between Jews and Poles in Lublin District after Liberation, 1944–1945." *East European Politics and Societies* vol. 20, no. 4 (2006): 598–621.

– *The Death Marches: The Final Phase of Nazi Genocide*. Translated by Ch. Galai. Cambridge: Harvard University Press, 2011.

Blustein, Jeffrey. "Traumatic Emotions." In *Emotions and Mass Atrocity. Philosophical and Theoretical Explorations*, edited by Thomas Brudholm and Johannes Lang. Cambridge: Cambridge University Press, 2018.

Bohus, Kata, Atina Grossman, Werner Hanak-Lettner, and Mirjam Wenzel, eds. *Our Courage – Jews in Europe 1945–48*. Berlin: De Gruyter Oldenbourg, 2020.

Bothe, A., M. Schärtl, and S. Schüler-Springorum, eds. *Shoah: Ereignis und Erinnerung*. Berlin: Hentrich & Hentrich, 2018.

Braddick, Michael J., and John Walter, eds. *Negotiating Power in Early Modern Society. Order, Hierarchy and Subordination in Britain and Ireland*. Cambridge: Cambridge University Press, 2001.

Broomhall, S. and S. Finn, eds. *Violence and Emotions in Early Modern Europe*. London: Routledge, 2016.

Brot, Rivka. *Be'eyzor haafor: hakapo hayehudi kemishpat*. Tel Aviv: The Open University Publishing House, the David Berg Institute for Law and History, 2019.

– "Everyday Justice: Legal Aid for Jewish Displaced Persons, Germany, 1945–1950." *Holocaust and Genocide Studies* vol. 136, no. 2 (2022): 224–41.

Browning, Christopher R. *Remembering Survival: Inside a Nazi Slave-Labor Camp*. New York: W.W. Norton, 2010.

– ""Alleviation' and 'Compliance': The Survival Strategies of the Jewish Leadership in the Wierzbnik Ghetto and Starachowice Factory Slave Labor Camps." In *Gray Zones: Ambiguity and Compromise in the Holocaust and its Aftermath*, edited by Jonathan Petropoulos and John K. Roth, 26–36. London: Berghahn Books, 2012.

Brudholm, Thomas, and Johannes Lang, eds. *Emotions and Mass Atrocity. Philosophical and Theoretical Explorations*. Cambridge: Cambridge University Press, 2018.

Burds, Jeffrey. "Sexual Violence in Europe in World War II, 1939–1945." *Politics and Society* vol. 37, no. 1 (2009): 35–73.

Cadiot, Juliette, and Tanja Penter. "Law and Justice in Wartime and Postwar Jahrbücher Für Stalinism." *Geschichte Osteuropas* vol. 61, no. 2 (2013): 161–71.

Cała, Alina. *Ochrona bezpieczeństwa fizycznego Żydów w Polsce powojennej. Komisje Specjalne przy Centralnym Komitecie Żydów w Polsce*. Warszawa: ŻIH, 2014.

Carlsmith, Kevin M. Daniel T. Gilbert, and Timothy D. Wilson. "The Paradoxical Consequences of Revenge." *Journal of Personality and Social Psychology* vol. 95, no. 6 (2008): 1316–24.

Cerovic, Masha. "'Au chien, une mort de chien.' Les partisans face aux 'traîtres à la Patrie.'" *Cahier du monde russe* 49, no. 2 (2008): 239–62.

Charmatz, Konrad. *Nightmares: Memoirs of the Years of Horror under Nazi Rule in Europe, 1939–1945*. Translated by Miriam Dashkin Beckerman. Edited by Matthew Kudelka. Syracuse: Syracuse University Press, 2003.

Christensen, Kit R. *Revenge and Social Conflict*. Cambridge: Cambridge University Press, 2016.

Cichopek-Gajraj, Anna. *Beyond Violence: Jewish Survivors in Poland and Slovakia, 1944–48*. Cambridge: Cambridge University Press, 2014.

Cohen, Yisrael, ed. *Sefer Buczacz: Matsevet Zikaron Le-kehila Kedosha*. Tel Aviv: Am Oved, 1956.

Dawidowicz, Lucy. *From That Place and Time: A Memoir, 1938–1947*. New York: W.W. Norton & Co Inc, 1998.

Deston, Yehudit Dori, and Dan Porat. "A Prisoner, Legislator, and Jurist: Joseph Lamm's Legal Legacy in Relation to the Nazis and Nazi Collaborators (Punishment) Law, 1950." *Holocaust and Genocide Studies* vol. 37, issue 1 (2023): 74–89.

Dulić, Tomislav. *Utopias of Nation: Local Mass Killing in Bosnia and Herzegovina, 1941–1942*. Uppsala: Uppsala universitet, 2005.

Dvorjetsky, Mark. "Adjustment of Detainees to Camp and Ghetto Life and Their Subsequent Readjustment to Normal Society." In *Yad Vashem Studies on the European Jewish Catastrophe and Resistance*, edited by N. Eck and A.L. Kubovy, 193–220. Israel: Yad Vashem, 1963.

Egit, Jakow. "'Cu a naj Leben' (Cwaj jor jidiszer jiszuw In Niderszlezje)." Wrocław: Niderszlezje.

Eisenberg, Avraham. "In the Forests and Reprisal Activities." Translated by Ala Gamulka. In *Rokitno (Volin) ve-ha-seviva; sefer edut ve-zikaron*, edited by E. Leoni. Tel Aviv: Former residents of Rokitno in Israel, 1967.

Engel, David. "Who Is a Collaborator? The Trials of Michał Weichert." In *The Jews in Poland*, vol. 2, edited by Sławomir Kapralski, 339–70. Kraków: Jagiellonian University, 1999.

Engelking, Barbara. "'Zupelnie zdani jesteśmy na nich.' Relacja ratujacych z ukrywanymi na przykładzie dziennika Feli Fischbein." *Zagłada Żydów. Studia i Materiały* 4 (2008): 144–69.

Engelking, Barbara, ed. *Sny chociaż mamy wspaniałe … Okupacyjne dzienniki Żydów z okolic Mińska Mazowieckiego*. Warszawa: Stowarzyszenie Centrum Badań nad Zagładą Żydów, 2016.

Engelking, Barbara, and Jan Grabowski, eds. *Dalej jest noc. Losy Żydów w wybranych powiatach okupowanej Polski. Tom 1–2*. Warszawa: Stowarzyszenie centrum Badań and Zagładą Żydów, 2018.

Epstein, Barbara. *The Minsk Ghetto 1941–1943. Jewish Resistance and Soviet Internationalism*. Berkeley: University of California Press, 2008.

Exeler, Franziska. "Reckoning with Occupation: Soviet Power, Local Communities, and the Ghosts of Wartime Behaviour in Post-1944 Belorussia." PhD diss., Princeton University, 2013. http://arks.princeton.edu/ark:/88435/dsp01gf06g2796.

– "The Ambivalent State: Determining Guilt in the Post-World War II Soviet Union." *Slavic Review* vol. 75, no. 3 (2016): 606–29.

– *Ghosts of War. Nazi Occupation and Its Aftermath in Soviet Belarus*. Ithaca: Cornell University Press, 2022.

Fialkov, Gitl. "In Destruction and Anguish." Translated by Kevin and Sara Allen. In *Ayaratenu Visotsk; sefer zikaron*, ed. Arie Fialkov. Haifa, Association of former residents of Visotsk in Israel, 1963.

Finder, Gabriel N. "'Sweep Out Evil from Your Midst': The Jewish People's Court in Post-War Poland." In *Beyond Camps and Forced Labour: Current International Research on Survivors of Nazi Persecution*, edited by. Johannes-Dieter Steinert and Inge Weber-Newth, 269–79. Osnabrück: Secolo, 2005.

– "The Trial of Shepsl Rotholc and the Politics of Retribution in the Aftermath of the Holocaust," *Gal-Ed* 20 (2006): 63–89.

Finder, Gabriel N., and Alexander V. Prusin, "Jewish Collaborators on Trial in Poland, 1944–1956," *Polin: Studies in Polish Jewry* vol. 20 (2007): 122–48.

– *Justice Behind the Iron Curtain: Nazis on Trial in Communist Poland*. Toronto: University of Toronto Press, 2018.

Finkel, Evgeny. *Ordinary Jews: Choice and Survival during the Holocaust*. Princeton: Princeton University Press, 2017.

Forecki, Piotr. "Fantazmat Julii Brystiger." *Środkowoeuropejskie Studia Polityczne* no 1 (2017): 47–69.

Friedman, Tuvia. *Nazi Hunter*. Translated by David C. Gross. Haifa, 2006.

Friling, Tuvia. *A Jewish Kapo in Auschwitz: History, Memory, and the Politics of Survival*. Translated by Haim Watzman. Waltham: Brandeis University Press, 2014.

Fulbrook, Mary. *A Small Town near Auschwitz. Ordinary Nazis and the Holocaust*. Oxford: Oxford University Press, 2013.

Gerth, H.H. and C. Wright Mills, eds. *From Max Weber: Essays in Sociology*. New York: Taylor & Francis, 1946.

Geva, Sahron. "'And Now You Are Married and You Have Two Children.' Female Witnesses at the Eichmann Trial." *Yad Vashem Studies* vol. 47, no. 2 (2019): 131–64.

Grabowski, Jan. *Hunt for Jews: Betrayal and Murder in German-Occupied Poland*. Bloomington: Indiana University Press, 2013.

Gringauz, Samuel. "Some Methodological Problems in the Study of the Ghetto." *Jewish Social Studies* 12, no. 1 (1950): 65–72.

Gross, Jan T. *Revolution from Abroad. The Soviet Conquest of Poland's Western Ukraine and Western Belorussia*. Princeton: Princeton University Press, 1988.

Grossmann, Atina. *Jews, Germans, and Allies. Close Encounters in Occupied Germany*. Princeton: Princeton University Press, 2007.

Grupińska, Anka. *Ciągle po Kole. Rozmowy z żołnierzami warszawskiego getta*. Warszawa: wielka litera, 2022.

Hagin, Pinhas, and Malkah, eds. *Sefer zikaron le-'ayarot Rafalowka ha-yeshenah, Rafalowka he-hadashah, Olizarka, Zoludzk veha-sevivah*. Tel Aviv: Tel-Aviv: Irgun yots'e Rafalovkah ha-yeshanah, Rafalovkah ha-hadashah, Olizarkah, Z'alutsk veha-sevivah, 1996.

Hájková, Anna. "'What Kind of Narrative Is Legal Testimony?' Terezín Witnesses before Czechoslovak, Austrian, and German Courts." In *Rethinking Holocaust Justice: Essays across Disciplines*, edited by Norman Goda, 71–99. New York: Berghahn, 2017.

Hanebrink, Paul. *A Specter Haunting Europe: The Myth of Judeo-Bolshevism* (Harvard University Press, 2018).

Haska, Agnieszka. "Dowody i zeznania. Świadectwa o Zagładzie w pierwszych latach powojennych." *Teksty drugie* no. 3 (2018): 361–72.

Himka, John-Paul. *Ukrainian Nationalists and the Holocaust: OUN and UPA's Participation in the Destruction of Ukrainian Jewry, 1941–1944*. Stuttgart: ibidem, 2021.

Holquist, Peter. *Making War. Forging Revolution. Russia's Continuum of Crisis, 1914–1921*. Cambridge: Harvard University Press, 2020.

Horowitz, Rosemary, ed. *Memorial Books of Eastern European Jewry: Essays on the History and Meanings of Yizker Volumes*. Jefferson: McFarland, 2014.

Huizinga, Johan. *The Waning of the Middle Ages: A Study of the Forms of Life, Thought and Art in France and the Netherlands in the XIVth and XVth Centuries*. England: E. Arnold, 1924.

Hulme, Kathryn. *The Wild Place*. Boston: Little, Brown, 1953.

Jakel, Elena. "Ukraine without Jews?" Nationality and Belonging in Soviet Ukraine, 1943–1948." PhD Diss., University of Illinois at Urbana-Champaign, 2014.

Janicka, Elżbieta. "Pamięć przyswojona. Koncepcja polskiego doświadczenia zagłady Żydów jako traumy zbiorowej w świetle rewizji kategorii świadka." *Studia Litteraria et Historica* nr ¾ (2015): 148–226.

Jockusch, Laura. *Collect and Record! Jewish Holocaust Documentation in Early Postwar Europe*. Oxford: Oxford University Press, 2012.

Jockusch, Laura, and Gabriel Finder, eds. *Jewish Honour Courts. Revenge, Retribution and Reconciliation in Europe and Israel after the Holocaust*. Detroit: Wayne State University Press, 2015.

Judt, Tony. "The Past Is Another Country: Myth and Memory in Post-War Europe." In *Memory and Power in Post-War Europe: Studies in the Presence of the Past*, edited by Jan-Werner Müller, 157–83. Cambridge: Cambridge University Press, 2009.

Kabalek, Kobi. "Edges of History and Memory: The 'Final Stage' of the Holocaust." *Dapim: Studies on the Holocaust* vol. 29, no. 3 (2015): 240–63.

Kalyvas, Stathis N. *The Logic of Violence in Civil War*. Cambridge: Cambridge UP, 2006.

Kanc, Shimon, ed. *Sefer Zikaron Czyzewo*. Tel Aviv: Former residents of Czyzewo in Israel and the USA, 1961.

Kantorowich, Naftali. "What Happened to Me When I Returned Home." Translated by Jerrold Landau. In *Rozhinoy; sefer zikaron le-kehilat Rozhinoy ve-ha-seviva*, edited by M. Sokolowsky. Tel Aviv: Former residents of Rozhinoy in Israel, 1957, 172.

Kerenji, Emil, ed. *Jewish Responses to Persecution: 1942–1943*, vol. IV. Lanham, MD: AltaMira Press in association with the United States Holocaust Memorial Museum, 2015.

Kermish, Joseph, ed. *To Live with Honor and Die with Honor!...: Selected Documents from the Warsaw Ghetto Underground Archives "O. S." ("Oneg Shabbath")*. Jerusalem: Yad Vashem, 1986.

Kerrigan, John. *Revenge Tragedy: Aeschylus to Armageddon*. Oxford: Clarendon Press, 1996.

Kivimäki, Ville, and Petri Karonen, eds. *Continued Violence and Troublesome Pasts: Post-War Europe between the Victors after the Second World War*. Helsinki: Finnish Literature Society, 2017.

Kleinman, Yehudit, and Nina Springer-Aharoni, eds. *The Anguish of Liberation. Testimonies from 1945*. Jerusalem: Yad Vashem, 1995.

Kobrin, Rebecca. *Jewish Bialystok and Its Diaspora*. Bloomington: Indiana University Press, 2010.

Kochanowski, Jerzy. *W polskiej niewoli. Niemieccy jeńcy wojenni w Polsce 1945–1950*. Warszawa: Wydawnictwo Neriton, 2001.

Königseder, Angelika, and Juliane Wetzel. *Waiting for Hope: Jewish Displaced Persons in Post-World War II Germany*. Evanston, Ill.: Northwestern University Press, 2001.

Konrád, Ota, Boris Barth, and Jaromír Mrňka, eds. *Collective Identities and Post-War Violence in Europe, 1944–48. Reshaping the Nation*. London: Palgrave Macmillan, 2022.

Kopciowski, Adam. "Przemoc antyżydowska w powojennej Polsce w świetle ksiąg pamięci." *Zagłada Żydów. Studia i Materiały* (2018): 212–47.

Kornbluth, Andrew. *The August Trials. The Holocaust and Post-War Justice in Poland*. Cambridge: Harvard University Press, 2021.

Kubicki, Leszek. *Zbrodnie wojenne w świetle prawa polskiego*. Warszawa: PWN, 1963.

Kwasik, K., J. Jaroszyński, and G. Łęcicki, eds. *Media wobec śmierci*, vol. 1. Warszawa: Elipsa, 2012.

Kwiek, Julian. *Nie chcemy Żydów u siebie. Przejawy wrogości wobec Żydów w latach 1944–1947*. Warszawa: Wydawnictwo Nieoczywiste, 2021.

Lang, Berel. "Holocaust Memory and Revenge: The Presence of the Past." *Jewish Social Studies* vol. 2, no. 2 (1996): 1–20.

Lavi, Shai. "'The Jews Are Coming': Vengeance and Revenge in Post-Nazi Europe." *Law, Culture and the Humanities* 1, no. 3 (October 2005): 282–301.

Leoni, E., ed. *Rokitno (Volin) ve-ha-seviva; sefer edut ve-zikaron*. Tel Aviv: Former residents of Rokitno in Israel, 1967.

Lewis Herman, Judith. *Trauma and Recovery: The Aftermath of Violence – From Domestic Abuse to Political Terror*. New York: Basic Books, 1992.

Libionka, Dariusz, and Alina Skibińska. '"I Swear to Fight for a Free and Mighty Poland, Carry Out the Orders of My Superiors, So Help Me God.' Jews in the Home Army. An Episode from Ostrowiec Świętokrzyski." *Holocaust Studies and Materials* (2008): 235–69.

Lityński, Antoni. "Ustawodawstwo karne w pierwszych latach Polski Ludowej." In *Wojna domowa czy nowa okupacja? Polska po roku 1944*, edited by Andrzej Ajnenkiel. Wrocław: Ossolineum, 1998.

Losh, L. ed. *Sefer zikaron le-kehilot Szczuczyn Wasiliszki Ostryna Nowy-Dwor Rozanka*. Tel Aviv: Former Residents of Szczuczyn Wasiliszki 1966.

Lower, Wendy. *The Ravine. A Family, A Photograph, A Holocaust Massacre Revealed*. London: Head of Zeus, 2021.

Machcewicz, Paweł and Andrzej Paczkowski. *Wina, kara, polityka. Rozliczenia ze zbrodniami II Wojny Światowej*. Kraków: Znak, 2021.

Magier, Dariusz. "Stosunek milicjantów powiatu radzyńskiego do komunizmu i Związku Sowieckiego na początku 1946 roku." *Radzyński Rocznik Humanistyczny* (2020): 55–72.

Mahler, R. *Shenstokhover Yidn*. NY: United Czestochower Relief Committee and Ladies Auxiliary, 1947.

Mankowitz, Zeev W. *Life Between Memory and Hope: The Survivors of the Holocaust in Occupied Germany*. Cambridge: Cambridge University Press, 2002.

May, Larry, ed. *War: Essays in Political Philosophy*. Cambridge: Cambridge University Press, 2008.

Milch, Baruch. *Testament*. Warszawa: Karta, 2001.

Mintzer, Oscar A. *In Defense of the Survivors: The Letters and Documents of Oscar A. Mintzer, AJDC Legal Advisor, Germany, 1945–46*. Berkeley: Judah L. Magnes Museum, 1999.

Morina, Christina, and Krijn Thijs. *Probing the Limits of Categorization: The Bystander in Holocaust History*. New York: Berghan Books, 2019.

Moss, Kenneth B. *An Unchosen People. Jewish Political Reckoning in Interwar Poland*. New Heaven: Harvard University Press, 2021.

Moss, Kanneth B., Benjamin Nathans, and Taro Tsurami, eds. *From Europe's East to the Middle East: Israel's Russian and Polish Lineages*. Philadelphia: University of Pennsylvania Press, 2021.

Muir, Simo. "Rumkowski's Scapegoat? The Case of Łódź Ghetto Functionary Maks Szczęśliwy at a Rabbinic/Honor Court in Helsinki, 1949–1953." *Holocaust and Genocide Studies* vol. 35, no. 2 (2021): 185–210.

Müller, Jan-Werner, ed. *Memory and Power in Post-War Europe: Studies in the Presence of the Past*. Cambridge: Cambridge University Press, 2009.

Murav, Harriet, and Gennady Estraikh, eds. *Soviet Jews in World War II: Fighting, Witnessing, Remembering*. Boston: Academic Studies Press, 2014.

Musial, Bogdan. *Sowjetische Partisanen 1941–1944: Mythos und Wirklichkeit*. Paderborn: Ferdinand Schöningh Verlag, 2009.

Myers Feinstein, Margarete. *Holocaust Survivors in Post-war Germany, 1945–1957*. Cambridge: Cambridge University Press, 2010.

Nalewajko-Kulikov, Joanna. *Strategie przetrwania. Żydzi po "aryjskiej" stronie Warszawy*. Warsaw: Neriton, 2004.

Olejnik, Leszek. *Polityka narodowościowa Polski w latach 1944–1960*. Łódz: Wydawnictwo Uniwersytetu Łódziego, 2003.

Owsiński, Marcin. *Lagrowi ludzie. Śledztwo i pierwszy proces stutthofski (1945–1946). Opowieść o przemianie*. Łódź: Księży Młyn, 2022.

Patt, Avinoam. *The Jewish Heroes of Warsaw. The Aftermath of the Revolt*. Detroit: Wayne State University Press, 2021.

Pawlicki, Artur. *Procesy osób oskarżonych o popełnienie zbrodni niemieckich w Kraju Warty przed polskimi sądami specjalnymi w latach 1945–1946*, t. 1. Poznań-Warszawa: Instytut Pamięci Narodowej, 2019.

Penter, Tanja. "Local Collaborators on Trial: Soviet War Crimes Trials under Stalin (1943–1953)." *Cahiers Du Monde Russe* 49, no. 2/3 (2008): 341–64.

Persak, Krzysztof. "Jedwabne before the Court. Poland's Justice and the Jedwabne Massacre – Investigations and Court Proceedings, 1947–1974." *East European Politics and Societies* vol 25, no. 3 (2011): 410–32.

Person, Katarzyna. *Warsaw Ghetto Police: The Jewish Order Service during the Nazi Occupation*. Translated by Z. Nowak Soliński (Ithaca: Cornell University Press, 2021).

Person, K., M. Trębacz, and Z. Trębacz, eds. *Archiwum Ringelbluma. Dzienniki z Getta Warszawskiego*. Warszawa: ŻIH, 2015.

Pinchevski, Amit. "The Audiovisual Unconscious: Media and Trauma in the Video Archive for Holocaust Testimonies." *Critical Inquiry* vol. 39 (2012): 142–66.

Pollin-Galay, Hannah, and Avrom Sutzkever. "Art of Testimony: Witnessing with the Poet in the Wartime Soviet Union." *Jewish Social Studies* vol. 21, no. 2 (Winter 2016): 1–34.

– *Ecologies of Witnessing: Language, Place, and Holocaust Testimony*. New Haven: Yale University Press, 2018.

Porat, Dina. *The Fall of the Sparrow. The Life and Times of Abba Kovner*. Stanford: Stanford University Press, 2009.

– *Li Nakam Veshilem: HaYishuv, Hashoah, Vekvutzat Hanokmim Shel Abba Kovner*. Haifa: Pardes Publishing, Haifa University Press, 2015.

Rabin, H., ed. *Voronova; sefer zikaron le-kedoshei Voronova she-nispu be-shoat ha-natsim*. Voronova Societies in Israel and the United States, 1971.

Reckwitz, Andreas. "Affective Spaces: A Praxeological Outlook." *Rethinking History. The Journal of Theory and Practice* vol. 16 (2012): 241–58.

Remba, Aizik, and Benjamin Halevy, eds. *Sefer zikaron le-kehilat Kolno*. Tel Aviv: Kolner Organization and Sifirat Poalim, 1971.

Rice, Monika. *"What! Still Alive?!" Jewish Survivors in Poland and Israel Remember Homecoming*. Syracuse: Syracuse University Press, 2017.

Ringelblum, Emmanuel. *Notes from the Warsaw Ghetto*. Translated and edited by Jacob Sloan. iBooks, 2006.

Roseman, Mark. "… but of Revenge Not a Sign. Germans' Fear of Jewish Revenge after World War II." In *Jahrbuch für Antisemitismusforschung* vol. 22 (2013): 79–98.

Rosen, Alan. *Sounds of Defiance. The Holocaust, Multilingualism and the Problem of English*. Lincoln and London: University of Nebraska Press, 2005.

– *The Wonder of Their Voices: The 1946 Holocaust Interviews of David Boder*. Oxford: Oxford University Press, 2010.

Rosen, Alan, ed. *Literature of the Holocaust*. Cambridge: Cambridge University Press, 2013.

Rothberg, Michael. *The Implicated Subject. Beyond Victims and Perpetrators*. Stanford: Stanford University Press, 2019.

Rykała, Andrzej. *W reakcji na powojenną przemoc antysemicką. Samoobrona Żydów w Łodzi – uwarunkowania społeczno-polityczne i przestrzenne*. Łódź: Wydawnictwo Uniwersytetu Łódzkiego, 2020.

Rzepliński, Andrzej. *Sądownictwo w PRL*. Londyn: Polonia, 1990.

Schatz, Jaff. *The Generation. The Rise and Fall of the Jewish Communists of Poland*. Berkeley: University of California Press, 1991.

Schmidt, Sibylle. "Perpetrators' Knowledge: What and How Can We Learn from Perpetrator Testimony?" *Journal of Perpetrator Research* vol. 1, no.1 (2017): 85–104.

Schneider, Wolfgang. "From the Ghetto to the Gulag, from the Ghetto to Israel: Soviet Collaboration Trials against the Shargorod Ghetto's Jewish Council." *Journal of Modern European History* vol. 17, issue 1 (2019): 83–97.

Schumann, Karina, and Michael Ross. "The Benefits, Costs, and Paradox of Revenge." *Social and Personality Psychology Compass* 4/12 (2010): 1193–1205.

Schwarz, Leo W. *The Redeemers: A Saga of the Years 1945–1952*. New York; Farrar, Straus and Young, 1953.

Seidman, Naomi. "Elie Wiesel and the Scandal of Jewish Rage." *Jewish Social Studies: History, Culture, and Society* 3/1 (Fall 1996): 1–19.

Semczyszyn, Magdalena. "Żydzi w sowieckich oddziałach partyzanckich na północno-wschodnich terenach Drugiej RP 1941–1944 – zarys problematyki," *Zagłada Żydów. Studia i Materiały* vol. 17 (2021): 139–71.

Shapira, Anita. *Land and Power. The Zionist Resort to Force, 1881–1948*. Translated by W. Templer. Stanford: Stanford University Press, 1992.

Shenker, Noah. *Reframing Holocaust Testimony*. Bloomington: Indiana University Press, 2015.

Shmueli-Schmusch, Nechama, ed. *Zabludow; dapim mi-tokh yisker-bukh*. Tel Aviv: Former Residents of Zabludow in Israel, 1987.

Shuval, Dov, ed. *Sefer zikaron le-kehilat Shebreshin*. Haifa: Association of Former Inhabitants of Shebreshin in Israel and the Diaspora, 1984.

Siegelman, Yitzhak, ed. *Sefer Kobylnik*. Haifa: Committee of former residents of Kobylnik in Israel, 1967.

Silverman, Joel. "Krieger v. Mittelman and Jewish Perception of the Refugee in the Early Cold War." *Judaism* 55, no. 1 and 2 (2006): 40–54.

Simyon, Mosheh, ed. *Sefer zikaron li-ḳehilat Horodoḳ (ʻa. y. Byalisṭoḳ)*. Tel Aviv: ha-Irgunim shel yots'e Horodoḳ be-Yiśra'el uve-Argenṭinah, 1963.

Skibińska, Alina. "The Return of Jewish Holocaust Survivors and the Reaction of the Polish Population." In *Jewish Presence in Absence: The Aftermath of the Holocaust in Poland, 1944–2010*, edited by Feliks Tych and Monika Adamczyk-Garbowska. Jerusalem: Yad Vashem, 2014.

Skorczewski, Dawn. "'You Want Me to Sing?' Holocaust Testimonies in the Intersubjective Field." *Dapim: Studies on the Holocaust* 32, no. 2 (2018): 112–27.

Slepyan, Kenneth. *Stalin's Guerrillas. Soviet Partisans in World War II*. Lawrence/KS: University Press of Kansas, 2006.

Smilovitsky, Leonid. "Antisemitism in the Soviet Partisan Movement, 1941–1944: The Case of Belorussia." *Holocaust and Genocide Studies* vol. 20, no. 2 (2006): 207–34.

Snopko, Jan. "Początki działalności powiatowego urzędu bezpieczeństwa w Augustowie." *Studia Podlaskie* tom XV: 273–317.

Snyder, Timothy. *The Reconstruction of Nations: Poland, Ukraine, Lithuania, Belarus, 1569–1999*. New Haven: Yale University Press, 2003.

Sokolowsky, M., ed. *Rozhinoy; sefer zikaron le-kehilat Rozhinoy ve-ha-seviva*. Tel Aviv: Former residents of Rozhinoy in Israel, 1957.

Solonari, Vladimir. *Purifying the Nation: Population Exchange and Ethnic Cleansing in Nazi-Allied Romania*. Washington/Baltimore: Woodrow Wilson Center Press/Johns Hopkins University Press, 2009.

Stankowski, Albert. "Nowe spojrzenie na statystyki dotyczące emigracji Żydów z Polski po 1944 roku." In *Studia z historii Żydów w Polsce po 1945 roku*, edited by Grzegorz Berendt, August Grabski, and Albert Stankowski, 103–51. Warszawa: Żydowski Instytut Historyczny, 2000.

Starowieyski, Łukasz. "Oprawcy na szafocie. Publiczne egzekucje w Polsce po II wojnie." https://dzieje.pl/wiadomosci/oprawcy-na-szafocie-publiczne-egzekucje-w-polsce-po-ii-wojnie

Statiev, Alexander. *The Soviet Counterinsurgency in the Western Borderlands*. Cambridge: Cambridge University Press, 2010.

Stein, Rachel. *Vengeful Citizens, Violent States: A Theory of War and Revenge*. Cambridge: Cambridge University Press, 2019.

Stockfish, David, ed. *Sefer Dokshitz-Parafianov*. Translated by Yariv Eldar and Daniella HarPaz Mechnikov. Tel Aviv: Association of Former Residents of Dokszyce-Parafianow in Israel, 1970.

Stola, Dariusz. "Jewish Emigration from Communist Poland: The Decline of Polish Jewry in the Aftermath of the Holocaust." *East European Jewish Affairs* vol. 47, no. 2–3 (2017): 169–88.

Stone, Dan. *The Liberation of the Camps: The End of the Holocaust and Its Aftermath*. New Haven and London: Yale University Press, 2015.

Sztejn A. Sh., and G. Wejszman, eds. *Pinkas Sochaczew*. Jerusalem, Former residents of Sochaczew in Israel, 1962.

Szymczak, Jakub. *Ja łebków nie dawałem! Procesy przed Żydowskim Sądem Społecznym*. Warszawa: Czarne, 2022.

Talmi, E., ed. *Kehilat Sierpc; sefer zikaron*. Tel Aviv: The former residents of Sierpc in Israel and abroad, 1959.

Tokarska-Bakir, Joanna. "The Polish Underground Organization Wolność i Niezawisłość and anti-Jewish pogroms, 1945–6." *Patterns of Prejudice* vol. 51, no. 2 (2017): 111–36.

– *Pogrom Cries – Essays on Polish-Jewish History, 1939–1946*. Frankfurt am Main: Peter Lang Publishing, 2017.

Tumblety, Joan, ed. *Memory and History. Understanding Memory as Source and Subject*. Abingdon: Routledge, 2013.

Tych, Feliks, and Monika Adamczyk-Garbowska, eds. *Jewish Presence in Absence: The Aftermath of the Holocaust in Poland, 1944–2010*. Jerusalem: Yad Vashem, 2014.

Waligórska, Magdalena, Yechiel Weizman, Alexander Friedman, and Ina Sorkina, "Holocaust Survivors Returning to Their Hometowns in the

Polish-Belarusian-Ukrainian Borderlands, 1944–1948." *Journal of Holocaust Research* (forthcoming).

Waxman, Zoe. *Writing the Holocaust: Identity, Testimony, Representation*. Oxford: Oxford University Press, 2005.

Wein, Abraham. "'Memorial Books' as a Source for Research into the History of Jewish Communities in Europe." *Yad Vashem Studies on the European Catastrophe and Resistance* vol. 9 (1973): 260–1

Wiesel, Elie. *Un di velt hot geshvign*. Buenos Aires: Tsentral-Farband fun Poylishe Yidn in Argentine, 1956.

Winter, Jay, and Emmanuel Sivan, eds. *War and Remembering in the Twentieth Century*. Cambridge: Cambridge University Press, 1999.

Wolfson, Leah, ed. *Jewish Responses to Persecution: 1944–1946*, vol. V. Lanham, MD: Alta Mira Press in association with the United States Holocaust Memorial Museum, 2015)

Wood, Nancy. *Vectors of Memory: Legacies of Trauma in Post-War Europe*. Oxford: Berg, 1999.

Woźniczka, Zygmunt. "Obóz pracy w Świętochłowicach- Zgodzie i jego komendant." *Dzieje Najnowsze* no. 4 (1999): 17–35.

Wyman, Mark. *DP: Europe's Displaced Persons, 1945–1951*. London: Associated University Presses, 1989.

Yablonka, Hanna. "The Eichmann Trial: Was It the Jewish Nuremberg?" *The Loyola of Los Angeles International and Comparative Law Review* 301: (2012).

Yerushalami, Eliezer, David Cohen, and Helen Cohn, eds. *Pinkas Novogrudok*. New York: Jewishgen, 2013.

Ziemba, Zdzisław Albin. *Prawo przeciwko społeczeństwu. Polskie prawo karne w latach 1945–1956*. Warszawa: Instytut Stosowanych Nauk Społecznych Uniwersytetu Warszawskiego, 1997.

Zigelman, Yitzchak, ed. *Sefer Radzyn*. Tel Aviv: Radzyn (Podlaski) Immigrants Association in Israel, 1957.

Zuckerman, Yitzhak. *A Surplus of Memory. Chronicle of the Warsaw Ghetto Uprising*. Translated by B. Harshav. Los Angeles: University of California Press, 1993.

Index

acquittals, 58, 61, 92
Adamczyk-Garbowska, Monika, 14–15, 124n35
affective spaces, 28
agency, 118–19
Aleksandrowicz, Chaim, 103
Aleksiun, Natalia, 28, 33, 36, 38
Allied Control Commission, 83
Altbauer, Hermann, 150n75
American Jewish Joint Distribution Committee, 95
anti-Jewish violence, 29–32, 40, 45–7; Jedwabne Pogrom (1941), 60–1; Kielce Pogrom (1946), 30, 45, 69
Apelfeld, Józef, 40
Appelbaum, Anne, 50
arms, illegal possession of, 92
Auerbach, Philip, 96
August 1944 Decree, 58, 61
Auschwitz-Birkenau concentration and extermination camp, 16, 79, 85, 116–17

Bad Ischl DP Camp, 89–90
banishment, 86–7, 92, 95–6
Barzion, Joseph, 116–17
Bauer, Leon, 66
Bauerowa, Bronisława, 66, 67, 68
Baumgarten, Sonia, 115
beit din (rabbinic courts), 114
Bełżyce, 110
Beresteczko, 40
Berger, Aleksander, 70
Berlin, postwar division into occupational zones, 83
Bloxham, Donald, 57
Boder, David, 15
Borowski, Tadeusz, 52
Botwinik, Mariasza, 37
Braddick, Michael J., 65
Brot, Rivka, 105, 148n39
Browning, Christopher, 5, 28
Brystiger, Julia, 50
Brzezińska, Franciszka, 81–2
Buczacz, 111
Budzyn concentration camp, 94, 98, 101–2
Buenos Aires, Zajfman trial in, 112–13
Bydgoszcz, 40–1
Byelorussians, as targeted for revenge, 8

Camp Herzog, 97
cemeteries, desecration of, 36, 134n107
Central Committee of Jews in Poland, 10, 66, 67. *See also* Jewish Civic Court

Central Committee of Liberated Jews, 93, 108, 153n3
Central Jewish Historical Commission, 10, 25, 57
children: and accusations against Regina Kupiec, 85; seeking revenge, 139n34
Churchill, Winston, 53
Cichopek-Gajraj, Anna, 39, 64
city, return to, 38–41
civic court. *See* Jewish Civic Court
collaborators: attacked in Israel, 115; and defense strategies in DP honour courts, 98–106; investigated by Jewish Civic Court, 67–8, 69; and justice in displaced persons camps, 88–92; killed by partisans, 19–20; methods of dealing with suspected, 77; positions in postwar community, 103; and rehabilitation requests in Jewish Civic Court, 78–82; rehabilitation requests of relatives of, 113; and revenge of Polish Jews in Germany, 84–8; in Soviet-occupied territories, 41–3; as targeted for revenge, 9, 37–8, 51; trials of, 57–65, 92–8; witness testimonies of, 146n9
collective memory, 11, 116
Communism, 7–8
community, and transnational trials, 116. *See also* Jewish community
concentration camps: Auschwitz-Birkenau concentration and extermination camp, 16, 79, 85, 116–17; Budzyn concentration camp, 101–2; Polish Jews' perception of, 84; post-liberation revenge at, 20–1, 24
continuum of vindictive violence, 117–18
core values, 4, 121n5
Criminal Codes, 58
Czapnicki, Mieczysław, 94

death marches, 20–1
"Declaration of German Atrocities," 53
denunciations: in displaced-persons camps, 107; motives for, 71–8; preceding migration, 107–8; and trials of suspected collaborators, 93–5. See also *meshorah* (informing)
displaced persons (DPs), 83; court martial of, 148n38; and defense strategies in DP honour courts, 98–105; emigration of, 105. *See also* displaced-persons camps; DP courts
displaced-persons camps, 83–4; Bad Ischl DP Camp, 89–90; closing of, 105; as communities of memories, 99; denunciations in, 107; Kupiec trial in, 84–8; Landsberg DP Camp, 89, 92–3; rules for, 148n38; system of justice in, 88–92; trials of suspected collaborators in, 92–8. *See also* displaced persons (DPs); DP courts
divine judgment, 35
Dołajczuk, 40
DP courts: defense strategies in, 98–105; as system of justice in displaced-persons camps, 88–92; trials of suspected collaborators, 92–8
Dvorjetski, Mark, 3–4
Dzierżoniów, 62

Egit, Jakub, 25
Eichmann, Adolf, 49; trial of, 3–4
Einhorn, Arnold, 96
Eizenberg, Izrael, 53
Engel, Masza, 79
Epshteyn, Shakhne, 130n58
executions, public, 54–5

Fakler, Runa, 113
family camps, 18
Federation of Polish Jews in Brazil, 113
Finder, Gabriel, 70
Finger, Berek, 109–10
Finkel, Evgeny, 17–18
First Polish Army, 25
Fischer, Fritz-Adolf, 55–6
Flayshker, Jakov, 97
Forecki, Piotr, 50
forest, as hiding place, 17–19
Frauenglass, Marian, 66–7, 68
Freidheim, Władysław, 98, 101–2, 103
Friedman, Tuviah (Tadeusz Jasiński), 49
Friling, Tuvie, 9
Frydman, Henryk, 94
Fulbrook, Mary, 8

gender, 37–8. *See also* women
"gentile, righteous," 41–5
German perpetrators, trials of, 52–7
Germany, postwar division into occupational zones, 83. *See also* displaced-persons camps; DP courts
Gertler, David, 101, 107–8
Gleiwitz, 62
Gliksman, Henryk, 152n99
God of Vengeance, 34–7
Goldberg, Lejb, 51
Górny, Jechiel, 20
Greiser, Arthur, 54–5
Gringaus, Samuel, 97–8
Gutmacher, Ludwik, 109

Hertz, Karol, 81
historishe komisye, 10
Hoch, Józef, 100, 150n72
honour courts: and collaboration, 9; creation of, 70–1; defense strategies in, 98–105; documentation from, 13; information exchange between Jewish civic courts and, 108; and justice in displaced persons camps, 88–92; and trials of suspected collaborators, 92–3
hope, through imagined revenge, 16–17
Huizinga, Johan, 29

imagined revenge, 16–20
individual memory, 10
International Military Tribunal (IMT), 53
International Refugee Organization (IRO), 84
Israel: and justice in displaced persons camps, 70–1, 88; as key scene of revenge-seeking, 114–16; and trials of displaced persons suspected of collaboration, 96–7. *See also* Zionism

Jaffe, Ludwik, 100–1, 102, 104
Janicka, Elżbieta, 8
Jasiński, Tadeusz (Tuviah Friedman), 49
Jaszuńska, Miriam, 42
JDC (Joint Distribution Committee), 84
Jedwabne massacre (1941), 60–1
Jewish Civic Court, 66–70; and denunciations, 71–8; limited punitive powers of, 75; and migration, 108–11, 113; mission of, 67; punishments issued by, 68; and rehabilitation requests, 78–82; as site of revenge and retribution, 70–1
Jewish community: denunciations' role in rebuilding postwar, 77–8; and transnational trials, 116

Jewish Historical Institute, 10, 113, 153n3
Jewish Order Service, 9, 63, 81–2
"Jewish revenge," 5–6
Jews: joining security apparatus, 47–50; postwar attacks on, 45–7; revenge by individual, against German perpetrators, 56–7; as targeted for revenge, 9; trials of, 57–65, 140n37; and trials of German perpetrators, 52–7. *See also* anti-Jewish violence
Jockusch, Laura, 70
Joint Distribution Committee (JDC), 84
Jolles, Norbert, 95
Jozwiak, Franciszek, 46
Judt, Tony, 21
Jungster, Chazciel, 152n105
justice, revenge versus, 4

Kahane, Dawid, 66
Kamińska, Ida, 66
Kanada, 86, 104
kapos: defense strategies in displaced-person honour courts, 99, 100, 101–2, 103–4; and justice in displaced persons camps, 89
Kerrigan, John, 6
Kestner, Heinrich, 56–7
Kielce Pogrom (1946), 30, 45, 69
Klejnman, Dovid, 92–3
Kluger, Ruth, 89
Knyszyńska, Rita, 82
Kolno, 97, 103
Koło, 69
Kopciowski, Adam, 14–15, 124n35
Korbin, Rebecca, 11
Kornbluth, Andrew, 29, 45
Kovner, Abba, 18
Koźmińska-Frejlak, Ewa, 81, 113
Kraków 30, 31–2, 38, 80
Kresy, 27
Krzesiny (Kreising), 62
Kubicki, Leszek, 57–8
Kupiec, Regina, 75, 84–8, 104

lamentation, 37
Landsberg DP Camp, 89, 92–3
landsmanshaftn, 11
La Paz, 113
Lerner, Icek, 46–7
Lewinstein, Nikolaj, 95–6
liberation, 20–4; joining Red Army following, 24–7; return to Poland following, 27–32; return to villages following, 32–4
Lisowski, Aleksander, 41
Łódź, 39, 40, 110
Lokiec, Uszer, 150n74
Lozowick, Yaacov, 20
Lviv, 100, 101, 131n67

Mandatory Palestine, as key scene of revenge-seeking, 114–16
Manifesto of the Polish Committee of National Liberation (1944), 52
Mazurek, Adam, 80
memorial books, 11–12, 14–15, 38, 124n35
memory: collective, 11, 116; individual versus public, 10
Mendelson, Jankiel, 58
Mercel, Leon, 104
Merin, Moishe, 100
Merin, Roman, 100
meshorah (informing), 9, 124n26. *See also* denunciations
migrations, 107–16
Milch, Baruch, 43
Milicja, 45–50. *See also* security apparatus
Military Courts, 95
Mittlemen, Majer, 114
mob justice, 53

Molczycki, Chaim, 115
Morel, Salomon, 50
Moscow Declaration (1943), 112
mourning, 116
Munzberg, Szlamo, 153n3

Nazi war criminals, prosecution of, 53–7
neighbours, as perpetrators of violence, 33–4
Nekama, 18
Neufeld, Daniel, 104
Night (Wiesel), 21, 129n39
NKVD, 41, 42, 43, 44–5, 89
NNCL (Nazis and Nazi Collaborators [Punishment] Law, 1950), 115–16
Nuremberg trial, 53

oral histories, 12–13
Organization of Ukrainian Nationalists, 89
Ostrowiec, 23, 112–13, 115

partisan groups: motivations for joining, 17–19; restrictions on, 42; and violence against collaborators, 41–2
Patt, Avinoam J., 84
Penter, Tanja, 44
Persak, Krzysztof, 60–1
Pinchas, Majer, 79–80
Plaszow concentration camp, 73, 93, 113
pogroms: Jedwabne Pogrom (1941), 60–1; Kielce Pogrom (1946), 30, 45, 69; postwar, 30, 40. *See also* anti-Jewish violence
Poland, return to, following liberation, 27–32
police forces, local, partisan groups' revenge actions against, 19
police officers, district, as agents of violence, 42–3
Polish courts, German perpetrators in, 53–7
Polish-Jewish Holocaust survivors: defined, 7; depiction of, in Jewish Civic Court defense, 75–6; as perceived as incapable of revenge, 5; repatriation of, 27–32, 83–4, 131n67; return to cities, 38–41; return to villages, 32–4; self-defense units organized by, 31–2; as target of violence, 29–32, 38–9. *See also* displaced persons (DPs); displaced-persons camps; DP courts
Polish Social Court, 148n47
Pollin-Galay, Hannah, 33, 130n58, 138n12
Porat, Dan, 114–16
posthumous revenge, 31
Prindyn, Eustachij, 56
public executions, 54–5
public memory, 10. *See also* collective memory

rabbinic courts, 114
Rajzman, Szmuel, 53
rape, 22–3
Rauch-Kwiatkowska, Estera, 89
Reckwitz, Andreas, 28
Red Army: revenge through joining, 24–7; and "righteous gentile," 41; and violence against collaborators, 42
Redlich, Shimon, 39
Rehabilitation Commission, 93, 94–5, 103
rehabilitation requests, 78–82; of collaborators' relatives, 113; of displaced persons suspected of collaboration, 94–6; and

migration, 110–11; tried in Polish Social Court, 148n47
resistance groups. *See* partisan groups
retribution, revenge versus, 5
revenge: defined, 4; denunciations and pursuit of, 74, 75–6; as duty, 23; gendered aspect of, 37–8; groups targeted for, 8–9; hope through, 16–17; imagined, 16–20; as interplay between local and transnational entities, 7; "Jewish revenge," 5–6; and liberation, 20–4; methodology of postwar, 4–5; motivations for, 3; perceptions of, 5; posthumous, 31; purpose and effects of, 6; and questions concerning civilized society, 118; reliance on God for, 34–7; in Scriptures, 35; security apparatus and acts of, 41–5; studying, 119; through joining security apparatus, 48–50; transnational aspect of search for, 111–13; as traumatizing, 24
"righteous gentile," 41–5
Ringelblum, Emanuel, 17
Roosevelt, Franklin D., 53
Rosenberg, Chaskiel, 113
Rothberg, Michael, 70
Rotkoph, Marian, 80
Rowiński, Stanisław, 71, 72
Rubin, Majer, 92
rural areas, 29
Rykała, Andrzej, 132n85
Rzeszów 30, 31

sacral spaces, desecration of, 36, 134n107
Salsitz, Norman, 3
Schachter, Henryk, 78
Schatz, Jeff, 137n165
Schmidt, Sibylle, 79
Schwarz, Leo W., 116–17, 155n41
security apparatus, 41–5; Jews joining, 47–50
self-defense units, 31–2
Senderowicz, David, 26–7
Shapira, Anita, 17, 125n40
Shema Israel, 3
Silberstein, Samuel, 71, 72
silence, 60
Silesia, 48
Skarżysko Kamienna forced labour camp, 97
Skibińska, Alina, 30
Skorczewski, Dawn, 12
Snyder, Timothy, 17
Sochaczew cemetery, 36
Sonderabteilung, 107
Special Commission by the Central Committee of Polish Jews, 31–2
Special Penal Courts, 58
state courts, 51–2; German perpetrators in Polish courts, 53–7; seeking revenge through, 4–5; and trials of German perpetrators, 52–3; trials of Jews and collaborators, 57–65
Stein, Rachel, 121n5
Stutthof trial and execution, 54
Sutzkever, Avrom, 53
Świętochłowice-Zgoda, 50
Szczęśliwy, Maks, 114
Szenderowicz, Naumi, 82
Szmit, Chawa, 80
Szwalb, Izaak, 95

Teichholtz, Bronisław, 148n47
Tkacz, Benisz, 103, 104
Tokarska-Bakir, Joanna, 31, 49–50, 63–4
train actions, 30, 45
trauma, trials as way of externalizing collective, 116

Ukrainian Insurgent Army (UPA), 43
Ukrainians: as targeted for revenge, 8; trials and executions of, 44
United Nations Relief and Rehabilitation Administration (UNRRA), 84
United Nations War Crimes Commission, 53
UNRRA (United Nations Relief and Rehabilitation Administration), 84

values, core, 4, 121n5
Velyki Mezhyrichi, 41–2
vengeance. *See* revenge
village, return to, 32–4
Vilnius 3, 8, 18, 19, 42, 53
"violent tenor of life," 29–30
visibility, as defense strategy in displaced-person honour courts, 101–2

Wachtel, H.J., 84–5
Walter, John, 65
Warsaw Ghetto 34, 81, 85, 98
Warsaw Ghetto Uprising (1943), 4, 12, 17, 85
Waxman, Zoe, 129n39
Webber, Rudolf, 59
Weber, Max, 52
Wein, Abraham, 126n50
Weizman, Yehiel, 36, 134n107
Wełyczko, 37–8
Wiesel, Elie, 12, 21, 129n39
witness testimonies, 108–9, 138n12, 146n9
women: accusations of collaboration against, 113; and gendered aspect of vengeance, 37–8; and rehabilitation requests in Jewish Civic Court, 81–2
Wood, Nancy, 10
World Jewish Congress, 108
Wrocław, 56

Yablonka, Hannah, 53–4
Yiddish, 99, 150n75

Zajfman, Abram, 112–13
Zajfman, Lejbusz, 112, 113
Zeigel, Juliusz, 103
Zionism, 7–8, 99–100
Zuckerman, Yitzhak, 4, 14